John McGaw Foster

Class of 1882 Baccalaureate Sermon, Class Day Oration, etc

John McGaw Foster

Class of 1882 Baccalaureate Sermon, Class Day Oration, etc

ISBN/EAN: 9783744746168

Printed in Europe, USA, Canada, Australia, Japan

Cover: Foto ©Paul-Georg Meister /pixelio.de

More available books at **www.hansebooks.com**

HARVARD COLLEGE.

Class of 1882.

Baccalaureate Sermon,

CLASS DAY ORATION, Etc.

CAMBRIDGE.
WM. H. WHEELER, PRINTER,
1882.

Baccalaureate Sermon.

BY FRANCIS G. PEABODY, B.D.

"The End of These Things."

Daniel, XII. 8. "*Then said I, Oh, my Lord, what shall be the end of these things?*"

We are brought in these days to the end of many things — the end of another year of learning and of teaching, the end of many intimate companionships and many personal relations, hopes and fears. One inevitable question presses at such times upon every thoughtful mind: What has it all amounted to? What has been gained? What is the outcome of it in permanent possessions and resources? While we were busy moving with the moving year the interest of details shut out the final view. Now the end tests the whole. We gather the fragmentary results of our work and our companionship together. We see the whole sweep of the life we have been leading and ask ourselves what there is left that will stay.

But this is not all. You, who are finding this time most completely an end are finding it still more completely a beginning. Your first thought may be what there is left of the years that are passed; your next or more anxious thought is what then is ready for the years that are waiting. That which seemed like an end turns out to be only a means to a larger end. That which looked like a climax in life becomes only a fresh starting point. The experiences and conflicts which appeared so much like real warfare now seem more like preparatory drill and skirmishes and the battle of life still waits. Thus the fragment of life you have lived here takes its place in the whole of life. You are lifted out of an absorbing relation with one part of life and consider its whole sweep and purpose. A new end announces itself and you ask yourself what it shall be. Ask yourself — do I say? Nay, I believe that in these days many of you are turning from your own ignorance to a better wisdom, and are laying before your God all the tendencies, pursuits, acquisitions and neglects of these years and are asking of him — it may be with an unspoken prayer — "Oh my Lord, what shall be the end of these things?"

Now what does this mood in which you find yourselves to-day really mean? What does it mean—this repeated reference of the parts of life to the end of life and then the transfer of each end as it is reached into a means to a larger end? What does it mean—this repeated broadening of the horizon of one's purposes as though one climbed what seemed a summit and saw on the one hand a larger world about him, and on the other hand a higher summit above? I ask you to see that it means a great deal. In the first place it is the secret of all sagacious, large, effective living. I suppose the very nature of a small life is its momentary fragmentary nature, its finding in piecemeal work a sufficient unity, its getting so bent down over one part of life that it cannot look up and see the breadth and beauty of the whole; and I suppose the very essence of a large life lies in this — that it is not overborne by details or absorbed in fragmentary interests, but that the scattered facts and materials of its experience take their place in the orderly structure of a permanent plan. Who is the small man of science? It is he to whom the acquisition of facts is everything and the meaning of facts is nothing; he to whom fragments of knowledge are sufficient and co-ordinated knowledge is a stranger. Such a man may be a learned man but he remains a small man. He is forever arranging his materials and collecting his specimens but he is in reality drying, pressing and labelling his own life among the rest. And who is the great naturalist? It is he who perceives in the slightest incidents of his pursuit not merely what they are but what they point to. Each aspect of Nature, however microscopic in itself, is eloquent with suggestions, each part ministers to the theory of the whole; each apparent accident reports the method of a general law. Such a student stands before the apparently trivial phenomena of the fertilization of a flower or the work of an earth-worm and inquires of them, like a Prophet of Israel: — What shall be the end of these things? Who is the small man of business? It is he for whom the immediate results of business are the complete results; for whom it is enough to gain and to thrive from day to day without much thought of what gaining and thriving are. Such a man is forever getting the means to live instead of living; and so it comes to pass that instead of a career broadening with his enlarging means he finds himself more and more shut in by narrowing and converging walk. He is like a fish swimming unconsciously into the labyrinth of a weir. The net-work of his occupation hems him in closer and closer, until even in the element where he thinks himself most free he is held a prisoner and the possessions which he thought he had got turn out to have got him. And who is the wise man of affairs? It is he who in the midst of details remains aware of the purpose which details should serve; who in the midst of his getting gets, as the Scripture says, understanding; for whom the parts of life minister to the whole of life. Such a man comes to the end of his work and there is something there. He has not buried all his resources of content in the tomb of professional eminence. The work of his life contributes to the larger needs of his life. He anticipates old age and provides for himself resources which will not then fail. He observes the drift of his vocation and corrects it by refreshing avocations. From the beginning he sees the end.

Here, then, is the most serious question one can ask himself when he faces the choice of a vocation. Is it likely, on the whole and in its general sweep, to enlarge life or to stunt it? Do its lines converge to narrowness or open into breadth? Is it to be a constant addition of permanent resources or a slow impoverishing of the soul? This is not a question of the vocation alone; it is a question of the man in relation to the vocation. It is the question which a crew on the river has to ask itself — a question of putting what weight one has on the precise point where it will most tell; of sparing wasted force and saving some strength to finish with. Many a pursuit looks insignificant at the outset, but grows great as a man puts his weight into it and settles — so to speak — to its stroke; and, after all, it is not the start but the finish which counts. And if anything ought to lead a man into a wise answer to this question I think it should be the experience of his college life. Many a man, I believe, if he were asked to sum up what he had gained among us here would be forced to confess that his permanent acquisitions had been very few. He would look back with equal amazement at the amount he used to know and the promptness with which he had forgotten it, at his capacity of accumulating information for a pressing emergency and his still more marvellous capacity of shedding it all when the emergency was past. But one thing, I think he would say, remained a permanent possession, — a certain demand upon life for resources beyond bare bread winning, and interest bred of discipline here in things which seemed to a large part of the world the merest rubbish, but which had given glow and color to his whole life, a sympathy for books, or research, or affairs and persons of intelligence, which had given meaning and use to his prosperity and soothed the sting of his reverses. He has had to work as hard as any man, he has been distanced by many; but the end of the work has not been wholly hidden from him. He has watched many another life starting, like a well-built vessel, on an apparently prosperous voyage. Swiftly she sails and quickly she arrives; yet when she draws up to the foreign dock and the hold is thrown open the voyage turns out to be a failure. For the hold is empty. It was all equipment and no result, all means and no end. Everything had been remembered except the cargo. No wonder that the fully-freighted vessel lagged behind.

What shall be the end of these things? I have spoken to you thus far as if this was no more than the question of worldly wisdom and prudent calculation; and it is the question of wisdom and prudence, — but it is much more than this. This view of life as given to use, as tested by its end, as strung with all its beads of many-colored circumstance upon one thread of a permanent design, — this is not only the wise, sagacious, effective view of life, it is in reality nothing less than the religious view, and it is wise and sagacious because it is religious. The view of Religion is precisely distinguished from all other views, either of the world without or of the life within, by this faith in a final Purpose linking the whole into a coherent unity. Religion sees in the outward Universe, not a chaos of straying atoms, but the Kosmos of an immanent God. Through the mechanism of physical phenomena runs one spiritual Purpose, through their apparent accidents are fulfilled the perfect laws of God. Religion sees the same thing in the inward life. The petty circumstances, the besetting details, the drudgery and trials of each human lot, — these are the interworking atoms through which each mikrokosm finds its life and motion. Looked at apart, each may seem the most blind and purposeless of forces. A section cut through a life at any one point may be as meaningless as the combinations of a kaleidoscope. Yet, beneath these atomic agitations, working in and through them, is the underlying, permanent immanent life of God. It takes up our purposes into its larger Purpose. It has a plan for each life and the wisdom of each life lies in discovering that plan. It is the life of God in us which is forever striving toward a plan, inquiring for the permanent, crying out for the end of things. If it were not for this indwelling, beckoning Purpose, true wisdom would be to live with as little fore-thought and anxiety as one could. Let us eat and drink, for to-morrow we die. If, on the other hand, it is true that a man's life is given to him to use, is a trust from God, then the way of wisdom becomes simply the way of obedience, and fragmentary, purposeless living becomes not merely practically foolish but religiously disloyal. Thus the view of Religion is simply this: My life is not my own. It has its part in a plan which holds its purposes, as the plan of a commander holds the faithfulness of each private in the ranks. If my body were my own, I might abuse it or defile it. But it is not my own. "Know ye not that ye are the temple of God? If any man defile the temple of God him shall God destroy. For the temple of God is holy, which temple ye are." If my daily work were my own I might well grow conceited in its success or despondent in its failure. But it is not my own. It is a much larger work than my own, a work in which my failures and my successes alike count for just what they are worth. If my joys and trials were for me to shape and for me to interpret, what a muddle my life would seem to be! But they are not all my own. Their disconnected incompleteness finds its meaning in a larger plan. Just as, in the life of nature about us each part ministers to the whole, and in the sequence of the seasons each in its turn serves its successor, so the successive experiences of life are taken up into the service of God's perfect purpose. One law controls the days of June and the days of January; one life invites the sap to climb and climb — the sap knows not why; — draws out the leaves to bud and spread — the leaves know not why; — touches them with frost and makes them tremble and fall — they know not why. One plan holds me with all the universe about me. Springtime and autumn are both alike its servants. Whether the leaves give shade above or enrich the earth below, they are still fulfilling their predestined part, and renewing the beauty and order of the whole.

I think you must see what a change and lift and transfiguration such a thought as this gives to the whole of life. The view of common sense and the view of Religion turn out to be one view. That which we have talked of as the part of wisdom becomes nothing less than loyalty to the life of God. Instead of saying that we are environed by a net-work of circumstances, we say, as we have sung to-day, that

> "Through the ceaseless web we trace
> His presence working all things well."

The very thought of a unity and plan in life reveals the whole of life as held in a larger unity, every man's life a plan of God, and underneath all life the everlasting arms.

And now turn back from these heights of contemplation to the common level of daily life and see what follows when we look at the whole sweep of life in this larger way. If life is wise so far as it is held to a definite purpose from end to end, and if, once more, this permanence of purpose is to be found only in the line of God's will, consider what this implies. It gives—does it not?—a wholly new meaning to the problems and decisions which beset us on any given day. They are to be estimated, not by what they seem, but by the course they indicate. Two ships sail side by side out of Boston Bay. No variation in their course or speed appears. Side by side they sink below the horizon. But—

> "When fell the night up sprung the breeze
> And all the darkling hours they plied,
> Nor dreamt but each the self-same seas
> By each was cleaving side by side."

Slowly, imperceptibly, their paths from day to day diverge, and when the one is beating up the Irish Channel, the other is yielding to the gentle current that sweeps her into the Mediterranean. Two lives may begin their voyage with this same parallelism and likeness here to-day. No human eye can see why they should not come side by side at the same moment to the same port; but it may be that at the end a continent shall divide them. It is not a question of to-day's course but of permanent tendency. Slowly may fulfil itself the most sad and solemn of human spectacles. The paths which seem one may divide. The wavering rudder, the divergent purpose, forces souls asunder whether they desire it or not; and while the one is still fighting its way against the whole sweep of God's commands the other is borne along upon the favoring current of His purpose. Thus day by day the course presages the port; and the most earnest cry that can be sent from one soul to another across the sea of life is the cry: Whither bound? Whither bound with all the sails of inclination set? It is an easy thing to shift the course; it is impossible to transform the end.

One word more. Here is not only the secret of wise undertakings and effective lives; it is, no less truly, the consolation of those whose mission it may be to bear and to wait. To some of you it will be given to reach all the results you can desire and to accomplish more than you now dream. Then, looking back, I believe you will say that it was the steady purpose, the unremitting loyalty, the vision of a worthy end from the very beginning, which led you on. But from some of you will be withheld the purpose to which you now impetuously turn. You will be immersed in drudgery or beset by lack of strength. The ideals of usefulness which are so bright to-day will seem dim and far away to you and your life will seem no more worthy of being called a plan of God. But this is the crowning wonder of God's Providences — that they fulfil themselves alike through apparent failures and through apparent successes. One life does its best and finds prosperity and reward; but the Christ does his best and finds — the Cross. Who can say where your victory may lie? Who can be sure that it is not the lesson of patient waiting, of large principles amid small duties — yes, and of giving up that which seemed the one thing worth your doing — which the world is waiting for you to teach? The accomplishing of one's own ends—that is the secret of human wisdom; the bringing of one's own ends into obedience to the will of God — that is the secret of eternal life and peace.

Fellow-students of the Graduating Class, I invite you to this large view of life. The University sends you into the world trained for usefulness and service, and each step you take counts for her honor or her hurt. She prophecies no soft things for you. She expects you to endure hardness, as good soldiers of a worthy cause. But think what it might be, for her and for yourselves and for the world, if a body of men like you could look together to-day through the whole range of life and distinguish in it the ends that are permanent from the ends that pass away. Think what might happen if you should commit yourselves together to a wise, large plan of life, and then think of the new power which would be added to you if you could see in this wise purpose of your own a plan of God for you and could translate your own self-discipline into loyalty to Him. Think what might come to pass if you could even now hear the voice of God saying to you: " Whom shall I send and who will go for us?" and could answer: " Lord, here am I: send me. My meat is to do the will of Him that sends me, and to finish the work which is given me to do."

Class Day Exercises,

June 23, 1882.

ORDER OF EXERCISES.

Music.

Prayer.
By REV. CHAS. C. EVERETT, D.D.

Oration.
By SHERMAN HOAR,
OF CONCORD.

Music.

Poem.
By JOHN McGAW FOSTER,
OF BANGOR, ME.

Ivy Oration.
By GEORGE LYMAN KITTREDGE,
OF ROXBURY.

Ode.
By FRANK EDWARD FULLER,
OF WEST NEWTON.

Class Day Oration.

BY SHERMAN HOAR.

CLASSMATES AND FRIENDS. — The class of '82 has gathered here to-day to say farewell to the college it has loved. No account of their indebtedness would appear adequate to those about to leave this place. Instruction and pleasure have here been mingled for our benefit. Doors have been opened through which we have caught glimpses of the garden where grow the tree of knowledge and the tree of life. A life spent in honoring such an *Alma Mater* would bring honor upon itself; but for most of Harvard's graduates keeping her fame unsullied is the only possibility. It should be our endeavor to keep the credit side of the account as large as possible.

To all who have been graduated here the history of four years at Cambridge must be well known; for, like the different parts of a sonata, the stories of the classes are but variations on the same theme. The victories of the Nine and Crew, the strong record of our class in every branch of athletics, the honors won by our scholars, have all received our praise and admiration. Our class has seemed — to us at least — the best class.

It is said that young ladies always find the party just over the most pleasant of the season; and perhaps it is something of the same kind of praise which each graduating class receives on Class Day. We receive it to-day and to-morrow it passes to our successors. But if in the times to come our class shall have won esteem by a record illuminated by honorable names and stanch virtues, then its existence can be called a success.

Success, — the one thing for which all men strive and which creates in all alike a common hope and ambition. Go where you will, the successes of men attract your attention. Temples and monuments everywhere proclaim what has been well done on earth. For some Fame's temple contains no tablet; but the progress of the world is a continual memorial to their good work.

When I think of the time needed to gain success, the early death of some once with us seems to me doubly sad. Some whom we have known as friends are not with us to-day. They passed away from earth before success or failure could be predicted for them. Their power for good or evil in this world had never been fully tested. When we consider the work done and the hopes raised, we may safely say that the struggles of life would have been entered upon manfully by them. But now they live on earth only in the sweet memories of their friends; their future is with God.

You, classmates, are about to enter this work and struggle for success. It is no easy undertaking which now confronts you; your future must always depend upon your past; and the builder, standing over his finished cellar walls, has hardly less control on the form of the superstructure, than have you over the life to come. Ornaments and embellishments you may add, but certain forms alone can rise over the foundations laid. Life can be but a succession of stories, the one built upon the other, and each taking its general characteristics from the last. A master mind was needed to place the Gothic on the Roman in those temples of the Middle Ages; a master soul alone can build truth upon falsehood, knowledge upon ignorance.

But, since this is a day of gladness, our past sorrows and failures are not perhaps the best themes on which to dwell. Looking forward is always more pleasant than looking behind. Let us, then, see what paths in life we may take that our strength of body and of mind may bring about the best results.

Burke said "The great men of a nation are the milestones of its progress." But they serve another purpose which makes them still more valuable to us,—they indicate the way chosen as well as the progress made. Study then the great men of the world that you may enjoy their influence upon your lives; study them, because the history of the world teaches you that it is good to do it; study them, because other people have done so before you and have prospered. Look at the Spartans admiring and copying the sternness of their king; look at those early Christians worshipping and trying to imitate the gentleness of their Saviour. Triumphs in peace and in war, in conquering and in yielding, have each in turn held as by fascination the whole world.

Great men are not simply to be admired. They are given to us to study and appreciate, and there is but one rule which will help you in your examination of them. Decide whether they help or hinder you; decide whether for you they point forward or backward. If they point forward, follow them, as did those shepherds that Bethlehem star. If they point backward, let them stay and turn to pillars before their own Sodom and Gomorrah. Mr. Lowell gives us the one question to be asked about a man's character. "Ask," he says, "what is the amount of this man's honest performance in the world." This is the question to ask; and, if you receive a true answer to it it will be of value to you through your whole life.

You, classmates, are Americans, and for you American examples are the best. In the history of your own country guiding characters are by no means wanting. A nation which in one year celebrates a victory by Washington and a financial success by Hamilton; a country which comes from the grave of Garfield to commemorate the birthday of Daniel Webster, — such a people need not seek far from home to find the pure gold of example. But do not expect to find absolute purity in great men, for there must be some alloy in all characters from nature's mint. If, as we grow older, our faith in certain fictitious virtues of Washington becomes less, admiration for the real excellences of the man becomes greater. If the end of Hamilton's life was in a cloud, the darkness did not extend beyond that one point; and it may be comforting for us to think that with this darkness the light went out forever, leaving no shadow to mingle in its brightness. To my mind Webster failed at last; but "I still live" was truly spoken by him, for his influence on the unity of this nation can never die.

Am I able to bring before you only statesmen? Is the public service the only one in which reputations have been made? Certainly not. Are you to be doctors? — you have your Bigelow and Jackson. Are you to be scientists? — you have your Franklin and Agassiz. Are you to be scholars? — do not forget your Prescott and Emerson. There is no business or profession that has not produced men of lasting fame.

It has been your good fortune to belong to a generation that venerates such men. To praise whatever is good and noble has become traditional with the American people. You have passed through your four years at college that you might learn of the best men their best thoughts. You have gained but little if you have learned only so much Latin or so much Greek; but if the books read and experiences undergone have given you powers to appreciate the measures and men you must meet in life, then you have indeed won a pearl without price.

Unfortunately there is a growing sentiment in this nation that book learning produces nothing lasting. Its origin is in the American desire to trace all greatness to humble beginnings. Those that have this feeling claim that no great change in society was ever started by such as had for constant companions refinement and education. They point to Webster, who as a boy at his father's inn, used to read the Psalms to those New Hampshire teamsters. They point to Garfield, walking along the tow-path of that canal and little dreaming of the high destiny that was to be his. "Surely," they say, "from such spheres in life comes the stuff of which great men are made!" To such minds our country owed its very existence to men who had but limited advantages for becoming educated; and freedom for the slave would never have been gained (according to them) had not the people demanded it.

This catalogue of falsehoods is too long for me to repeat. If the principles on which it is based were true, our mouths were safer closed, for education would have little honorable to point to as its results. But these principles are not true, neither are the examples quoted just and fair. Sometimes it has been the common people who have appealed to a higher law than that of their masters, but never until their masters sank beneath them in all that constitutes men. Such was the cry of those French revolutionists against a class that had sunk so low that even the horrors of '93 could not arouse them. When leaders are so debased, human nature must assert itself, and the common people become uncommon as they are forced to think and act for themselves. Such occasions are, however, rare; and it is the influence of educated men which gives the motive power to all great reforms. The people of Europe had not thought of purifying the Roman church till Martin Luther stirred them. He educated them until they saw the evils known to him long before.

But why seek in foreign lands for instances to disprove a theory so thoroughly refuted in our own times. If it was the American people who first overcame British aggression, if it was the farmers and mechanics who first founded this country, it was due to the exertions of such men as John Adams, James Madison, and Alexander Hamilton that this country lasted more than one decade. The people did desire liberty; but they soon forgot that all liberty must be based upon law; and that constitutional convention which met and decided that there was to be a republic in this western hemisphere, decided as it did because of the exertions of educated men. Do you suppose that if John Quincy Adams and his successors, Sumner and Wilson, had not used their exertions for the suppression of slavery, the people would ever have demanded its abolishment out of their own sense of right and justice?

The examples I have quoted are from a history full of instances of such work by educated men. The strength of the action may lie with the people, but the brains that guide and formulate must be finely cast and well trained.

Let us look at the very men quoted as examples of greatness despite their humble early life. In all but a few cases their native powers were made available for the world's good by the training and discipline of an American education. Webster may have gained his strength from the hills, but the power to apply it he won at a New England college. There was no vulgarity in Garfield's life at home. His college life was but a higher continuation of the training begun at home. A distinguished citizen whatever his origin; and such, not because his estate was humble, but because in education he saw the true path to the usefulness and assistance that was to be required of him.

It is not strange that some men, who have never enjoyed the benefits of education, should delight in the fact that some men have succeeded even without its influences. A few men like Abraham Lincoln and old John Brown of Ossawatomie show that nature alone is often strong. But when men who owe their position in the world to education and its fruits, when such men exert the very power conferred by it to undermine its foundations, then we should stop and think to what lengths their advice may lead us.

One who in this cool north kindled a fire that consumed slavery; one whose name is almost a synonyme for reform,—that man fails to recognize the source of his own great powers when he declaims against the books from which he draws his most beautiful illustrations. He says that "New England learned more of toleration from Sumner, Emerson, George William Curtis, and Edwin Whipple refusing to speak in a hall unless a negro could pass into it as freely as another, than she could from all the treatises on free-thinking from Milton or Aristotle, from Locke down to Stuart Mill." Was it not their appreciative attention to these best masters and their thought that gave Emerson and Sumner, in common with this very man, such powers for good. Some men, like Robert Burns, have a native sense of justice which no amount of book-learning could make stronger. Such men can come forward and claim for nature that when her powers are strong they shall be placed high in the scale of human qualities; all men have a right to say that education without action is as nothing; and he is but poorly educated who has not been taught to act; but when a man, standing before an ordinary audience, declaims against education and its fruits, it is wholly and entirely wrong; for his power of evil goes farther than he knows, and those who need the education he derides are often turned away from its benefits by the influence of his words.

The people of France had the same love of liberty as our fathers; but in '93 no culture was allowed to stand before the ravages of that populace. Education was treated as a laughing-stock. The people kindled that fire. That it did not consume more than it did, that its fumes did not poison other lands, was due to the exertions of men like Pitt and Burke, Stein and Hardenberg. They reverenced the educational privileges which had been theirs. Religion, property, and education were thrown away as mere ornaments by those French insurgents: that our fathers kept them as sacred, accounts for much of our present happiness and prosperity.

Our forefathers came to this country looking for liberty—liberty in religious and political action; but one of their first acts was to unite liberty and education. This college of ours was the first born of that union. Our fathers sought for liberty in political action, but they soon found that was impossible as long as the people were not educated to exercise the right of suffrage properly. They desired liberty in religious action; but they found it impossible as long as the people, into whose ears the gospel was to flow, were not ready to receive and appreciate it. Religion, liberty, and education,—this the trinity our fathers sought here to establish; these the idols before whose shrines we all should worship. Treat with consideration those less favored than you, but guard as a part of your birthright the education you have enjoyed.

To-morrow, classmates, you will enter the world as educated men; if you are not such, still the world will receive and judge you as such. Show then to the world that you will act as educated men; show to the world that you will honor education and educated men; show it that you will denounce with all your powers those who would degrade educational influences. If you do this—if you follow the precepts received here at Harvard—if you live true and noble lives—then the world will honor you while you are here and will miss you when you have passed away.

Class Day Poem.

By John McGaw Foster.

An Orient garden, bright with flowers, springing
    In summer freshness all the changing time ;
A tropic breath across its bosom, bringing
    New life and beauty from a kinder clime.
Rich lawns that sweep to southward, groups of shade
And many an arbor, many a silent glade.

A garden filled with richest fruitage, lading
    Low arching bowers, gently bending trees ;
Fountains whose waters fill with life unfading
    The velvet lawns and verdant waving leas :
Fields ripe for harvest, fruitful pasture land,
And landscape glimpses spread on either hand.

This is our Harvard—here our happy dwelling,
    Four sunny years these summer skies beneath ;
Four happy years the buds of springtime swelling
    To fullest splendor for the summer's wreath,
Have charmed our senses with their fragrance sweet,
And cast their Autumn fruits before our feet.

Now, as we linger ere the word is spoken
    That calls us forth to fairer, larger fields ;
To pledge our faith, fain would we weave as token
    The rarest garland that our garden yields.
Strip of its choicest fruit each loaded vine,
And lay our wreath, Fair Harvard, at thy shrine.

If all the great deeds that have ever been shown
On this round earth of ours since was cast the first stone
O'er the head of Deucalion which, fable relates,
Renewed our lost race, or since first from the gates

Of Eden our parents were sent with a curse—
If all these great doings were sung of in verse,
Greek dactyls or English with syllables ten,
What a wonderful epic we'd have to read then!
The heroes who struggled so long about Troy
Were eclipsed long ago by one Patrick Maloy;
And descents to Avernus can't hold up a bit
To the tale of those Freshmen who went to the pit
—Of the theatre—the Globe—on one mem'rable night
(See old Heralds or Globes if you want for more light)
And banquets ambrosial — three dollars a plate,
Or sometimes but one—but I anticipate—
I only will say 'tis enough to make clear
How it happens to be that our college life here
Is a great epic poem — and how, if you want to,
You can call each division a separate canto;
And as the prim ancients were wonted to choose
For their subject of singing some goddess or muse,
And sang to Euterpe or Clio, so we
May choose some fair guardian to smile on our glee;
As we've no modern muses to whom we may sing,
In default of a better aërial thing,
And as our own nation an eagle has taken
As a sort of a sprite its fond harp to awaken,
This worthy example we've rather preferred,
And taken as muse some respectable bird?

Canto one — Called the Freshman — so simple — so sweet;
The lines limp along in slow, faltering feet;
Beginning so softly — alas for the bard —
With crashing crescendo the ending is *hard*.
And its guardian angel — oh! what is the use
Of naming the bird — you all know it's a goose!

Canto second is opened with much of an air,
And a spice of its own that is hard to compare —
A little in fact of about everything.
Its lines move along with a vast deal of swing;
And in full blaze of splendor, with feathers outspread
Its guardian peacock keeps watch o'er its head.

Canto three, or the Junior, is solemn and slow ;
In dignified measure the syllables go,
Yet by no means unmixed with a fresh air of ease
A kind of that blest *savoir faire*, if you please,
That says "Well we know that our guardian fowl
Is nothing less solemn or wise than an owl."

Canto four — 'tis the Senior, sad, sombre, subdued,
To be sung to slow music in dignified mood,
Maestoso adagio non viva mente;
Of dignity some — of indifference plenty,
And through these slow verses our steps to conduct
We'll take — well, a chicken — that's easily plucked.

Thus in varying measure, my classmates, we tell
Our tale of these years, in fond accents that swell
With loving regret as we fain would prolong
In lingering fervor the strains of our song ;
To tell with glad voice of the labor we've done
And shout to the glory of victories won —
Of the memories bright that shall render us true
To our Harvard for aye, and our own Eighty-two !
    Yet in the joyous chorus that we raise
Exultant in our happy college days,
Some voices that have joined ours oft before
In that glad paean echo never more ;
Till strong hearts falter, and the passioned cry
Of loss and pain is breathed, and borne on high.

When fresh the morning scatters o'er the earth
    Its brilliant gems with golden lustre gleaming,
When heart and limb, strong in their newer birth
    Press nobly on — and, o'er the fancy streaming,
Glad hopes point up to Honor's shining crest,
The heart throbs strong response — what care we then for
    rest ?

O, brothers, taken from our side before
    Our road's beginning we had walked together ;
Ere yet dark rain-clouds gathered lowering o'er,

Or future's sunlight gloomed in stormy weather —
Borne from the untried toil to glad release,
We at our labor still — you in eternal peace.

He who first gave you to us knoweth best —
  His all-wise love hath judged on whom the burden
Must even now a little longer rest —
  And whose life-toil has won the victor's guerdon ; —
And while the parting pains, yet in accord
We bless the hand that gives the worthy their reward.

In ancient times with moss o'ergrown,
Ere yet to mortal hearts were known
The mystic syllables which tell
Of all those things we love so well,
Whose mem'ries thrill us through and through
Whene'er we shout for Eighty-two :
Before the swelling cheer had rung
To greet that name, from many a tongue,
Those tongues that shout to-day, then bound
In childish faltering, lisped the sound
Not full and strong as e'en to-day,
But in a trembling, hoping way.
  But now for four full years we've known
Those cherished numbers as our own ;
In loving harmony those years
We've raised that name in all our cheers,
Since first when as a harmless mass
Of human things, we formed our class,
Till now, when, like a well scrubbed shoe,
We show the *polish* of Eighty-two !
We went our several quiet ways,
That band of us, those early days —
Those ways that led, I don't know where,
To College House, perhaps, or Thayer,
Whose tomb has many a Freshman held
Who couldn't get in Grays or Weld.
And all these devious by-ways centred
From the very day on which we entered
In number thirteen or three or five

(From which none hoped to come alive).
Or fragrant rooms in Boylston Hall
Where weird enchantment made us crawl,
Or where with voices fair and fresh
We raised the chorus βρεκεκεχ.
Then lectures were not voluntary
And many a luckless wight unwary
Got two and thirty marks of censure
As penalty for some bold venture;
Or else was summoned unawares
For coming in too late to prayers.
 But as we went to take our places
As brave contestants in the races
On Jarvis Field, that Freshman fall,
We showed such prowess in them all,
'Twas said there never came to pass
Such promise in a Freshman class,
And other strugglers in the field
To Eighty-two the palm must yield.
Say you we've lost this reputation?
I pray you take consideration:
In every contest, every race
Brute force must e'er succumb to grace;
And, in the latest winter's meet,
Our class by no means strove to beat
In things disgraceful, harsh and grating,
But took to contests elevating —
Deeds airy, light and not nerve-jarring,
Club-swinging, fencing, light-weight sparring!
 But more of this anon — 'tis here
Our place to sing of Freshman year.
There ne'er was Freshman class as yet
A more refined example set.
When 'twas proposed that, just for fun,
We do the same as Eighty-one
And have a punch, upon the score
'T would gratify the Sophomore,
We said, "Ye tempters all begone;
A Freshman punch we do but scorn;

But then perhaps 't will not be wrong,
To help good fellowship along,
By giving, if we will be good,
To a little play — 'Babes in the Wood.'
We must be quiet while we're gay,
And not steal signs along the way."

With such a stirring and commotion
We first were launched on Harvard's ocean.
We came in an auspicious day,
To see our College walk away
With all the honors won from Yale,
And if our lot has been to fail
In later strife for these — why then
We've naught to do but start again.
I pause — I see the anxious crowd —
I hear the cheers that echo loud
Across the Thames's silver breast.
"Let every man pull for his best!"
I see the flush that crimsons o'er
The cheek of beauty—and, what's more,
The netted lashes droop so far
Over the bright eye's radiant star
They shut out every trace of *blue*,
Till when, to greet *our* winning crew,
In glad response they open wide,
And speak their joy in Harvard's pride.
I cast my gladdened glance on high,
Where, fair beneath the summer sky,
The Crimson waving o'er the Blue,
Adds new renown to Eighty-two!

May this our pleasant prophesy
Meet its fulfilment perfectly!
But prophesy comes not alone
To bear us glory, for we own
A record so with glory fraught,
Of future's hopes the need we've naught.
Twice has the cheer that sounded far
To greet each winning college tar,
Who pulled along the winning crew,

Borne the refrain of "Eighty-two."
Oh! memories of the happy past,
That throng across our minds so fast,
The sunny visions that we dreamed,
The host of trials that have seemed
So dark at first — yet, like the shades
That swiftly flit o'er sunlit glades
Were but the darkenings here and there
To make the whole seem far more fair;
Have all these memories naught to show.
To guide our footsteps as we go
Through future's untried ways!
May not in coming days
Our hearts be girt and strengthened for a lifetime's
    grander frays?
Ah! Classmates, there's a destiny
Laid for us in eternity,
Leading through many a maze and storm.
A destiny we've helped to form
For one another while we've lingered here.
Each day, each changing year,
Marked how the grasp of friendship stronger grew
Each for his brother — all for Eighty-two —
Dear Eighty-two! the fervor that that name
Warms in our heart shall ever glow the same;
Ever the fondest memories awake
In joyous praise for Eighty-two's dear sake;
For we must say farewell — we who have passed
These happy college hours have known the last.
The lingering grasp of parting hopes that throng
For future's good, would fain the hours prolong;
But all are tokens, telling every one
Our college day — our happy day — is done!

  The day is done — the trailing shadows falling
      O'er eastward slopes, their slender length extend;
  The evening breezes bear the amorous calling
      Of feathered mates, and breeze and voices blend
  In one sweet burst of song that fades away
  In fitful faltering — and ceases with the day.

The happy day — whose morning rose to brighten
    With softened light the unattempted way
Where hearts beat full, and strong hopes came to lighten
    The easy load we bore — that summer day
Is passing — in its fading light we rest
And know not yet what hides within to-morrow's breast.

Perchance the rose that tints the western heaven
    Shall be the promise of a fairer dawn;
Perchance the glad foretelling of the even
    May be o'ershadowed by a sombre morn —
We hope and doubt, our spirits fear and pray
While with dimmed eyes we watch the passing of the day.

The shadows fade — the golden barriers vanish
    Slow, one by one, from yonder western sky;
A sombre veil falls o'er the land to banish
    The distant hill-tops from our following eye;
Classmates, our day is done, dusk falls the night—
But see! the star of promise, rising into splendor bright.

Ivy Oration.

BY GEORGE LYMAN KITTREDGE.

You will find my text in the 17th chapter of the Acts of the Apostles, verse 22: "Then Paul stood in the midst of Mars' Hill and said: Ye men of Athens, I perceive that in all things ye are too superstitous." Superstition, beloved, has been defined in many different ways, and manifested to the world in many different forms. Some learned Thebans have regarded as the extreme of superstition for a Freshman to believe that four years of solid application to the classics will enable him to read with any ease the Ciceronian inscription above my head; others declare the acme of superstition to be that form of idol-worship in which all Harvard bows down before the omnipotent janitor; and still others have maintained, with some show of reason, that nothing in this world can be more superstitious than to pull a man out of bed at the unheard-of hour of 8.30 A. M., no matter if the highest medical authorities of the State insist that it is death for him to get up before 10, — to drag him into chapel whether he feels devout or not, and to force him to look for ten minutes at a preacher he cannot hear, and to listen for five minutes to a choir he cannot see, wishing all the time the conditions were reversed so that he could hear the minister rather than see him, and see the choir rather than hear it. (Out of regard for your feelings, I say nothing of that agitated and agitating instrument in the loft, — that nameless something, which, if it could speak, and should speak truly, would squeak out the watchword of the New York Tribune in the Grant and Greeley campaign: "This is not an organ.")

The superstition, however, of which I am to speak is none of these. Dark and sombre it spread its shades over us when we were Freshmen in the cradle; it darkened our young lives, when, as Sophomores, we were learning to walk by the help of a cane;

it dimmed the lustre of all that perfect happiness which Class Day affords the Junior; and now, when gray and decrepit Seniors, we totter on the verge of the grave of alumniship, it casts its baleful shadow over our departing hours. I mean the unhappy superstition that good classes run by odd numbers, that *even* years are *off* years, that, because, like sensible men, we are divisible by 2, therefore we are inferior to '81, inferior to '83, inferior to '85, inferior to '87. I call upon you, classmates, in the name of common sense and justice, to stamp out this absurdity, to prove that the even classes are in no wise inferior to the odd.

"By their fruits ye shall know them: Do men gather grapes of thorns and figs of thistles?" Not in Cambridge. I do not ask you to believe my word when I talk of the greatness of '82. What was Harvard when we came here four years ago? If there is a man of '78 still living I call him to witness that I speak truth. Harvard was a howling wilderness. Cambridge supplied the wilderness, and an unhappy body shut up in an unventilated room in Boylston very near the Organic Laboratory, furnished the howling. We Freshmen used to hold our ears and set our teeth as we rounded the corner of Boylston. Once we asked a Junior what it was. He said, in Spenser's phrase, "It is 'the cursed river Phlegethon wherein the damnéd ghosts in torments fry.'" We asked a Senior. He said, "It is the Chapel Choir." Such was Harvard in '78, — a damp, dreary, desolate dungeon. No lamps smoked on the corners of the buildings, — all was darkness! no steam-radiators warmed the entries of Thayer and Middlesex, — all was cold; no brick paths and plank walks covered the quagmires of the quadrangle, — all was mud. The Library was not open on Sundays, recitations were involuntary, Sever Hall consisted of but two sticks to mark its foundation, the *Harvard Echo* had not yet begun to reverberate and to misprint. Our athletes still knocked their heads against the roof, and whanged their knuckles against the sides of the Old Gymnasium in the vain endeavor to find room according to their strength; the *Harvard Register* still slumbered in the brain of its royal projector; the Annex was just raising the feeble wail of doubtful infancy; the Co-operative Society and the Total Abstinence Alliance did not exist. This, then, was the melancholy state of Harvard when we came here. '78. — Enter '82. — Look you now what follows! First we said the Library must be open on Sundays. Other classes may be content to loaf away their Sabbath days, but not so we. What! shall we not have *one* day out of seven for study? So we appealed to the President, and he said he would see to it at once. So he referred the matter to the Library Council, and the Library Council deliberated, and the Library Council referred the matter to the Faculty, and the Faculty deliberated, and the Faculty referred the matter to the Corporation, and the Corporation deliberated, and the Corporation referred the matter to the President and Fellows, and the President and Fellows deliberated, and the President and Fellows referred the matter to the Board of Visitors, and the Board of Visitors deliberated, and the Board of Visitors referred the matter to the Librarian, and the Librarian deliberated, and the Librarian referred the matter to Mr. Kiernan, and Mr. Kiernan deliberated, and Mr. Kiernan referred the matter to the library-boys, and the library-boys deliberated, and the library-boys referred the matter to the Janitor, and the Janitor said he was willing if the President was, and the President said he was willing if the Janitor was; so the Library was opened on Sunday. All this took time, but in the mean time the O. K. generously threw open to the reading public the treasures of its well-stocked library, so that the demand for Sunday reading was in a great measure supplied.

Then Mr. Hemenway took council with himself. "What," said he, " is '82 in college, cabin'd, cribb'd, confin'd in that irregular octo-hepto-dodecagon, familiarly known as the Gas House? This must not be." And the Gymnasium rose as if by magic and took some of the cold look off the L. S. S. next door. Then the friends of higher education for women bethought them, "Oh! '82 has entered Harvard!" and at once the wilderness of the Annex began to blossom as the rose; its halls were crowded with students; and our instructors began to tell us, " If I don't get here till six minites past the hour I shall have to ask you to wait for me. I am occasionally detained." All this from '82. About this time we began to complain of the cold, and we besought the college, "Give us steam radiators in the entries or we perish!" And the powers that be heard our cry, and they said, " Soon we will give you steam pipes. In the mean time warm yourself at this, — and lo! THE HARVARD REGISTER." And it did keep us warm for a time. First a postal card,—"Will you subscribe?" Then a postal card, — " Won't you subscribe?" Then another, — " Do you know anybody that will subscribe, or anybody that won't? If not, why so; and if so, why not? Please answer and oblige. Busiris Rex, Harvard College." And thus they came till most of us hired a man to intercept Billy when he brought the mail and ask him. "Have you anything from the *Register or the Registrar?*" and if he had we never saw it. All this from '82.

One thing alone in the way of reforms even '82 has not accomplished. We haven't been able to get a ferry established between the Library and the inhabited portions of the Yard. The Class of '85 kindly offered the use of their shell for a ferry-boat, as they had no further use for it. But nothing satisfactory has yet been suggested.

To turn from these feats in the reformatory line to our other triumphs,—how they scoffed at us when we were Freshmen, called us lazy and said we never could do anything in athletics. I can't begin to tell you how we redeemed our Freshman laziness, how we showed on the river last year that we could beat '81 or anything else there was afloat, and that too under the most trying circumstances. We then demonstrated that broken slides and iron cushions had no adverse effect on the pluck of '82; and, classmates, I don't doubt that, if our shell had been swamped, our Crew would have swum over the course in time to win the race. As it was, we got there so much ahead of '81 that the latter wasn't visible, even per telescope, and the last heard of her was that she was being carried up the river by the tide, spite of the frantic efforts of her crack oarsmen; and this, friends, is the class that proclaimed last year, "We let '82 have the class races because we saw she couldn't get anything else."

Besides, '82 has the credit of turning her athletics to use in deeds of practical heroism. Who that saw it will ever forget the Wadsworth fire? When that old gray building, which has recently been treated to a fresh coat of shingles, and which may some time be treated to a fresh coat of paint, was in imminent danger of falling a prey to the greedy jaw of the relentless fire-fiend. Smoke issued from between those musty shingles, and already insidious tongues of ruddy flame were caressing the aged and careworn cheek of the venerable house with kisses whose touch is death. Far in the distance, roused by the discordant clang of the jangling bells, and the belligerent bellow of the Brighton bull, an ancient horse attached to an antediluvian watering-cart crawled rapidly along attended by three men, with two helmets between them, and one old coat in the crowd,—each man armed with an axe and a watering-pot. Their eyes flashed fire. The populace thronged to see them as they passed, calling out with accents of frenzied admiration, "The Cambridge Fire Department! The Cambridge Fire Department!" Meanwhile the Borsair was not idle. Rising superior to all fear, with a garden hose he scaled the perilous edge of the building and appeared on the roof in the midst of smoke and flame. He seized the hose and he began to pump. But there was no water. "Water, water!" shrieked the baffled hero, in the tones of despair. Then was the genius and the heroism of '82 displayed. While others stood aloof at Bartlett's, some shouting, some turning pale, some wondering why Wadsworth, innocent Wadsworth should be taken, and U. 5, where their prayer-cuts were recorded, should be left,—at this trying moment a head and a bucket appeared at a window of the burning edifice. The head was the head of an '82 man, the bucket, —alas! its name, like what song the Sirens sung, is gone forever. How they got there, who knows? Some think they gained the place by a leap; some assert that they flew; others, dull souls, conjecture that they went up by the staircase. At all events, there they were: and thus the head addressed the perspiring Borsair:—

"Thy orders, Borsair, gladly would we fill,
But not a dealer in all Cambridge has 'em;
I cannot give the water, but instead
Accept a little Fresh Pond protoplasm."

But why delay? The Borsair seized the bucket and emptied the protoplasm upon the raging flames. The fire-fiend quailed. Mere water he could stand; but Cambridge water, Fresh Pond water, was one too many for him, and with a shriek he departed. The Fire Department three hours after arrived, and proceeded to wet down the shrubbery in the front yard; then the hose broke and they adjourned to Adam's to talk it over. But Wadsworth was saved,—saved for future generations. Let him bear the palm who has deserved it; and that is the editor of the *Echo*, who shall be nameless.

Somewhere about the middle of the year many of us began to be scared at the aspect of our friends. Lean, hollow-eyed, haggard, famished, we feared to be alone with them, for we saw

"The longings of the cannibal arise
(Although they spoke not) in their wolfish eyes."

When we asked what ailed them, they always replied,—if not too weak to answer,—"I board at Memorial Hall." Of course this set '82 to thinking, and the Steward of the Castle was investigated, as well as his system of blood-money, or head-money, or whatever he calls it. We forced Mr. Frank Er to become franker in his dealings with us. I will not dwell on the subject. Suffice it to say that, since '82 took hold of the matter the cases of death have been reduced from fifty in the hundred to not more than ten.

With like determined resistance to oppression, we set ourselves against the Chinese Bill. President Arthur was vacillating; he waited for some clarion voice of public opinion. It came. Over the wires to Washington, over the telephone to the chamber of the Executive, flashed the news: "The English 6 section has decided adversely." Quickly followed another telegram: "The Harvard Union votes the Chinese Bill an outrage on human rights." No longer did the President hesitate. He seized a pen and wrote a message of veto (which, to be sure, he afterwards very gracefully took back). And who presided over the Harvard Union when it rendered this decision, so fraught with influence in the councils of a great nation? "Where,"—as a college paper once said.—"where in the roll-call of history shall he take his seat?" More than once has he raised his voice and brought down his gavel in the counsels of '82. More than once may he do it in assemblies more august (if that be possible). I shall not tell you his name. I shall only quote a familiar line of a familiar poem. Listen, for therein is mystery:—

"All things come out at last to them that *Wait*."

There is but one thing to regret. All the time the Union was deliberating there lay in the vaults of the senate-house a corpse, a fair young corpse, a gory-bleeding corpse, with an *I move* trembling on its pallid lips, and 37½ cents balance in its trousers pocket,—the corpse of the Harvard Legislature.

But let us turn to brighter themes. I have tried hard to get some trustworthy information for you about the college press. I have tackled the President of the *Crimson*; I have tackled the President of the *Advocate*. But they are both '83 men; and '83 men, as you know, though some of them are very good-looking, *will tell lies*. Baffled, I betook myself to the Great American Traveller, and bargained for three yards of his best heoric poetry, and here it is:—

The *Aberrate* and the *Crime's-own*
  Are papers wise and witty,
They're publish*èd* at Cambri-idge,
  Which some folks call a city.

They got so mad about Shakespere
  They poured out ink by gallons,
They hit each other with stuffed clubs,
  They *fit* with claws and talons.

But now the fight is over and
  The combatants are cooler;
Each owns that he was full himself,
  But surely *one* was *Fuller*.

  Who killed the *Lampoon?*
  "I," said the graduate,
  "I left him to his fate,
  "I killed the *Lampoon*."

  Who resurrected him?
  "We," answered '82.
  "Had nothing else to do;
  We resurrected him."

And everybody likes Lampy, even the Momus of the *Echo*. May he grow better and funnier (I mean *even* funnier) as he grows older, and may his fame spread all over Christendom, or, as the proverb has it, "through all Christendom, and Kent, too."

Now, Muse, let's sing the office. When we were young we looked at the sun, and said, what keeps it there? We gazed upon the moon, and said likewise. We meditated the stars, and each star inspired us with the same question. Then came a still, small voice, that whispered, "My children, it is very simple: it is the law of universal gravitation, which operates through space inversely in proportion to the square of the distance. They hold each other up." Then were we satisfied, and returned to our rattle and our tin-trumpet, to our rocking-horse and our A B C blocks, and wondered no more about the matter, for did we not know the secret of the universe? Universal gravitation, — they hold each other up. So, friends, when, infants of a larger growth, we have exchanged our A B C blocks for a Livy, our tin whistle for a Horace (Bohn's ed.), and our go-cart for a Wheeler's Trigonometry, then another wonder comes over us. We go forth into the Yard, we sit down under the beech-tree or upon the dark, mysterious, iron cover of the drain; we recline upon the steps of University, or we hang ourselves over the top of the pump, — we gaze, we ponder, we admire. What is it that supports the dignity of the office of *For the Registrar?* Who gives it the authority to summon us from our peaceful repose, to harrow our hearts as we sit at meat? Who is it who allows this mysterious being (or essence) to send round to us those innocent missives which look like postal cards, but are not. Who allows that essence to get us, all trembling, into the outer court of its den, and then, as we stand expecting nothing less than special probation, to ask us with much severity, "Why did you not dot your i's in your last petition"? What mystic chain supports him—the priest of the inner shrine — a word from whom means business, whose summonses are nothing if not matter of fact, to whom all things (including doctor's certificates) are tolerably evident? And what power — and our steps are slow as we approach the inmost adytum of the temple — keeps up the high-priest and guardian of our morals, whose voice is that of the muezzin, who cries (as he rings his bell by proxy), "To prayers, ye faithful. There is no God but Allah, and your cuts are all gone. To prayers! to prayers! You have exhausted your allowance, and Mahomet is his prophet!" As we learn and meditate these things, and wonder till our minds are dim and our souls are sick, comes gliding to our side a gentle figure with the mien of Demosthenes and the words of Cicero, but a hat, a coat, and an accent entirely and peculiarly his own. "Ask me not who I am," says the figure; " I am a man who has lost thousands of dollars by unprincipled men turned out bad; I am a man who counts his prose by the yard, his poetry by the square foot; I am a great man, though I have not money enough to buy the salt to put on an animalcule's eyeball. I can tell you the mystery which is wearing out your young life." "Speak, sage!" we cry, and he speaks. "Universal gravitation holds up the sun, my child, and the moon, and the countless hosts of little twinkling stars. So in the office. It is the same principle. They hold each other up. Only in the universe it is gravitation, in the office it is red tape. My son, can you lend me five cents?" And you give the sage his dole, and you get up next morning and find a summons waiting for you, and you receive it joyfully, and you say not. with Oscar Wilde. "Seek no more the secret of life, for the secret of life is art;" but you say, "Seek no more the secret of Harvard, for the secret of Harvard is red tape."

But all things must have an end,—even Ivy Orations. I should like to say to the scores of kind friends who have been suggesting things to me for the last three months as good jokes for the Ivy Oration, that I should like to use their contributions, but conscience forbids. I have tried most of these contributed witticisms on the lower animals, as experimenters try poisons, and they have been fatal in every case. The following jest, e. g., which *is a bona fide* '82 effort, and was really suggested to me by a man sitting over there in the first gallery, has been the death of more dogs and cats in Cambridge than would suffice the hydrophobia experiments of Pasteur for three months: The Freshman Class is the only bird which, as soon as it is hatched, proceeds to purchase a shell. This is the sort of thing I have been enduring for three months. I respectfully suggest to future classes a law for the relief and protection of distressed Ivy Orators.

But all this is over. We are going — going. Who can fill our places? We shall be missed (shall we) at prayers; we shall be missed on the river; we shall be missed in Sever; we shall be missed on the ball-field. They will miss us at Carl's, at Adam's, and at Memorial Hall, but nowhere will they so much miss us as at the Office. Even now, methinks, I hear a siren voice from the wreck-strewn shore of U. 5, singing sadly her farewell song, and the words, as it seems to me, are these: —

   Friends, Harvard would thrive
    Without '85,
  She would live some years more
    Without '84,
  Much better would be
    Without '83,
  But what *will* she do
    Without '82?

CLASS ODE.

I.

As a traveller discerns thro' the mist, far away,
    But the tempest-blown robes of the sea,
So to us who look forth from the shores of to-day
    Come brief glimpses of life-times to be.
Tho' the lips of the ages be dumb and the eyes
    Of the centuries blinded with tears,
Yet the hopes we now cherish forever shall rise —
    Distant beacons to shine thro' the years.

II.

And we linger to-day in this mid-arch of time
    And thro' infinite vistas behold
A light on the face of that future, sublime
    As some sea-morning's splendour of gold;
And we walk forth to meet it — ah! mother, again
    Ere we go, hear our reverent vow, —
Whatever befall, we must think of thee then
    With the same love we bear to thee now!

CLASS SONG. Concluded.

Harvard College.

Secretary's Report.

Class of 1882.

I.

July, 1882.

Wheeler, Printer, Brighton St., Cambridge.

CLASS COMMITTEE.

RUSSELL WHITMAN.
ARTHUR PRESCOTT LOTHROP.
FRANKLIN ARTHUR DAKIN.

Class Secretary.
ALFRED EUGENE MILES.

INTRODUCTION.

To the Class of 1882:

I have the honor to present to you my first report as your Secretary. In the preparation of it I have followed quite closely the reports of the last two years, making but one change of any importance. The first list of the class on pages 5, *et seq.* has formerly contained the names of those who were regular members of the class during Senior year. Formerly no list has been given of those who received degrees. In this report the first list is of those who received degrees. To this fact the double column entitled Class of 1882 in the statistics (probable occupation, etc.) is due. The first half of this column gives the statistics of those who were regular members of the class during the Senior year, the second the statistics of those who received degrees. Thus our class may be compared with preceding classes and also the statistics of our class, as composed of those who received degrees, may be examined. I imagine that eventually the statistics of graduating classes given by secretaries will be of those graduating, and with this idea in mind I have made the change. At any rate it seems to me that the report ought to contain a list of those who graduate.

For the errors I trust you will pardon me, remembering that in many cases the statistics here presented were obtained from men who from mere carelessness, totally ignored or for a long time neglected to answer my questions.

From the part entitled "Temporary Members" you will get an idea of what the triennial report will be, and I trust my requests for information will be more promptly granted than they have been. At any rate please keep me informed of your addresses, and if any of you can inform me of the addresses of those " not heard from," I shall be much obliged to you.

We shall entertain the graduating class next commencement at Holworthy, the room to be announced hereafter. Notices will be published in the Boston Advertiser, Post, and Transcript, and the more important ones in the New York Times.

With the best wishes for you all, I am

Your classmate,

ALFRED E. MILES.

CLASS OF 1882.

Alfred Marston Allen
Luther Stetson Anderson
Charles Walker Andrews
Andrew Preston Averill
James Woods Babcock
Robert Tillinghast Babson
Charles Franklin Bacon
James Hayward Bacon
Chambers Baird
Edward Wild Baker
Charles Adolphe Baldwin
Clarence Bancroft
George Francis Barlow
Joseph Henry Beale
†††John Remsen Bishop
†††William Allen Blair
James Williams Bowen
Alexander Boyd
Charles Edgar Boynton
Richards Merry Bradley
Charles Jerome Brown
John Sweeney Bryant
George Clifford Buell
John Eliot Bullard
William Henry Burnham
Charles Dean Burt
Frederick Russell Burton
Walter Nelson Bush
Godfrey Lowell Cabot

Henry Gardner Chapin
Heman Lincoln Chase
Walter Greenough Chase
Edwards Cheney
Joseph Payson Clark
Hazen Clement
John McGregor Cochrane
Robert Codman
Frank Nelson Cole
Arthur Messinger Comey
Frank Gaylord Cook
Joseph Austin Coolidge
Charles Townsend Copeland
Frank Leonard Creesy
Morton Stimson Crehore
Montgomery Adams Crockett
Robert Cumming
Henry Winchester Cunningham
William de Lancey Cunningham
Charles Francis Cutler
Ralph Pomeroy Dabney
Franklin Arthur Dakin
William Henry Danforth
Wendell Phillips Davis
Clarence Randall Dean
Richard Delaney
†George Washington Dickerman
Charles Denston Dickey
George Bradford Dunbar

† Joined the Class Sophomore Year. †† Joined the Class Junior Year.
††† Joined the Class Senior Year.

William Harrison Dunbar
George Herbert Eaton
Charles Eliot
†††Albert Danner Elliot
William Gordon Fellows
Frederic Atherton Fernald
Burton Monroe Firman
William Boyd Fiske
Joshua Gardner Flagg
John McGaw Foster
George Hills Francis
Harry Cormerais French
Frank Edward Fuller
Homer Gage
Joseph Peabody Gardner
†††David Claiborne Garrett
John Gillespie
Henry Hale Gilman
Frederick Norton Goddard
Charles Henry Goldthwaite
Xanthus Henry Goodnough
Lysson Gordon
James Jay Greenough
Asaph Hall
Frederick Stanley Hall
Henry Winthrop Hardon
Henry Williams Harlow
George Trumbull Hartshorn
Frank Spangler Haupt
William Hale Herrick
Frank Everett Heywood
Sherman Hoar
James Hughes Hopkins
Albert Andrew Howard
Henry Reese Hoyt
Harry Mascarene Hubbard
Frederick Thayer Hunt
Charles Green Rockwood Jennings
William Jones
Charles Hallam Keep
William Winthrop Kent
Albert Benjamin Kingsbury
Benjamin Rufus Kittredge
George Lyman Kittredge
Charles Francis Swift Knowles
Albert French Lane

Heyward Gibbons Leavitt
Arthur Prescott Lothrop
Robert Luce
†††Thomas William Ludlow
John Plumer Lyons
Arthur Fred McArthur
†Walter Irving McCoy
Edward Valentine McDonald
†††Richard Hayes McDonald
William Henry McKendry
William Thomas McKone
William Hobbs Manning
Charles Frank Mason
John Whiting Mason
George Lowell Mayberry
Edward Percival Merritt
Alfred Eugene Miles
Sam Henry Morrill
Garrett Edward Nagle
Oliver Allen Olmsted
Henry Thomas Oxnard
†††William Enoch Page
Robert Treat Paine
Ivan Nikolayevitsh Panin
Elliott Hunt Pendleton
Edmund Sehon Perin
††George William Perkins
John Walter Perkins
†Ernest Perrin
McLaurin Jameson Pickering
Whipple Nahum Potter
John Preston
William Lowell Putnam
Frederic William Rhinelander
Charles Moen Rice
George Morey Richardson
Herbert Augustus Richardson
Lucien Moore Robinson
†††William Armstrong Rogers
William Joseph Rushmore
John Russell
Harold Marsh Sewall
Henry Hamilton Sherwood
Horace Emmet Smith
Charles Armstrong Snow
George Frederick Spalding

Charles Herbert Stevens
Edward Knights Stevens
Frederic Mather Stone
William Enos Stone
John Humphreys Storer
Thomas Chandler Thacher
Roland Thaxter
George Warren Towne
Stephen Van Rensselaer Townsend
Gustavus Tuckerman
Edward Livingston Underwood
William Cushing Wait
Guy Waring
Henry Eldridge Warner

Frederic Warren
Frederic Leonard Washburn
Philip Moen Washburn
John Sydney Webb
Evert Jansen Wendell
Elmer Ellsworth Wentworth
†††Isaac Spalding Whiting
Russell Whitman
Samuel Williston
Owen Wister
Frederick Clinton Woodbury
Herbert Grafton Woodworth
Joseph Ruggles Worcester

— 177

An asterisk (*) is used to denote deceased members.

Herbert Austin[1]
Charles Sidney Averill[1]
René Bache[1]
Charles Hammatt Bartlett[2]
George Edwin Bachelder[2]
Charles Wesley Birtwell[4]
William Ashley Blodgett[4]
Frank Taylor Brown[1]
William Chalfant[3]
Stephen Cutter Clark[3]
James Pendleton Cruger[1]
John Pomeroy Dabney[1]
Hiram Irving Dillenback[2]
James Joseph Dooling[2]
Hiland Hulburd Dunlevy[1]
Charles Hamlin Dunton[2]
Clinton Johnson Edgerly[1]
Frederick Larnac Eldridge[1]
Frederick Ware Emerson[4]
Daniel Butler Fearing[1]
Edwin Thayer Fearing[1]
Edward Ashley Ferguson[1]
John Quincy Adams Griffin[2]
Almon Whiting Griswold[1]
Ramon Benjamin Guiteras[1]
Percival Smith Hill[2]
Francis Marion Holden[1]

Charles Harvey Holman[4]
Frank Whitehouse Howe[1]
William Addison Howe[1]
Woodbury Kane[4]
*George Clark Kennett   *1879
William Amos Lamprey[2]
Courtney Langdon[1]
Prescott Lawrence[1]
George Henry Leatherbee[4]
*Clinton Hill Lord   *1880
Charles Washington Luck[3]
Albert Matthews[4]
George William McColl[3]
Charles Herbert McFee[3]
Charles Henry Mahon[3]
Ernest Homer Mariett[2]
Charles Andrews Mitchell[1]
John Kearsley Mitchell[2]
Sollace Mitchell[1]
Henry Whiting Munroe[2]
Hugh Kinsley Norman[1]
Richard Chappell Parsons[1]
William Herbert Prescott[1]
Frederick Henry Prince[1]
Hazen Kimball Richardson[2]
Herbert St. Pierre Ruffin[1]
Edward David Scott[1]

The superior figures indicate the year of leaving the Class.

Henry Dwight Sedgwick[3]
Archibald Lowery Sessions[1]
Henry Shippen   1879
Denison Rogers Slade[3]
Eliot Dawes Stetson[4]
Charles Inches Sturgis[1]
William Eldredge Thayer[3]
Frank Harrison Thompson[2]
Edward James Tilton[1]
Charles Everett Torrey[1]
George Macbeth Trenholm[1]
*George Chrystie Van Benthuysen
                          1882*

Charles Michael Van Buren[2]
Mars Edward Wagar[1]
William Bernard Waring[1]
J. Edward Weld[4]
†††Edward Freeman Wells[4]
Gordon Wendell[1]
Alfred Jerome Weston[1]
Henry White[1]
George Walton Williams[1]
Frank Herbert Young[1]
                — 76 = 253

Note.—The first list is of those who received degrees, the second of the others who at some time have been members of the Class. No list is given of men who tried for degrees and failed to get them.

NUMBER IN THE CLASS.

Freshman Year.

Admitted previous to 1878	11
" in July, 1878	178
" in September, 1878	31
" from the class of 1881	14
	234
Left during Freshman Year	43
	191

Sophomore Year.

Of original number	191
Admitted during Sophomore Year	5
	196
Left during Sophomore Year	16
	180

Junior Year.

Admitted from Sophomore Year	180
Admitted from Class of 1880, 1; 1881, 3; 1883, 1; 1872, 1;	6
	186
Left during Junior Year	12
	174

Senior Year.

Admitted from Junior Year	174
Admitted from 1883, 1; others, 8;	9
	183
Left during Senior Year	2
Membership Commencement Day, 1882	181
Other candidates for degree of A. B.	6
Total number of candidates for degrees	187
Received degrees Commencement Day	177
Whole number connected with the Class	253

BIRTHPLACE AND RESIDENCE.

	Birthplace.	Residence.
Alabama	1	0
Azores	1	1
California	4	2
District of Columbia	1	2
England	1	0
Florida	0	1
France	1	0
Georgia	1	0
Illinois	4	5
Indiana	1	1
Iowa	1	1
Maine	10	6
Massachusetts (Boston) 32, 23	106	110
Michigan	2	0
Minnesota	0	2
Missouri	1	0
New Hampshire	4	4
New Jersey	1	1
New York (New York City. 6, 13)	20	27
North Carolina	1	2
Ohio	5	4
Pennsylvania	3	2
Rhode Island	1	3
Russia	1	0
Scotland	1	0
South Carolina	1	1
Syria	1	0
Vermont	3	2
	177	177
New England	124	125
Middle States	24	30
Western States	18	15
Southern States	5	6
Outside the United States	6	1
	177	177

PROBABLE OCCUPATION.

	Class of 1872.	Class of 1878.	Class of 1879.	Class of 1880.	Class of 1881.	Class of 1882.	Class of 1882.
Business	29	14	22	28	38	55	54
Law	31	21	68	73	44	48	46
Undecided	41	14	44	29	38	23	21
Medicine	46	13	21	14	26	20	20
Teaching	7	10	22	13	20	11	11
Ministry	4	4	9	3	10	5	6
Chemistry	1	0	0	1	6	6	6
Journalism	1	3	0	0	2	5	5
Study	1	3	4	3	6	1	1
Architecture	1	0	0	0	2	0	0
Art	0	0	1	0	1	0	0
Farming	0	1	0	0	1	0	0
Physical Science	0	0	0	0	1	1	1
Publishing	0	0	0	0	1	0	0
Library work	0	0	0	1	1	0	0
Others	0	4	7	6	0	6	6
Not heard from	0	72	0	0	0	0	0
	112	159	198	171	197	181	177

RELIGIOUS VIEWS.

	Class of 1872.	Class of 1878.	Class of 1879.	Class of 1880.	Class of 1881.	Class of 1882.	Class of 1882.
Undecided	14	18	35	28	25	25	24
None	0	4	6	13	2	8	8
Liberal	0	2	8	16	3	7	6
Agnostic	1	1	0	2	15	4	4
Christian	1	2	2	0	1	3	3
Non-sectarian	0	0	0	4	13	1	1
Rationalism	0	0	0	0	1	0	0
Deist	0	0	0	0	1	1	1
Theist	0	0	0	0	1	0	0
Uncertain	0	0	0	0	1	0	0
	16	27	51	63	63	49	47
Episcopalian	27	18	36	34	48	37	36
Unitarian	38	18	42	34	32	34	34
Congregationalist	10	8	32	22	31	29	29
Baptist	5	2	11	2	7	7	7
Presbyterian	3	4	1	4	2	7	7
Swedenborgian	2	1	3	1	4	1	6
Catholic	3	0	3	3	2	0	4
Methodist	2	1	3	0	3	4	1
Universalist	3	1	4	1	3	7	0
Jewish	0	0	0	0	1	0	0
Dutch Reform	1	0	0	1	1	0	0
Various others	2	7	12	5	0	6	6
Not heard from	0	72	0	1	0	0	0
	112	159	198	171	197	181	177

NUMBERS, RESIDENCE AND AGE.

Numbers.

	Class of 1872.	Class of 1878.	Class of 1879.	Class of 1880.	Class of 1881.	Class of 1882.
Membership, Freshman Year	131	197	251	232	240	234
Membership, Senior Year	112	167	203	171	198	181
Received degrees at Commencement	112	144	189	162	182	177
Whole number connected with the Class	146	229	276	252	268	253

Residence.

New England	96	143	112	134	125
Middle States	34	33	35	36	30
Western States	20	16	15	21	15
Southern States	8	5	8	4	6
Outside the United States	1	2	1	2	1

Age at Commencement.

	Class of 1872.		Class of 1878.		Class of 1879.		Class of 1880.		Class of 1881.		Class of 1882.	
	Yrs.	Mos.	Yrs.	Mos.	Yrs.	Mos.	Yrs.	Mos.	Yrs.	Mos.	Yrs.	Mos.
Average	21	10.9	22	3.3	22	2.83	22	1	22	11.7	22	6.28
Oldest	27	2	31	5	28	4	31	1	31	11	31	5
Youngest	20	8	18	11	18	1	19	7	19	5	19	6

Over 25	2	9	13	5	17	10
Between 22 and 25	49	70	90	94	98	96
Between 20 and 22	61	86	98	69	80	72
Under 20	0	2	2	3	3	3
	112	167	203	171	198	181

ELECTIVES.*

	Fresh.	Soph.	Jun.	Sen.	Total.
Ancient Languages	0	9	5	7	21
Chemistry	1	64	54	44	163
English	1	43	65	88	197
Fine Arts	3	10	30	58	101
French	7	87	50	42	186
German	12	131	80	50	273
Graduate Courses	0	0	5	58	63
Greek	19	170	54	65	308
History	1	109	143	195	448
Italian	0	9	29	22	60
Latin	23	181	51	40	295
Mathematics	3	54	29	22	138
Music	4	28	26	17	75
Nat. History	6	76	103	97	282
Philosophy	1	72	104	62	239
Physics	0	28	20	23	71
Pol. Economy	0	19	87	49	155
Spanish	1	4	5	17	27
Roman Law	0	0	0	21	21

* This table includes extras.

MEASUREMENTS OF THE CLASS.

The measurements of the last three classes made by Dr. Sargent are much more accurate than those of the previous classes, and comparison would therefore be unfair.

		Class of 1879.[1]	Class of 1880.[2]	Class of 1881.[3]	Class of 1882.[4]
CHEST.		In.	In.	In.	In.
Average	Natural	35.94	33.7	33.9	34.79
	Inflated	37.66	36.3	36.4	36.63
Largest	Natural	43.	38.6	39.4	38.24
	Inflated	45.5	41.5	42.5	40.62
Smallest	Natural	32.	28.6	27.2	29.54
	Inflated	33.25	31.1	29.9	30.75
UPPER ARM.					
Average		12.45	12.17	11.7	11.83
Largest		14.75	14.6	14.2	13.43
Smallest		10.	9.4	8.7	9.5
FORE-ARM.					
Average		11.14	10.3	10.2	10.35
Largest		13	12.4	12.1	11.75
Smallest		9.5	8.9	8.5	8.54
HEIGHT.		Ft. In.	Ft. In.	Ft. In.	Ft. In.
Average		5 9	5 6.5	5 8.5	5 8.23
Tallest		6 3.75	6 3.7	6 2.1	6 0.5
Shortest		5 2.5	5 2.3	5 2.8	5 1.5
WEIGHT.		Lbs.	Lbs.	Lbs.	Lbs.
Average		150.35	145.6	142.3	137.30
Heaviest		205.	217.2	185.2	201.
Lightest		110.	107.6	95.9	105.

[1] Height and weight from 115 men; other measurements from 109 men.
[2] "   "   "   "   110   "   "   "   108 "
[3] "   "   "   "   142   "   "   "   130 "
[4] "   "   "   "   87   "   "   "   81   "

RANK OF THE CLASS.

	Class of 1878.	Class of 1879.	Class of 1880.	Class of 1881.	Class of 1882.
FRESHMAN YEAR.					
Over 90 per cent	5	3	1	6	3
Between 80 and 90 per cent	11	17	18	24	18
Over 67 per cent	58	61	71	73	70
Number in the class	168	215	187	211	206
SOPHOMORE YEAR.					
Over 90 per cent	5	2	5	15	6
Between 80 and 90 per cent	18	24	35	28	22
Over 67 per cent	62	81	91	105	87
Number in the class	166	200	171	188	181
JUNIOR YEAR.					
Over 90 per cent	6	7	5	13	10
Between 80 and 90 per cent	30	38	33*	30	36
Over 67 per cent	77	100	94	105	110
Number in the class	157	193	165	192	175
SENIOR YEAR.					
Over 90 per cent	16	22	12	26	15
Between 80 and 90 per cent	32	43	42	60	48
Over 67 per cent	104	139	114	151	126
Number in the class	159	198	169	197	181
FOR THE FOUR YEARS.					
Over 90 per cent	4	3	2	7	4
Between 80 and 90 per cent	18	30	29	29	24
Over 67 per cent	70	81	83	100	104

HONORS.

	Class of 1878.	Class of 1879.	Class of 1880.	Class of 1881.	Class of 1882.
Deturs	32	30	32	33	28
Second-year Honors	19	22	32	36	28
Final Honors	13	15	17	28	27
Honorable Mention	—	—	70	108	85
Commencement Parts	26	36	74	101	85

PRIZES.

LEE PRIZES FOR READING.

FRESHMAN YEAR.

Burton Monroe Firman, Clinton Hill Lord,
Henry Winthrop Hardon, William Hobbs Manning,
Samuel Williston.

SOPHOMORE YEAR.

Charles Townsend Copeland, Clinton Hill Lord,
Frederick Atherton Fernald, George Chrystie Van Beuthuysen,
Charles Harvey Holman, Samuel Williston.

BOYLSTON PRIZES FOR ELOCUTION.

JUNIOR YEAR.

First Prize. — Edmund Sehon Perin.
Second Prizes. — Burton Monroe Firman, Gustavus Tuckerman.

SENIOR YEAR.

First Prizes. — Sherman Hoar, Burton Monroe Firman.
Second Prize. — George Herbert Eaton.

BOWDOIN PRIZE DISSERTATIONS.

JUNIOR YEAR.

George Lyman Kittredge: "Burke as a Statesman."
Frank Gaylord Cook: "Burke as a Statesman."

SENIOR YEAR.

George Lyman Kittredge: "Thomas Carlyle as an Historian."
George Lyman Kittredge: "Democracy in the Greek and in the Modern State compared."
George Lyman Kittredge: "Translation into Attic Prose from John Henry Newman."
Robert Luce: "Transmission of Power by Electricity."

DETURS.

Freshman Year.

Alfred Marston Allen.
Joseph Henry Beale.
Charles Wesley Birtwell.
Richards Merry Bradley.
Frank Nelson Cole.
Frank Gaylord Cook.
Franklin Arthur Dakin.
William Harrison Dunbar.
Frederic Atherton Fernald.
William Boyd Fiske.
Homer Gage.
Joseph Peabody Gardner.
Asaph Hall.
Albert Andrew Howard.
Charles Hallam Keep.
George Lyman Kittredge.
Albert French Lane.
Clinton Hill Lord.
Arthur Prescott Lothrop.
John Whiting Mason.
Charles Andrews Mitchell.
Ivan Nicolayevitsch Panin.
William Lowell Putnam.
Charles Moen Rice.
Lucien Moore Robinson.
Roland Thaxter.
Russell Whitman.
Joseph Ruggles Worcester.

HONORS.

SECOND-YEAR HONORS IN CLASSICS.

Sophomore Year.

Highest Honors.

George Lyman Kittredge.
Albert French Lane.
William Hobbs Manning.
George Morey Richardson.

Honors.

Alfred Marston Allen.
Joseph Henry Beale.
Richards Merry Bradley.
Franklin Arthur Dakin.
Clarence Randall Dean.
Frederick Stanley Hall.
Charles Harvey Holman.
Albert Andrew Howard.
William Jones.
Charles Herbert McFee.
Edward Percival Merritt.
Charles Armstrong Snow.
Frederic Mather Stone.
Herbert Grafton Woodworth.

JUNIOR YEAR.

Honors.

Frank Gaylord Cook.   Charles Henry Goldthwaite.
                   Russell Whitman.

SECOND-YEAR HONORS IN MATHEMATICS.

SOPHOMORE YEAR.

Highest Honors.

Joseph Henry Beale.   John Whiting Mason.
Frank Nelson Cole.   William Lowell Putnam.

Honors.

Asaph Hall.   James Jay Greenough.
                 Joseph Ruggles Worcester.

FINAL HONORS.
CLASSICS.

Highest Honors.

George Lyman Kittredge.   George Morey Richardson.

Honors.

Franklin Arthur Dakin.   Albert French Lane.
Charles Henry Goldthwaite.   William Hobbs Manning.
Albert Andrew Howard.   Russell Whitman.
William Jones.   Herbert Grafton Woodworth.

PHILOSOPHY.

Highest Honors.

Russell Whitman.

Honors.

William Henry Burnham.

HISTORY.

Highest Honors.

Arthur Prescott Lothrop.   William Cushing Wait.

Honors.

Alfred Marston Allen. Homer Gage.
Frank Gaylord Cook. Philip Moen Washburn.

MATHEMATICS.

Highest Honors.

Frank Nelson Cole. John Whiting Mason.

Honors.

Asaph Hall. William Lowell Putnam.

CHEMISTRY.

Honors.

Godfrey Lowell Cabot. Edward Knights Stevens.

MUSIC.

Highest Honors.

Frederick Russell Burton. Owen Wister.

Honors.

Samuel Henry Morrill.

HONORABLE MENTION.

Alfred Marston Allen, *Political Economy, History.*
Luther Stetson Anderson, *French, German.*
Charles Walker Andrews, *History.*
James Woods Babcock, *Natural History.*
Chambers Baird, *History.*
Clarence Bancroft, *Chemistry.*
George Francis Barlow, *Philosophy.*
Joseph Henry Beale, *Music, Mathematics, English Composition, Greek.*
Alexander Boyd, *History.*
Charles Edgar Boynton, *Chemistry, History.*
Richards Merry Bradley, *Political Economy, History.*

John Eliot Bullard, *Philosophy.*
William Henry Burnham, *Philosophy, English Composition.*
Frederick Russell Burton, *Music.*
Godfrey Lowell Cabot, *Chemistry.*
Edwards Cheney, *Music.*
Joseph Payson Clark, *English.*
Frank Nelson Cole, *Mathematics.*
Arthur Messinger Comey, *Chemistry.*
Frank Gaylord Cook, *Philosophy, History, Greek, Political Economy.*
Joseph Austin Coolidge, *German.*
Charles Townsend Copeland, *History.*
Montgomery Adams Crockett, *Natural History.*
Robert Cumming, *Music.*
Charles Francis Cutler, *History.*
Franklin Arthur Dakin, *Greek, Latin, English Composition.*
William Henry Danforth, *Natural History.*
Wendell Phillips Davis, *Music, German.*
Richard Delaney, *History.*
George Washington Dickerman, *Philosophy, Greek.*
Charles Denston Dickey, *History.*
George Bradford Dunbar, *Natural History.*
William Harrison Dunbar, *History, Political Economy.*
George Herbert Eaton, *Philosophy.*
Frederick Atherton Fernald, *Chemistry.*
Burton Monroe Firman, *Philosophy, English Composition.*
William Boyd Fiske, *Natural History, Chemistry.*
John McGaw Foster, *English Composition.*
Harry Cormerais French, *Natural History.*
Frank Edward Fuller, *English, English Composition.*
Homer Gage, *History.*
Frederick Norton Goddard, *French.*
Charles Henry Goldthwaite, *Greek, Latin.*
James Jay Greenough, *Mathematics, Physics.*
Asaph Hall, *Mathematics.*
Henry Winthrop Hardon, *Greek.*
George Trumbull Hartshorn, *Chemistry.*
Albert Andrew Howard, *Greek, Latin.*
Harry Mascarene Hubbard, *Natural History.*
Charles Greene Rockwood Jennings, *Chemistry.*
William Jones, *Greek, Latin.*

George Lyman Kittredge, *English, Greek, Latin, English Composition.*
Albert French Lane, *Greek, Latin, English Composition.*
Hayward Gibbons Leavitt, *Chemistry.*
Arthur Prescott Lothrop, *Political Economy, History.*
Robert Luce, *History, Political Economy, English Composition.*
Thomas William Ludlow, *Greek.*
Walter Irving McCoy, *Philosophy.*
William Hobbs Manning, *Greek, Latin, History.*
John Whiting Mason, *Mathematics.*
George Lowell Mayberry, *Physics, Philosophy.*
Alfred Eugene Miles, *Philosophy.*
Samuel Henry Morrill, *Music.*
Edmund Seabon Perin, *Natural History.*
George William Perkins, *Natural History.*
John Walter Perkins, *Natural History, Political Economy.*
McLaurin Jameson Pickering, *History.*
William Lowell Putnam, *Mathematics.*
Charles Moen Rice, *Mathematics.*
George Morey Richardson, *Greek, Latin.*
Lucien Moore Robinson, *Physics, History.*
William Joseph Rushmore, *History, English Composition.*
Harold Marsh Sewall, *History, English Composition.*
Horace Emmet Smith, *History.*
Charles Armstrong Snow, *Greek, Philosophy.*
Edward Knights Stevens, *Chemistry.*
Frederick Mather Stone, *Greek.*
Roland Thaxter, *Natural History, English Composition.*
William Cushing Wait, *Political Economy, History.*
Guy Waring, *Natural History.*
Philip Moen Washburn, *History.*
Russell Whitman, *Philosophy, Greek, Latin.*
Owen Wister, *Music, Philosophy, English Composition.*
Herbert Grafton Woodworth, *Greek.*
Joseph Ruggles Worcester, *Mathematics.*

COMMENCEMENT PARTS.

ORATIONS.

George Lyman Kittredge.
Frank Nelson Cole.
Albert French Lane.
Arthur Prescott Lothrop.
George Morey Richardson.

William Cushing Wait.
Russell Whitman.
John Whiting Mason.
Frederick Russell Burton.
Owen Wister.

DISSERTATIONS.

Joseph Henry Beale.
Thomas William Ludlow.
Franklin Arthur Dakin.
Charles Hallam Keep.
Frank Gaylord Cook.
William Harrison Dunbar.
William Lowell Putnam.
Asaph Hall.
Homer Gage.
George Washington Dickerman.
William Boyd Fiske.
Charles Moen Rice.
Lucien Moore Robinson.
John Eliot Bullard.
Alfred Marston Allen.

Roland Thaxter.
George Lowell Mayberry.
Frederick Atherton Fernald.
Albert Andrew Howard.
Luther Stetson Anderson.
Charles Henry Goldthwaite.
William Hobbs Manning.
William Jones.
Godfrey Lowell Cabot.
William Henry Burnham.
Philip Moen Washburn.
Edward Knights Stevens.
Samuel Henry Morrill.
Herbert Grafton Woodworth.

DISQUISITIONS.

Richards Merry Bradley.
Ivan Nicolayevitsch Panin.
Robert Luce.
Joseph Ruggles Worcester.
John Walter Perkins.
Frederick Clinton Woodbury.
John Plummer Lyons.
Joseph Payson Clark.
John McGaw Foster.
Clarence Bancroft.
Charles Armstrong Snow.

Charles Eliot.
Alfred Eugene Miles.
John McGregor Cochrane.
George Herbert Eaton.
George William Perkins.
Arthur Messinger Comey.
Frederick Norton Goddard.
Montgomery Adams Crockett.
Charles Denston Dickey.
William Henry Danforth.
Henry Winthrop Hardon.

Joseph Austin Coolidge.
James Woods Babcock.
Charles Edgar Boynton.
Wendell Phillips Davis.
Frank Edward Fuller.
Horace Emmet Smith.
Robert Cumming.
Charles Green Rockwood Jennings.
William Joseph Rushmore.
Frederick Mather Stone.
George Trumbull Hartshorn.
James Jay Greenough.
Edwards Cheney.
Charles Townsend Copeland.
Harry Cormerais French.
George Bradford Dunbar.
McLaurin Jameson Pickering.
Charles Walker Andrews.
Richard Delaney.
Chambers Baird.
Harold Marsh Sewall.
Charles Francis Cutler.
George Francis Barlow.
Guy Waring.

The following parts were delivered:

LATIN ORATION.

Franklin Arthur Dakin: Alumnis et Fautoribus Universitatis gratulabitur.

DISQUISITIONS.

Harold Marsh Sewall: "Centralization in Our Government."
Charles Townsend Copeland: "Jane Austen and Charlotte Brontë."
Frank Edward Fuller: "Swift and Sterne."
Frederick Russell Burton: "Wagner's Theory of the Opera."

DISSERTATION.

George Lowell Mayberry: "The Poet of the Future."

FRESHMAN CLASS OFFICERS.

President	William Hobbs Manning.
Vice-President . . .	McLaurin Jameson Pickering.
Secretary	Edward Livingston Underwood.
Captain of the Crew .	Charles Hammatt Bartlett.
Captain of the Nine .	Daniel Butler Fearing.

The Captain of the Nine resigned before the end of the year and Henry Gardner Chapin was elected.

At a meeting held at the beginning of the Sophomore year, the following officers were elected:

Vice-President . . .	Elliott Hunt Pendleton.
Secretary	James Williams Bowen.

Those who held the other offices were reelected.

At the beginning of the Junior year the Captain of the Crew left college, and in his place was elected Clarence Randall Dean.

CLASS DAY AND CLASS OFFICERS.

The meeting for electing these officers was held in Boylston Hall on the evening of Monday, November 21, 1881, and resulted in the choice of the following: —

Orator	Sherman Hoar.
Poet	John McGaw Foster.
Ivy-Orator	George Lyman Kittredge.
Odist	Frank Edward Fuller.
Chorister	Frederick Russell Burton.
First Marshal	William Hobbs Manning.
Second Marshal . . .	Elliott Hunt Pendleton.
Third Marshal	James Woods Babcock.
Class Day Committee .	{ Evert Jansen Wendell. William Cushing Wait. Thomas Chandler Thacher.
Class Committee.	{ Russell Whitman. Franklin Arthur Dakin. Arthur Prescott Lothrop.
Secretary . . .	Alfred Eugene Miles.

FUNDS.

Class Fund.

	Total Subscriptions.	Average Subscription.	Number connected with Class.	Number of Subscribers.
Class of 1878	$4,965	$62.06	229	80
" 1879	9,035	48.84	276	185
" 1880	8,605	48.34	252	178
" 1881	6,150	48.04	268	128
" 1882	9,595	63.69	253	149

Our Fund was subscribed as follows: —

1	subscription of	$350.	$350.
3	" "	250.	750.
1	" "	200.	200.
5	" "	150.	750.
3	" "	125.	375.
32	" "	100.	3200.
5	" "	75.	375.
1	" "	60.	60.
46	" "	$50.	2300.
3	" "	40.	120.
2	" "	30.	60.
34	" "	25.	850.
4	" "	20.	80.
6	" "	15.	90.
3	" "	10.	30.
1	" "	5.	5.

149 Subscriptions, ... 9595.
Balance from sale of Class Day Tickets . . . 663.88

Total amount 10,258.88

Amount due May 1, 1882, 1-5 of $9,595. . . . . . . $1919.
" of first instalments paid . . . . 1104.
" " " due and unpaid . . . . . 815.

First instalments, paid . . . . 1104.
Five subscribers have paid in full anticipating . . . . . 332.
1 Subscriber ($50.) has paid $25 " . . . . . 15.
1 " ($10.) " $4 " . . . . . 2.

Total amount paid to date. July 8 . . . . . . 1453.

ACCOUNT OF CLASS FUND.

Rec'd as per statement	$1453.00	For Class Dinner	$328.00
" for stamps	1.59	Pictures for Secretary and Class Day Committee	150.70
		Printing Class Day Book	83.75
		W. A. Bancroft (Crew)	70.00
		W. H. Wheeler, Advanced on Class Report	50.00
		Collation for Election Night	30.00
		John Wilson & Son, Printing	24.00
		Class Life blanks	21.00
		Printing, Stamps, Advertising, etc., etc.	85.16
			842.61
		Balance, July 11, 1882	611.98
	1454.59		1454.59

It will be seen that our Fund is a large one, and we are particularly fortunate in receiving a large balance — over $600 — from the Class Day Committee. In comparing our Fund with that of other classes, this amount should not be counted, since we do not know how much other Secretaries have received or have paid out on the Class Day account. The balance $611.98 will be diminished about $150 for the printing of this report, and somewhat more by a few small bills which must be incurred before I get the Report distributed.

COLLEGE FUND.

	Total Subscriptions.	Average Subscription.	Number connected with Class.	Number of Subscribers.
Class of 1878	$1,630	$54.33	229	30
" 1879	3,425	48.93	276	70
" 1880	2,620	45.97	252	57
" 1881	855	50.30	268	17
" 1882	700	50.00	253	14

Our Fund was subscribed as follows: —

2 subscriptions of	$100.		200.
8	"	"	50.	400.
1	"	"	30.	30.
2	"	"	25.	50.
1	"	"	20.	20.
14				700.

Amount due June 1, 1882, 1-10 of $700. . . . . $70.00
    " of first instalments paid to date, July 11 . . . . . 52.50
    "   "   "   " due and unpaid 17.50

First instalments paid $52.50
1 Subscriber ($50.) has paid in full anticipating 45.00
1   "   ($25.)   " $5.   " 2.50
1   "   ($20.)   " $4.   " 2.00

Amount paid to date $102.00

COLLEGE FUND ACCOUNT.

Received as per statement	$102.00	Paid for expenses in canvassing for Subscriptions and in printing and postage	$2.00
		Balance	100.00
	$102.00		$102.00

The $2. charged for expenses I have been obliged to estimate. Several circulars have referred to both funds and I believe $2. to be a fair estimate of the expenses incurred by me on account of the College Fund. I am sorry the Fund is so small and trust that you will subscribe more liberally through me, or will make up to the College by individual gifts what it has failed to receive from you as a class.

CLASS LIVES.

To write a sketch of his life is the only thing requiring any effort I have asked each one of you to do. And yet from a class of 181 members I have received only 61 lives. To obtain an autograph sketch of the life of each one of you, I deem the most important part of my duty that is now unfulfilled. It is not very difficult to keep track of you while you are in college, and you have so many associations at college, kept up by constant intercourse, that you are apt to fail to realize the pleasure you will feel in after years, when you learn of the success of your classmates. In order to be able to keep myself informed of the life of each of you, I want an account of what you did before I met you, and to obtain this I have distributed to you these blanks. Two-thirds of you have totally ignored my request. Not only to me are the lives indispensable, but they will be of great value in the preparation of the book on Harvard graduates. I hope and trust therefore that those of you who have not written your lives will do so at once and send them to my address.

CLASS SUPPERS.

SOPHOMORE YEAR.

The Sophomore class supper took place at Young's Hotel, Boston, on the evening of March 10, 1880. The officers of the occasion were:—

President	W. H. Manning.
Orator	I. N. Panin.
Poet	J. M. Foster.
Chorister	E. H. Pendleton.
Toast-Master	C. J. Edgerly.
Musical Committee	Owen Wister.
	F. R. Burton.
	E. H. Pendleton.
Committee on Arrangements .	F. M. Stone.
	Guy Waring.
	J. H. Storer.

About 80 men were present. The usual toasts were given and Mr. Sewall spoke for the Advocate, Mr. Fuller for the Crimson, Mr. Kane for the ladies, and the Captains of the different class athletic organizations were heard from as the Class Crew, Nine and Eleven were toasted.

JUNIOR YEAR.

A class supper known as the "dollar supper" was held at the Revere House on the evening of May 16, 1881. The committee of arrangements nominally consisted of ten, but practically the committee consisted of Messrs. Buell, Blodgett, and W. G. Chase. Mr. George L. Kittredge served as toastmaster, and Mr. W. H.

Manning presided. The dinner was well attended and was a peculiarly pleasant one, for two days before, our crew had won the Class Races, and our University Nine had defeated Yale at Cambridge. Few class suppers have been held at times so favorable, and "the dollar supper" will be remembered for a long while by those who attended.

Senior Year.

The Senior class supper was held at Parker's on the evening of June 27th, 1882. 122 men were present, among them some who long ago left college, but came back to join in this, our last undergraduate supper.

Mr. George L. Kittredge served as toastmaster, and Mr. W. H. Manning presided. The arrangements were made by the Class Committee, and the Chorister of the Class, Mr. F. R. Burton, led the singing.

A pleasant feature of the supper was the kindness of the class of 1869, which was dining in a neighboring room, and sent its compliments to us with a bottle of excellent wine. After we had sent our thanks with a "magnum," the class of 1869 came to offer their congratulations in a body with a "maximum," and the drinking of each others health by the alumni of thirteen years' and the graduating class, was a pleasant spectacle not often witnessed at a class supper.

CLASS CRADLE.

All who received degrees with 1882 are eligible for the class cradle. As soon any one of you presents a claim, it will be duly examined by the Secretary and Class Committee, and the happy father who presents the first just claim will receive for his fortunate child the cradle and well wishes of the Class of 1882.

ORGANIZATIONS.

ATHLETIC.

BICYCLE CLUB, 1879.

Baldwin, Bowen, Buell, Bullard, Cabot, Codman, Comey, Creesy, Crehore, Crockett, Dabney, G. B. Dunbar, W. H. Dunbar (*sec'y*), Dean, Edgerly, D. B. Fearing, Fellows, French, Gardner, Hardon, Herrick, Kane, Kent, Lawrence, Matthews, Norman, Oxnard, Putnam, Sherwood, Storer (*pres't*), Thacher, Thaxter, Underwood, Waring, E. J. Wendell, Williston (*capt.*), Woodbury, Woodworth. — 38

CLASS CREW.

Babcock, Baldwin, Bartlett (*capt.*), Blodgett, Chalfant, Clark, Crehore, Cruger, W. de L. Cunningham, Dean (*capt.*), Goodnough, Hoar, Hoyt, Hubbard, Jennings, Kane, Lawrence, Luck, E. V. McDonald, Pendleton, G. W. Perkins, Sherwood, G. Waring, Warren. — 24

CLASS FOOTBALL ELEVEN.

Blodgett, Boyd, Crehore (*capt.*), Eldridge, Kane, Leatherbee, Manning, Perin, Sedgwick, Thacher, Warren, Williams. — 12

CLASS NINE.

Andrews (*R.*), Burt (*A.*), Chapin (*S.*) (*capt.*), D. B. Fearing (*capt., resigned*), E. T. Fearing (*subs.*), F. S. Hall (*M.*), Knowles (*P.*), Perin (*L.*), H. A. Richardson (*B.*), Snow (*C.*), C. H. Stevens (*H.*). — 11

CRICKET TEAM.

Andrews, Dickey, D. B. Fearing, Kane (*capt.*). — 4

LACROSSE TWELVE.

Bradley, Creesy, Sturgis. — 3

UNIVERSITY CREW.

Chalfant, Warren. — 2

UNIVERSITY CRICKET CLUB.

Dickey (*pres't*), Kane (*vice-pres't*).

UNIVERSITY FOOTBALL ELEVEN.

The superimposed figure shows the number of years.
Boyd[2], Dabney[1], Eldridge[1], Leatherbee[2], Manning[4] (*capt.*), Perin,[2] Sedgwick,[1] Thacher,[4] Warren.[2] — 9

UNIVERSITY NINE.

Burt (*A.*), F. S. Hall (*M & H.*), Leavitt (*R.*), Olmsted (*capt.*) (*L.*), H. A. Richardson (*S.*), Snow, (*C.*) — 6

COLLEGE PAPERS.

ADVOCATE, 1866.

Copeland, Foster (*sec'y*), Firman (*sec'y, resigned*), Hardon, Kent (*resigned*), G. L. Kittredge (*pres't*), Leavitt (*resigned*), Lord, Miles, Sewall (*resigned*), F. M. Stone (*business*). — 11

CRIMSON, 1873.

Bowen (*sec'y*), Buell (*resigned*), Fuller (*pres't*), Lyons, Manning (*vice-pres't*), J. K. Mitchell (*resigned*), Panin (*resigned*), Pendleton, Perin, Waring (*pres't, resigned*), E. J. Wendell. — 11

ECHO, 1879.

Burton, W. G. Chase, Dillenback, Holman, Luce, Panin. — 6

New Management, 1880.

Babcock (*resigned*), Bradley (*pres't*), Kingsbury, Putnam, Storer (*business*), P. M. Washburn (*resigned*), Warren (*resigned*), Wister (*resigned*). — 7

HERALD, 1881.

Associate Editors, Baird (*resigned*), W. G. Chase. — 2

LAMPOON, 1876.

First Series. — Kent.
Second Series. 1881. —Buell. Crehore (*business*). Kent (*pres't*). Wister, Woodworth. — 5

LITERARY, SOCIAL, ETC.

A. D. CLUB, 1867.

Baldwin. Buell, Chapin, Crehore, Fellows. Gardner, Goddard. Leavitt, Pendleton, F. M. Stone, Warren. Webb, E. J. Wendell.
— 13

A. Δ. Φ., 1879.

Baldwin. Bradley. Bullard, Codman, Dickey, Gardner, Goddard. Manning, Paine, Stetson, F. M. Stone. Storer, Warner (*pres't*). P. M. Washburn. E. J. Wendell (*sec'y*). Wister. — 16

ART CLUB, 1878.

Baldwin, Bowen, Crehore. W. de L. Cunningham, Dickey (*treas.*), Emerson, Fellows. Goddard, Hoyt, Kane, Leavitt, Manning, Sedgwick, F. M. Stone, Townsend (*sec'y*). Warren. — 16

B. Θ. Π., 1880.

Baird, Blodgett, Cole, Holman (*resigned*). Hunt, McFee, McKendry, Potter. Van Benthuysen, Underwood. — 10

CHAPEL CHOIR.

First Tenor. — Jones, Weld.
Second Tenor. — Chalfant, Haupt, Morrill, Smith, Tuckerman.
First Bass. — Burton, Chapin, Pendleton.
Second Bass. — C. F. Mason. — 11

CHESS CLUB, 1879.

Delaney, W. H. Dunbar, Gage, Greenough, Harlow, Hubbard (*treas.*), Keep, Luce, Putnam, Rice. — 10

CHRISTIAN BRETHREN, 1802.

Birtwell, C. J. Brown, Burnham, Bush, Cook (*pres't*), Dakin, Dickerman (*treas.*), Eaton, Gillespie, Luce, Potter, Robinson, Woodbury, Woodworth. —14

Δ. Y., 1881.

Allen (*pres't., sec'y*), Birtwell, Burnham, Cook (*pres't*), Dickerman, C. A. Mitchell. — 6

EVERETT ATHENÆUM, 1868.

Allen, Babcock, Baker, Beale, Blodgett, Burton, H. L. Chase, W. G. Chase, Cheney, Cochrane, Cole, Cook, Cumming, Dooling, Fernald, Fiske, Foster, Goodnough, Haupt, Holman, Langdon, Luce, C. A. Mitchell, Morrill, Olmsted, Potter, Preston, Rushmore, Van Benthuysen, Wait, Worcester. — 31

FINANCE CLUB, 1878.

Birtwell (*pres't*), Boyd (*sec'y*), Bradley, Bullard, W. H. Dunbar, Eaton, Gage, Gardner, Hoar, Lane, Lothrop, Manning, Miles, Perin, Wait, Whiting. — 16

GLEE CLUB, 1858.

Active Members.

First Tenor. — Jones, Tuckerman, Weld.
Second Tenor. — Bowen (*vice pres't*), Burton, Smith.
First Bass. — Chalfant, Pendleton (*pres't*).
Second Bass. — Chapin (*pres't, leader*), C. F. Mason. — 10

Associate Members.
(*Before Consolidation with the Pierian.*)

Buell, Crehore, Kane, Leavitt, Miles, Perin, G. Waring, Warren, Webb, E. J. Wendell, — 10

HARVARD UNION, 1880.

Allen, Baird, Barlow, Burton, Bradley, Beale, Babcock, Blair, Bancroft, Bush, Baker, Cabot, Cheney, Cole, Copeland, Cumming, Cook, H. L. Chase, Delaney, W. H. Dunbar, Dickerman, Eaton, Fernald, Firman, Foster, Fuller, Gage, Hardon, Holman, Hoar (*sec'y*), Hopkins, Herrick, Luce, C. F. Mason, Oxnard, Panin, Perrin, Putnam, Preston, Robinson, G. M. Richardson, Storer, Sewall, Sherwood, Spalding, Towne, Van Benthuysen, Wait

(*pres't*), Warner, Warren, Washburn, Washburn, E. J. Wendell,
Weld, Whiting, Whitman, Williston. — 57

Hasty Pudding Club, 1795.

Andrews, Babcock, Babson, Baldwin, Bowen (*vice pres't*), Boyd,
Bradley, Buell, Bullard, Burt, Cabot, Chalfant, Chapin, Clark,
Codman, Crehore, Cunningham, Cunningham, Dabney, Dean,
Dickey, Dunbar, Dunbar, Emerson, Fellows, Foster, Francis,
French, Gardner, Goddard, Goodnough, Greenough, F. S. Hall,
Hardon, Hartshorn, Hoar, Hoyt, Hubbard, Kane, Kent (Kp.
artist), Kingsbury, Lane, Leatherbee, Leavitt, Manning, Matthews,
McCoy, Merritt (*chorister*), Miles (*chorister*), Olmsted, Oxnard,
Paine, Pendleton (*pres't*), Perin, Putnam, Rhinelander, Russell,
Sedgwick, Sewall, Sherwood, Spalding, Stetson, C. H. Stevens,
F. M. Stone (*pres't*), W. E. Stone, Storer, Thacher, Thaxter,
Tuckerman, Townsend, G. Waring, Warner, Warren, P. M.
Washburn, Webb, Weld, E. J. Wendell (*sec'y*), Whitman (*treas.*),
Wister, Woodbury. — 80

Historical Society, 1880.

Andrews, W. H. Dunbar (*sec'y*), Gage, Lothrop, Matthews,
Sewall, Smith, Wait, P. M. Washburn. — 9

Institute of 1770, 1770.

Andrews, Baldwin, Bartlett, Bowen, Boyd, Buell, Bullard,
Cabot, Chalfant, Chapin, Clark, Codman, Crehore, Cunningham,
Cunningham, Danforth, Dean, Dickey, Edgerly, Emerson, D. B.
Fearing, Fellows, Francis, French, Gardner, Goddard, Greenough,
Hardon, Harlow, Hoyt, Kane, Kennett, Kent, Kingsbury, Kittredge, Kittredge, Lane, Lawrence, Leavitt, Lord, Manning,
Matthews, Merritt, Miles, Munroe, Norman, Oxnard, Paine, Parsons, Pendleton, Perin, Prince, Putnam, G. M. Richardson, Russell, Sedgwick, Sewall, Stetson, Stone, Stone, Storer, Sturgis,
Thacher, Thaxter, Townsend, Tuckerman, G. Waring, Warner,
Warren, P. M. Washburn, Webb, E. J. Wendell, Whitman, Wister, Woodbury. — 75

K. N. 1876.

Allen, Babcock (*pres't*), Beale, Birtwell, Burton, Cheney (*sec'y*),
Cole, Eaton, Firman, Foster (*pres't*), Fuller (*pres't*), Gage,
Lane, Lyons, McKone, Mariett (*sec'y*), C. F. Mason, Panin,
J. W. Perkins, G. M. Richardson, Wait. — 21

HARVARD DINING ASSOCIATION, 1875.

DIRECTORS.

Freshman Year. — Whitman, Williams (*resigned*).
Sophomore Year.—Boyd, P. M. Washburn (*resigned*), E. V. McDonald.
Junior Year. — Fuller, Panin (*vice-pres't*), Sewall.
Senior Year. — Babcock (*pres't*), Beale, Burt, Heywood (*resigned*). — 12

NATURAL HISTORY SOCIETY, 1837.

Buell, Cabot, H. W. Cunningham, Dabney, G. B. Dunbar, W. H. Dunbar, Eliot, Fiske, Foster, Francis, Greenough, Hardon, B. R. Kittredge, McCoy, Oxnard, Putnam, W. E. Stone, Storer, Thacher, Thaxter, Waring, Washburn, Washburn. — 23

O. K. 1858.

Babcock, Bradley, Bullard, Copeland, Foster (*treas.*), Fuller (*librarian*), Hardon, Gardner (*sec'y*), Kent, Kingsbury, G. L. Kittredge (*pres't*), Manning, Townsend, Tuckerman, Wait, Wister. — 16

Π. H. 1865.

Allen (*vice-pres't*), Anderson, J. H. Bacon, Baker, Bancroft, Beale, Boynton, Burton, Bush, Cheney, Comey, Coolidge, Cumming, Dakin, Fernald (*treas.*), Fuller (*pres't*), Gordon, Howard (*resigned*), Jones, Luce, C. F. Mason, Preston, Rice (*resigned*), H. A. Richardson, Rogers, Smith, Wentworth, Weston. — 28

PHILOLOGICAL SOCIETY, 1880.

Bullard, Hardon, Howard (*treas.*), Kingsbury, G. L. Kittredge (*sec'y*), Lane, Manning (*pres't*), G. M. Richardson, Woodworth.
— 9

PHILOSOPHICAL SOCIETY, 1878.

Barlow, Birtwell, Firman, C. F. Mason, Panin, Tuckerman.
— 6

PIERIAN SODALITY, 1808.

Blodgett (*second violin and bass drum*), Boyd (*triangle*), H. L. Chase (*piccolo*), Cheney (*horn*), Comey (*flute*), Cumming (*trom-*

bone), Danforth (*clarionet*), Hartshorn ('*cello*, *sec'y and vice-pres't*), (*resigned*), Merritt (*piano and leader*), Miles (*piano and pres't*), Perrin (*piano*.) — 11

PORCELLIAN CLUB, 1791.

Bowen, Dickey, Emerson, Kane, Paine, Sedgwick, Townsend, G. Waring, Wister. — 9

READING ROOM ASSOCIATION.

Directors. — Beale, G. B. Dunbar, Hubbard, Lord, Wait.
— 5

RIFLE CLUB, 1879.

Buell, Leatherbee. — 2

SIGNET, 1870.

There was no Signet from 1882.

ST. PAUL'S SOCIETY, 1861.

Babson (*treas.*), Baldwin (*resigned*), Clark, Codman (*librarian, sec'y and vice-pres't*), Crehore (*resigned*), W. de L. Cunningham (*resigned*), Dickey, Dunlevy, Edgerly, Eldridge, D. B. Fearing, Fellows (*resigned*), Gardner (*librarian*), Garrett, Greenough, Herrick, Hoyt, Kane (*resigned*), Langdon, Lawrence, Matthews (*resigned*), G. M. Richardson, Rhinelander, Robinson, Sedgwick, W. E. Stone, Storer (*treas.*), Tuckerman (*chorister*), P. M. Washburn, Webb, Wendell, Wendell, Wister (*chorister*). — 33

Φ. B. K. 1781.

Allen, Beale, Birtwell, Bullard, Cole, Cook, Dakin, Dickerman, W. H. Dunbar, Fernald, Fiske, Gage, A. Hall, Keep, G. L. Kittredge (*sec'y*), Lane, Lothrop, Ludlow, J. W. Mason, Putnam, Rice, G. M. Richardson, Robinson, Wait, Whitman. — 25

PIERIAN AND GLEE CLUB ASSOCIATE MEMBERS, 1881.

The Associate Members of the Glee Club, 10, and the following: Andrews, Baldwin, H. W. Cunningham, Emerson, Fellows, Goddard, Hoar, Kent, Lane, Leatherbee, Manning, Oxnard, F. M. Stone, Stetson, Townsend, Warner. — 16. — 26

Z. Ψ. 1882.

Babcock, Chapin, Crehore, Goodnough, Kane, Olmsted, Perin, Sherwood, Webb, E. J. Wendell. — 10

ATHLETIC RECORD.

BOATING.

FRESHMAN YEAR, 1878-79.

Officers II. U. B. C.

W. TRIMBLE, '79, President.
W. N. GODDARD, '79, Vice-President.
E. L. BAYLIES, '79, Treasurer.
F. H. ALLEN, '80, Secretary.
R. TRIMBLE, '80, Captain.

SCRATCH RACES. — November 9, 1878. Boat-house Course. First race was between three Freshman sixes.

Six-oared Race.

First Crew. — Jacobs, '79, *stroke;* Smith, '79; Trimble, '80; Trimble, '79; Brandegee, '81; Atkinson, '81, *bow;* Agassiz, *coxswain.* Time, 6 min. 50 sec.

Second Crew. — Peabody, L. S., *stroke;* Bancroft, L. S.; Freeland, '81; Hammond, '81; Watson, '79; Thomas, '79, *bow;* Browne, '81, *coxswain.*

Single-scull Race.

Goddard, '79, rowed over the course on time in 6 min. 46 sec.

Four-oared Race.

First Crew. — Jacobs, '79, *stroke;* Trimble, '80; Brandegee, '81; Atkinson, '81; Agassiz, *coxswain.* Time, 7 min. 30 sec.

Second Crew. — Bancroft, L. S.; Peabody, L. S.; Goddard, '79; Hammond, '81; Hoyt, '82, *coxswain.*

There were no fall club races.

SCRATCH RACES. — May 3, 1879. Boat-house Course.

In the single sculls, Peabody, L. S., went over the course on time in 6 min. 43 sec.

Canoe Race.

1. Gardiner, '80; Foster, '80. Time, 7 min. 2. Felton, '79; Evans, '79.

Four-oared Race.

First Crew.—Swan, '81, *bow;* Hemenway, '81; Danforth, L. S.; Peabody, L. S., *stroke.* Time, 7 min.

Second Crew.—Atkinson, '81, *bow;* Hammond, '81; Donaldson, '79; Trimble, '80, *stroke.* Time, 7 min. 10 sec.

Junior Single Sculls.

1. A. L. Hall, '80. Time, 7 min. 15 sec. 2. Gilley, '80. Time, 7 min. 25 sec. 3. Wolff, '79 (withdrew).

SINGLE-SCULL RACE.—Lake Quinsigamond, Worcester, May 9, 1879. One mile and return.

1. Warren N. Goddard, '79, Harvard. Time, 14 min. 30 sec. 2. Edmund P. Livingstone, '79, Yale. Time, 14 min. 50 sec.

CLASS RACES.—May 17, 1879. Charles River Course. For singles one mile and return; for eights, one mile and seven-eighths straight away.

Senior Single Sculls.

1. Goddard, '79. Time, 14 min. 34¾ sec. 2. Peabody, L. S. 14 min. 57 sec.

Junior Single Sculls.

1. A. L. Hall, '80. Time, 6 min. 21 sec. 2. Gilley, '80. 3. Ellis, '80.

Eight-oared Race.

Seniors, '79.—Cowdin, *bow;* Meyer; Burr; C. O. Brewster; T. Lee; Preston, *captain;* Ives; Crocker, *stroke;* Cadwell, *coxswain.* Average weight, 152. Time, 9 min. 9 sec.

Sophomores, '81.—Atkinson, *bow;* Swan; Hammond, *captain;* Hemenway; C. H. W. Foster; Freeland; Howard; Brandegee, *stroke;* Browne, *coxswain.* Average weight, 152.9. Time, 9 min. 10 sec.

Law School.—Boutelle, *bow;* Davis; Marvell; Danforth; Walker; Hooper; Cole; Peabody, *stroke and captain;* Cheney, *coxswain.* Average weight, 157.6. Time, 9 min. 19 sec.

Juniors, '80. — W. G. Taylor, *bow;* H. H. Morgan, *captain;* Hatch; Holden; W. Hooper; Bacon; Simmons; C. Ware, *stroke;* F. H. Allen, *coxswain.* Average weight, 155.5. Time, 9 min. 28 sec.

Freshmen, '82. — Blodgett, *bow;* Luck; Dean; Hoar; Cruger; Warren; Chalfant; Bartlett, *stroke and captain;* Oxnard, *coxswain.* Average weight, 160. Time, 9 min. 35 sec.

Referee. — C. H. Williams, U. B. C.

UNIVERSITY RACE. — June 27, 1879. Thames River, New London. Four miles straight away.

Harvard. — R. Trimble, '80, *bow and captain* (158.5); N. M. Brigham, '80 (178); F. Peabody, Jr., L. S. (168); M. R. Jacobs, '79 (169); V. D. L. Stow, '80 (196.5); W. H. Schwartz, '79 (190); F. W. Smith, '79 (185.2); W. A. Bancroft, L. S., *stroke* (161.5); F. H. Allen, '80, *coxswain.* Time, 22 min. 15 sec.

Yale.—J. B. Collins, '81, *bow* (159.7); T. H. Patterson, L. S. (164.5); C. B. Storrs, '82 (169.2); O. D. Thompson, '79, *captain* (171.5); J. W. Keller, '80 (184.5); G. B. Rogers, S. S. S. (181.7); H. W. Taft, '80 (173.2); P. C. Fuller, '81, *stroke* (158); A. Fitzgerald, *coxswain.* Time, 23 min. 58 sec.

Judges. — R. C. Watson, '69, Harvard; F. Wood, Yale.

Time-keepers. — G. Willis, '70, Harvard; H. St. J. Sheffield, Yale.

Referee. — Professor Alex. Agassiz, '55, Harvard.

SOPHOMORE YEAR, 1879–80.

Officers H. U. B. C.

C. WARE, '80, President.
F. H. WHEELAN, '80, Vice-President.
W. R. THAYER, '81, Treasurer.
P. EVARTS, '81, Secretary.
R. TRIMBLE, '80, Captain.

CLASS RACES. — October 25, 1879. Charles River Course. One and three-quarter miles straight away. In barges.

Juniors, '81. — Atkinson, *bow;* Swan; Hammond, *captain;* Hemenway; Otis; Freeland; Howard; Brandegee, *stroke;* Browne, *coxswain.* Average weight, 158.25. Time, 8 min. 30 sec.

Seniors, '80. — W. G. Taylor, *bow;* C. Ware; W. Hooper; Welling; Simmons; N. M. Brigham; Stow; Trimble, *stroke and captain;* F. H. Allen, *coxswain*. Average weight, 169.25. Time, 8 min. 38 sec.

Sophomores, '82. — Waring, *bow;* Hoyt; Baldwin; McDonald; Dean; Lawrence; Chalfant; Bartlett, *stroke and captain;* Oxnard, *coxswain*. Average weight, 155.25. Time, 8 min. 55 sec.

Referee. — C. H. Williams, U. B. C.

SINGLE SCULL RACE. — May 5, 1880. Charles River Course. One mile and return.

1. Ellis, '80. 2. Gilley, '80.

CLASS RACES. — May 15, 1880. Charles River Course.

Junior Single Sculls.

1. Holder, '81. Time, 8 min. 46 sec. 2. G. H. Williams, '81. Time, 8 min. 51 sec.

Senior Single Sculls.

1. A. L. Hall, '80. 2. Griswold, '80. Griswold upset at the start, and Hall rowed over the course alone.

Eights.

Freshmen, '83. — Sherwood, *bow;* Chapman; Burch; Sawyer; Belshaw; C. M. Hammond, *captain;* E. T. Cabot; Curtis, *stroke;* Buchman, *coxswain*. Average weight, 164.1. Time, 10 m. 41 sec.

Sophomores, '82. — Crehore, *bow;* Hoyt; Goodnough; Blodgett; Lawrence; Warren; Chalfant; Bartlett, *stroke and captain;* Oxnard, *coxswain*. Average weight, 160. Time, 11 min. 4 sec.

Juniors, '81. — A. S. Thayer, *bow;* Swinburne; Mueller; Swan; C. H. W. Foster; Brewer; Hammond, *captain;* Hemenway, *stroke;* Browne, *coxswain*. Average weight, 151.75. Time, 11 min. 5 sec.

Seniors, '80. — Cabot, *bow;* Miller; Dodd; C. Morgan; Stow; Simmons; Hatch; C. Ware, *stroke and captain;* F. H. Allen, *coxswain*. Average weight, 167. Time, 11 min. 15 sec.

Referee. — C. H. Williams, U. B. C.

UNIVERSITY RACE. — July 1, 1880. Thames River, New London. Four miles straight away.

Yale. — J. B. Collins, '81, *bow* (166.5); P. C. Fuller, '81 (157.2); F. W. Rogers, '83 (177); N. T. Guernsey, '81 (175); L. K. Hull, '83 (187.2); G. B. Rogers, L., '82, *captain* (195); C. B. Storrs, '82 (174.2); H. T. Folsom, '83, *stroke* (168.5); Mun

Yew Chung, *coxswain*. Average weight, 175. Time, 24 min. 24 sec.

Harvard. — E. W. Atkinson, '81, *bow* (153) ; W. Freeland, '81 (162.5); H. B. Howard, '81 (172.5) ; E. D. Brandegee, '81 (168) ; J. Otis, '81 (180) ; N. M. Brigham, '80 (177.2) ; R. Bacon, '80 (181) ; R. Trimble, '80, *stroke and captain* (165) ; S. P. Sanger, '83, *coxswain*. Average weight, 171.1. Time, 25 m. 9 s.

Judges.—R. C. Watson, '69, Harvard. G. A. Adee, '67, Yale.
Timekeepers.—W. A. Bancroft, '78, Harvard. F. Wood, '76, Yale.
Referee. — Professor A. M. Wheeler, Yale.

FRESHMAN RACE.—July 7, 1880. Thames River, New London. Two miles straight away.

Harvard, '83. — Sherwood, *bow;* Keith ; Burch ; Sawyer ; E. T. Cabot ; C. M. Hammond, *captain;* Belshaw ; Chapman, *stroke;* Buchman, *coxswain*. Average weight, 156.25. Time, 11 min. 32 sec.

Columbia, '83. — Eldridge, *bow;* Banks ; Fitzgerald ; Rossiter ; Reckhart ; Lynch ; Pupke ; Cowles, *stroke;* Benjamin, *coxswain*. Average weight, 143.5. Time, 11 min. 37 sec.

Referee. — R. Trimble, '80, Harvard.

NATIONAL AMATEUR OARSMEN'S ASSOCIATION. — July 7, 1880. Schuylkill River, Philadelphia. One mile and a half straight away.

College Singles.

1. A. L. Hall, '80, Harvard. Time, 10 min. $10\frac{3}{4}$ sec. 2. J. A. Powers, Renns. Polyt. Inst. 3. J. A. Devereux, Princeton.

JUNIOR YEAR. 1880–81.

Officers H. U. B. C.

S. HAMMOND, JR., '81, President.
W. CHALFANT, JR., '82, Vice-President.
F. M. STONE, '82, Treasurer.
C. P. CURTIS, JR., '83, Secretary.
E. D. BRANDEGEE, '81, Captain.

SCRATCH RACES. — October 16, 1880. Boat-house Course.

Single-scull Race.

1. Holder, '81. 2. Agassiz, '84. 3. Pendleton, S. S.

The next race was between two Freshmen eights, coxswained respectively by Browne, '81, and Oxnard, '82.

Eight-oared Race.

First Crew. — Hammond, '81, *stroke;* Howard, '81; Hemenway, '81; C. H. W. Foster, '81; Perin, '82; Burch, '83; Kip, '83; Sherwood, '83, *bow;* Browne, '81, *Coxswain.*

Second Crew. — Curtis, '83, *stroke;* Chalfant, '82; Luck, '82; H. L. Chase, '82; E. T. Cabot, '83; Lawrence, '82; Winthrop, '83, *bow;* Oxnard, '82, *coxswain.*

Third Crew. — Brandegee, '81, *stroke;* Otis, '81; Freeland, '81; A. S. Thayer, '81; Hoyt, '82; Pendleton, '82; Luce, '82; Jones, '82, *bow;* Sanger, '83, *coxswain.*

Fourth Crew. — C. M. Hammond, '83, *stroke;* Swan, '81; Mueller, '81; Baldwin, '82; Hubbard, '82; Lee, '83; Sawyer, '83; Goodnough, '82, *bow;* Buchman, '83, *coxswain.*

CLASS RACES. — October 23, 1880. Charles River Course.

Seniors, '81. — C. H. W. Foster, *bow;* Swan; Hemenway; Hammond, *captain;* Otis; Howard; Freeland; Brandegee, *stroke;* Browne, *coxswain.* Time, 9 min. 4½ sec.

Sophomores, '83. — Sherwood, *bow;* Perin; Burch; Sawyer; Belshaw; C. M. Hammond, *captain;* E. T. Cabot; Curtis, *stroke;* Buchman, *coxswain.* Time, 9 min. 5½ sec.

Juniors, '82. — W. de L. Cunningham, *bow;* Luck; Pendleton; Hubbard; Goodnough; Lawrence; Chalfant; Hoyt, *stroke;* Oxnard, *coxswain.*

Referee. — W. A. Bancroft, '78.

CLASS RACES. — May 14, 1881. Charles River Course.

Juniors, '82. — Crehore, *bow;* Hoyt; Sherwood; Babcock; Dean, *captain;* Warren; G. W. Perkins; Goodnough, *stroke;* Oxnard, *coxswain.* Average weight, 157.1. Time, 11 min. 18 sec.

Seniors, '81. — C. H. W. Foster, *bow;* Swan; Hammond, *captain;* Atkinson; Otis; Freeland; Howard; Hemenway, *stroke;* Browne, *coxswain.* Average weight, 159.6. Time, 11 m. 28 s.

Sophomores, '83. — Sherwood, *bow;* Lee; Keith; Jacobs; Burch, *captain;* Hubbard; Baxter; Perin, *stroke;* Buchman, *coxswain.* Average weight, 153.75. Time, 11 min. 55 sec.

Freshmen, '84. — Bryant, *bow;* Le Moyne; Wesselhoeft; Goodwin; Mumford; Hutchinson; E. A. S. Clarke; Perkins, *stroke and captain;* Davis, *coxswain.* Average weight, 163.5. Time, 12 min. 42 sec.

Referee. — Mr. Eaton, U. B. C.

UNIVERSITY RACE. — June 27, 1881. Thames River, New London. Four miles straight away.

Harvard. — E. D. Brandegee, '81, *bow and captain* (169) ; F. L. Sawyer, '83 (170) ; E. T. Cabot, '83 (179) ; C. M. Hammond, '83 (181) ; O. J. Pfeiffer, M.S. (177) ; S. I. Hudgens, '84 (182) ; W. Chalfant, '82 (178) ; C. P. Curtis, Jr., '83, *stroke* (152) ; Buchman '83, *coxswain* (95). Time, 21 min. 45 sec.

Columbia.—Moore, *bow* (160) ; Eldridge (150) ; Reckhart (164) ; Lynch (176) ; Montgomery (177) ; Van Sinderen (173) ; Muller (163) ; Cowles, *stroke;* Benjamin, *coxswain* (88). Time, 21 m. 58 s.

Judges.—R. C. Watson, '69, Harvard. J. T. Goodwin, Columbia.

Referee. — F. G. Brown, Nassau B. C., New York.

FRESHMAN RACE.—June 30, 1881. Charles River Course. One and seven-eighths miles straight away.

Harvard, '84. — Bliss, *bow;* Le Moyne ; Bryant ; Goodwin ; Mumford ; Hutchinson ; Clarke ; Perkins, *stroke and captain;* Davis, *coxswain*. Average weight, 163. Time, 9 min. 5¾ sec.

Columbia, '84.—Rapallo ; Ketchonne ; Wainwright ; Fishburn ; Reckhart ; Wheeler, *captain;* Merrill ; Dowling, *stroke;* Walker, *coxswain*. Average weight, 152. Time, 9 min. 21⅞ sec.

Referee. — A. G. Baxter, U. B. C.

UNIVERSITY RACE. — July 1, 1881. Thames River, New London. Four miles straight away.

Yale.—J. B. Collins, '81, *bow and captain* (166) ; P. C. Fuller, '81 (170) ; F. W. Rogers, '83 (178) ; N. T. Guernsey, '81 (184) ; L. K. Hull, '83 (180) ; G. B. Rogers. L., '82 (184) ; C. B. Storrs, '82 (184) ; H. T. Folsom, '83 (166) *stroke;* Mun Yew Chung, *coxswain*. Time, 22 min. 13 sec.

Harvard. — Same as in Columbia Race. Time, 22 min. 19 sec.

Judges.—R. C. Watson, '69, Harvard. G. A. Adee, '67, Yale.

Time-keepers.—R. Trimble, '80, Harvard. F. Wood, '76, Yale.

Referee and Starter. — Professor Alex. Agassiz, '55, Harvard.

SENIOR YEAR, 1881–82.

Officers H. U. B. C.

W. CHALFANT, JR., '82, President.
C. P. CURTIS, JR., '83, Vice-President.
GUY WARING, '82, Treasurer.
C. P. PERIN, '83, Secretary.
C. M. HAMMOND, '83, Captain.

There were no scratch races nor class races in the fall.

CLASS RACES. — May 19, 1882. Charles River Course.

1. *Senior Crew.* — Crehore (154) *bow;* Hoyt (143) ; Sherwood (150) ; Babcock (159) ; Dean (148) *captain;* Clark (152) ; G. W. Perkins (160) ; Goodnough (149) *stroke;* Oxnard (115) *coxswain.* Time, 12 min. 46 sec.

2. *Junior Crew.* — Sherwood (150) *bow*; Binney (149) ; Burch (151) *captain;* S. Smith (153) : Keith (153) ; Hubbard (164) : Belshaw (177) ; Perin (162) *stroke;* Sanger (95) *coxswain.* Time, 12 min. 50 sec.

3. *Sophomore Crew.* — Agassiz (140) *bow;* Hutchinson (162) ; Bliss (175) ; Wesselhoeft (165) ; Bacon (163) ; Woodward (172) ; Mumford (179) ; Bryant (150) *stroke and captain;* Davis (103) *coxswain.* Time, not taken.

4. *Freshman Crew.* — McCook (151) *bow and captain;* Barnes (155) ; Storrow (157) ; Howard (158) ; Kollock (176) ; Gilman (170) ; Read (159) ; Keefe (153) *stroke;* Whiteside (89) *coxswain.* Time, not taken.

Referee. — C. H. Williams, U. B. C.

UNION BOAT CLUB REGATTA. — June 17, 1882. Charles River Course.

1. *University Crew.* — E. T. Cabot, '83 (172) *bow;* Sawyer, '83 (169) ; Perkins, '84 (179) ; C. M. Hammond, '83 (181) *captain;* E. A. S. Clark, '84 (177) ; Hudgens, '84 (180) ; Chalfant, '82 (180) ; C. P. Curtis, '83 (152) *stroke;* S. P. Sanger, '83 (96) *coxswain.* Time, 11 min. 30 sec.

2. *Narragansett Crew.* — Rice (145) *bow and captain;* Burbank (148) ; Tingley (132) ; Davis (169) ; Cattamach (165) ; Moore (157½) ; Kirby (160) ; Livermore (136) *stroke;* Boyd (68) *coxswain.* Time, 11 min. 59 sec.

3. *Freshman Crew.* — McCook (142½) *bow and captain;* Hanson (154) ; Read (159) ; Barnes (149) ; Kollock (175) ; Gilman (171) ; Storrow (159) ; Keefe (150) *stroke;* Whiteside (94) *coxswain.* Time, 12 min. 5 sec.

Referee. — C. H. Williams, U. B. C.

UNIVERSITY RACE. — June 29, 1882. New London. Four miles straight away.

1. *Harvard.* — W. W. Mumford, '84 (165) *bow*; F. L. Sawyer, '83 (167) ; R. P. Perkins, '84 (175) ; C. M. Hammond, '83 (178)

captain; E. A. S. Clark, '84 (174) ; S. I. Hudgens, '84 (186) ; W. Chalfant, '82 (177) ; C. P. Curtis, '83 (151) *stroke;* S. P. Sanger, '83 (90) *coxswain.* Average weight, 171.50. Time, 20 min. 47½ sec.

2. *Yale.* — H. R. Flanders, '85 (161) *bow;* J. R. Parrott, '83 (182) ; F. W. Rogers, '83 (172) ; N. T. Guernsey, L. S. (176½) ; L. K. Hull, '83 (180) *captain;* W. H. Hyndman, '84 (182) ; C. B. Storrs, '82 (182) ; H. T. Folsom, '83 (151) *stroke;* D. R. Plesson, '85 (86) *coxswain.* Average weight, 176. Time, 20 min. 50½ sec.

Referee. — Prof. A. Agassiz, Harvard.

FRESHMAN RACE. — July 1, 1882, at New London. Four miles straight away.

1. *Columbia '85.* — Sanders (130) *bow;* Middletown (130) ; Crowell (130) ; Hunt (134) ; R. L. Lee (145) ; Whitman (160) ; G. B. Lee (150) ; Peet (140) *stroke;* Donnitzer (99) *coxswain.* Time, 10 min. 56 sec.

2. *Harvard '85.* — McCook (130) *bow;* Hauser (146) ; Read (156) ; Howes (150) ; Hallack (169) ; Gilman (165) ; Storrow (156) ; Keith, (151) *stroke;* Whiteside (93) *coxswain.* Time, 11 min. 10 sec.

Referee. — C. D. Moore, Columbia, '75.

UNIVERSITY RACE. — New London. The race with Columbia was postponed to July 3, 1882, on account of the drowning of the coxswain of the Columbia crew. The hour at which it should be rowed was not settled. Finally, the Harvard crew, supposing the race had been abandoned, went out of training and left New London. The Columbia crew then rowed over the course, and the referee, R. C. Watson, Harvard, '69, declared Columbia the winner. As there was no contest, neither the names nor time of the Columbia crew are given.

BASE BALL.

CLASS MATCHES.

FRESHMAN YEAR, 1878-9

Manager . . . . . G. W. Williams, *resigned*.
H. H. Dunlevy.

Captain . . . . . D. B. Fearing, *resigned*.
H. G. Chapin.

1. '82 *vs.* Yale '82, at New Haven. April 26, 1879. Yale '82 victorious, 19—11. Knowles, p.; C. H. Stevens, h.; Burt, a.; H. A. Richardson, b.; Leatherbee, c.; Chapin, s.; F. S. Hall, l.; Snow, m.; Andrews, r.

2. '82 *vs.* Adams' Academy, at Quincy, Mass. May 13, 1879. '82 victorious, 18—3. H. A. Richardson, p.; Olmsted, b.; Snow, c.; Perin, l.; F. S. Hall, m.; others same as in 1.

3. '82 *vs.* Brown '82, at Providence, R. I., May 17, 1879. Brown '82 victorious, 4—3. H. A. Richardson, b.; Knowles, p.; other positions same as in 2.

4. '82 *vs.* Brown '82, at Cambridge. May 24, 1879. Brown '82 victorious, 7—5. Nine same as in 3.

5. '82 *vs.* Yale '82, at Cambridge. May 31, 1879. Yale '82 victorious in 10 innings, 6—5. Olmsted, l.; Perin, m.; other positions same as in 4.

Games played, 5; won, 1; lost, 4.

UNIVERSITY MATCHES.

Freshman Year, 1878-79.

Manager . . . . Le Roy, '79.
Scorer . . . . Bates, '79.
Captain . . . . . . Wright, '79, *resigned.*
Winsor, '80.

1. Harvard *vs.* New Bedford, at New Bedford. April 12. 1879. New Bedford victorious, 25—2. Nunn, '79, s.; Coolidge, '81, b.; Folsom, '81, p.; Winsor, '80, m. and h.; J. S. Howe, '81, l.; Dalzell, '79, r.; Harding, '78, a.; Cohen, L. S., c.; Delano, '79, h. and m.

2. Harvard *vs.* Boston, at Boston. April 14, 1879. Boston victorious, 16—1. Nunn, '79, s.; Coolidge, '81, b.; Tyng, L. S., p.; Winsor, '80, h.; J. S. Howe, '81, l.; Olmsted, '82, a.; Harding, '78, r.; Cohen, L. S., c.; Delano, '79, m.

3. Harvard *vs.* Beacon, on Jarvis Field. April 16, 1879. Harvard victorious, 5—4. Nunn, '79, s.; Coolidge, '81, b.; Winsor, '80, r.; J. S. Howe, '81, l.; Olmsted, '82, a.; Cohen, L. S., c.; Delano, '79, m.; Stevens, '82, h.; Knowles, '82, p.

4. Harvard *vs.* Beacon, on Jarvis Field. April 23, 1879. Harvard victorious, 7—6. Nunn, '79, s.; W. A. Howe, '81, h.; Coolidge, '81, b.; Winsor, '80, r.; J. S. Howe, '81, l.; Olmsted, '82, a.; Cohen, L. S., c.; Eliot, '82, m.; Knowles, '82, p.

5. Harvard *vs.* Dartmouth, at Hanover. April 26, 1879. Harvard victorious, 5—2. Nunn, '79, s.; W. A. Howe, '81, h.; Coolidge, '81, b.; Folsom, '81, m.; J. S. Howe, '81, l.; Winsor, '80, p.; Olmsted, '82, a.; Eliot, '81, r.; Cohen, L. S., c.

6. Harvard *vs.* Beacon, on Jarvis Field. May 1, 1879. Beacon victorious, 3—1. Nunn, '79, s.; Coolidge, '81, b.; Folsom, '81, m.; J. S. Howe, '81, l.; Winsor, '80, p.; Olmsted, '82, a.; Cohen, L. S., c.; Knowles, '82, r.; Stevens, '82, h.

7. Harvard *vs.* Brown, at Providence. May 3, 1879. Brown victorious, 21—5. Nunn, '79, s.; Ernst, '76, p.; Coolidge, '81, b.; Folsom, '81, r.; W. A. Howe, '81, m.; Winsor, '80, p.; Olmsted, '82, a.; Cohen, L. S., c.; Stevens, '82, h.

8. Harvard *vs.* Clinton, at Clinton. May 6, 1879. Clinton victorious, 17—5. Nunn, '79, s.; Coolidge, 81, b.; Folsom, '81, m.; Howe, '81, l.; Winsor, '80, p.; Olmsted, '82, a.; Alger, '79, h.; Cohen, L. S., c.; Hanks, '79, r.

9. Harvard vs. Clinton, at Boston. May 8, 1879. Clinton victorious, 8—0. Nunn, '79, s.; Tyng, '76, h.; W. A. Howe, '81, m.; Coolidge, '81, b.; Winsor, '80, r.; Olmsted, '82, a.; Alger, '79, p.; Cohen, L. S., c.; Hanks, '79, r.

10. Harvard vs. Yale, at New Haven. May 10, 1879. Yale victorious, 11—5. Base hits: Harvard, 8; Yale, 19. Errors: Harvard, 7; Yale, 8. Nunn, '79, s.; W. A. Howe, '81, m.; Wright, '79, a.; Coolidge, '81, b.; Winsor, '80, r.; Holden, '81, h.; Olmsted, '82, l.; Cohen, L. S., c.; Alger, '79, p.

11. Harvard vs. Yale, on Jarvis Field. May 17, 1879. Harvard victorious, 2—0. Base hits: Harvard, 4; Yale, 6. Errors: Harvard, 4; Yale, 4. Winsor, '80, r.; Tyng, L. S., h.; Ernst, M. S., p.; W. A. Howe, '81, m.; Nunn, '79, s.; Coolidge, '81, b.; Olmsted, '82, a.; Alger, '79, l.; Cohen, L. S., c.

12. Harvard vs. Brown, on Jarvis Field. May 21, 1879. Brown victorious, 6—2. Winsor, '80, r.; Tyng, L. S., h.; Ernst, M. S., p.; Nunn, '79, s.; Coolidge, '81, b.; Wright, '79, a.; Olmsted, '82, m.; Alger, '79, l.; Cohen, L. S., c.

13. Harvard vs. Princeton, at Princeton. May 23, 1879. Princeton victorious, 5—2. Winsor, '80, s.; Tyng, L. S., p.; Howe, '81, m.; Coolidge, '81, b.; Wright, '79, a.; Olmsted, '82, l.; Alger, '79, h.; Hanks, '79, r.; Cohen, L. S., c.

14. Harvard vs. Princeton, at Princeton. May 24, 1879. Harvard victorious, 8—2. Winsor, '80, s.; Tyng, '76, h.; Howe, '81, m.; Ernst, '76, p.; Coolidge, '81, b.; Alger, '79, r.; Wright, '79, a.; Olmsted, '82, l.; Cohen, L. S., c.

15. Harvard vs. Dartmouth, at Cambridge. May 27, 1879. Harvard victorious, 11—3. Winsor, '80, r.; Tyng, L. S., m.; Ernst, M. S., p.; Coolidge, '81, b.; Nunn, '79, s.; Alger, '79, h.; Wright, '79, a.; Olmsted, '82, l.; Cohen, L. S., c.

16. Harvard vs. Princeton, at Cambridge. June 2, 1879. Six innings. Harvard, 3; Princeton, 3. Coolidge, '81, b.; Tyng, L. S., m.; Ernst, M. S., p.; Folsom, '81, h.; Wright, '79, a.; Olmsted, '82, l.; Cohen, L. S., c.; Hanks, '79, r.; Eliot, '82, s.

17. Harvard vs. General Worth, at Stoneham. June 11, 1879. General Worth victorious, 11—4. Coolidge, '81, b.; Tyng, L. S., p.; Holden, '81, r.; Winsor, '80, m.; Nunn, '79, s.; Olmsted, '82, l.; Wright, '79, a.; Alger, '79, h.; Cohen, L. S., c.

18. Harvard vs. Utica, at South Boston. June 13, 1879. Utica victorious, 6—4. Coolidge, '81, b.; Tyng, L. S., p.; Winsor, '80,

m.; Nunn, '79, s.; Wright, '79, a.; Holden, '81, r.; Olmsted, '82, l.; Alger, '79, h.; Cohen, L. S., c.

19. Harvard vs. General Worth, at Stoneham. June 14, 1879. Harvard victorious, 9—5. Coolidge, '81, b.; Tyng, L. S., h.; Ernst, M. S., p.; Winsor, '80, r.; Nunn, '79, s.; Wright, '79, a.; Olmsted, '82, l.; Cohen, L. S., c.; Folsom, '81, m.

20. Harvard vs. Campello, at Campello. June 17, 1879. Harvard victorious, 7—2. Coolidge, '81, b.; Tyng, L. S., h.; Ernst, M. S., p.; Winsor, '80, r.; Wright, '79, a.; Nunn, '79, s.; Olmsted, '82, l.; Alger, '79, c.; Holden, '81, m.

21. Harvard vs. Worcester, at Worcester. June 18, 1879. Worcester victorious, 13—7. Coolidge, '81, b.; Ernst, M. S., p.; Cohen, L. S., r.; Wright, '79, a.; Nunn, '79, s.; Olmsted, '82, l.; Alger, '79, h.; Holden, '81, c.; H. A. Richardson, '82, m.

22. Harvard vs. King Philip, at Rockland. June 21, 1879. Harvard victorious, 18—5. Seven innings. Coolidge, '81, b.; Tyng, L. S., h.; Ernst, M. S., p.; Wright, '79, a.; Nunn, '79, s.; Olmsted, '82, l.; Holden, '81, c.; Cohen, L. S., r.; Berry, '81, m.

23. *Harvard* vs. *Yale, at New Haven. June 23, 1879. Yale victorious, 9—5. Base hits: Harvard 9; Yale, 10. Errors: Harvard, 10; Yale, 5. Coolidge, '81, b.; Tyng, L. S., h.; Ernst, M. S. p.; Wright, '79, a.; Olmsted, '82, l.; Winsor, '80, m.; Nunn, '79, s.; Cohen, L. S., r.; Holden, '81, c.*

24. *Harvard* vs. *Yale, on Jarvis Field. Commencement, June 25, 1879. Harvard victorious, 7—3. Base hits: Harvard 6; Yale, 8. Errors: Harvard, 4; Yale, 5. Nine same as in No. 23.*

25. Harvard vs. Holyoke, on Jarvis Field. June 26, 1879. Drawn game, 0—0. Thirteen innings. Base hits: Harvard, 4; Holyoke, 9. Errors: Harvard, 1; Holyoke, 8. Coolidge, '81, b.; Tyng, L. S., h.; Ernst, M. S., p.; Wright, '79, a.; Winsor, '80, m.; Olmstead, '82, l.; Nunn, '79, s.; Cohen, L. S., c.; Holden, '81, r.

26. *Harvard* vs. *Yale, at Providence. June 28, 1879. Harvard victorious, 9—4. Base hits: Harvard, 15; Yale, 7. Errors: Harvard, 4; Yale, 10. Coolidge, '81, b.; Tyng, L. S., h.; Ernst, M. S., p.; Wright, '79, a.; Winsor, '80, m.; Olmsted, '82, l.; Nunn, '79, s.; Cohen, L. S., r.; Holden, '81, c.*

Games won, 11; Games lost, 13; Drawn games, 2.

Sophomore Year, 1879-80.

Captain . . . . Winsor, '80.
Manager . . . . Townsend, '80.
Scorer . . . . Townsend, '82.

27. Harvard *vs.* Picked Nine, on Jarvis Field. April 6, 1880. Harvard victorious 2—1.

28. Harvard *vs.* Worcester, at Worcester. April 8, 1880. Worcester victorious, 9—5. Six innings. Shattuck, L. S., p.; Nichols, '83, h.; Folsom, '81, a.; Coolidge, '81, b.; Burt, '82, c.; Wright, s.; Washburn, '82, l.; Leavitt, '82, m.; Fearing, '83, r.

29. Harvard *vs.* Boston, on Boston Grounds. April 10, 1880. Boston victorious, 23—10. Coolidge, '81, b.; Shattuck, L. S., p.; McCullar, s.; Nichols, '83, m.; Folsom, '81, h. and c., Richardson, c. and h.; Fearing, '83, r. and a.; Burt, '82, l.; Brinsmade, '81, a. and r.

30. Harvard *vs.* Boston, on Boston Grounds. April 21, 1880. Boston victorious, 14—0. Coolidge, '81, b.; Shattuck, L. S., p.; Olmsted, '82, l.; Leavitt, '82, m.; Nichols, '83, h.; Folsom, '81, a.; Snow, '82, c.; Burt, '82, r.; H. A. Richardson, '82, s.

31. Harvard *vs.* Beacon, on Jarvis Field. April 22, 1880. Beacon victorious, 5—4. Coolidge, '81, b.; Shattuck. L. S., p.; Nichols, '83, h.; Winsor, '80, s.; Olmsted, '82, l.; Ranney, '83, r.; Folsom, '81, a.; Holden, '81, c.; H. A. Richardson, '82, m.

32. Harvard *vs.* Picked Nine, on Jarvis Field. April 24, 1880. Harvard victorious, 5—4. Coolidge '81, b.; Shattuck, L. S., a.; Richardson, h.; Snow, '82, s.; Olmsted, '82, l.; H. A. Richardson, '82, m.; Holden, '81, c.; Folsom, '81, p.; Fisher, '81, r.

33. Harvard *vs.* Beacon, on Jarvis Field. April 28, 1880. Beacon victorious, 7—4. Coolidge, '81, b.; Shattuck, L. S., p.; Nichols, '83, h.; Winsor, '80, s.; Olmsted, '82, l.; Richardson, '82, m.; Holden, '81, c.; Folsom, '81, a.; Fisher, '81, r.

34. Harvard *vs.* Boston, on Boston Grounds. April 29, 1880. Boston victorious, 13—9. Coolidge, '81, b.; Shattuck, L. S., p.; Nichols, '83, m.; Winsor, '80, s.; Olmsted, '82, l.; Jennison, '83, h.; Holden, '81, c.; Folsom, '81, a.; Fisher, '81, r.

35. Harvard *vs.* Brockton, at Brockton. May 5, 1880. Brockton victorious, 3—2. Coolidge, '81, m.; Shattuck, L. S., p.; Nichols, '83, h.; Winsor, '80, s.; Olmsted, '82, l.; Leavitt, '82, r.; Holden, '81, c.; Folsom, '81, a.; Fisher, '81, b.

36. Harvard *vs.* Beacon, on Jarvis Field. May 6, 1880. Har-

vard victorious, 7—3. H. A. Richardson, '82, b.; Shattuck, L. S., p.; Nichols, '83, m.; Winsor, '80, s.; Olmsted, '82, l.; Leavitt, '82, r.; Holden, '81, c.; Folsom, '81, a.; Jennison, '83, h.

37. Harvard *vs*. Dartmouth, at Hanover, N. H. May 8, 1880. Dartmouth victorious, 13—5. Coolidge, '81, b.; Shattuck, L. S., p.; Nichols, '83, h.; Winsor, '80, s.; Olmsted, '82, l.; Leavitt, '82, r.; Holden, '81, c.; Folsom, '81, a.; Alger, M. S. m.

38. Harvard *vs*. Amherst, at Amherst. May 12, 1880. Harvard victorious, 14—9. Coolidge, '81, b.; Shattuck, L. S., p.; Nichols, '83, h.; Winsor, '80, h. and s.; Olmsted, '82, l. and s.; Leavitt, '82, r.; Folsom, '81, a.; Elliott, L. S. S., c.; Fuller, '83, m.

39. *Harvard* vs. *Yale, at New Haven. May* 15, 1880. *Yale victorious*, 21—4. *Base hits: Harvard*, 10; *Yale*, 21. *Errors: Harvard*, 10; *Yale*, 6. *Coolidge*, '81, *b.; Shattuck, L. S., p.; Nichols*, '83, *m.; Winsor*, '80, *s.; Olmsted*, '82, *l.; Leavitt*, '82, *r.; Folsom*, '81, *a.; Alger, M. S., h.; H. A. Richardson*, '82, *c.*

40. Harvard *vs*. Princeton, at Princeton. May 21, 1880. Princeton victorious, 19—6. Coolidge, '81, b.; Shattuck, L. S., a. and p.; Nichols, '83, m.; Winsor, '80, h. and s.; Olmsted, '82, l.; Leavitt, '82, r.; Folsom, '81, p. and a.; Alger, M. S., c.; Jackson, L. S., s.

41. Harvard *vs*. Princeton, at Princeton. May 22, 1880. Princeton victorious, 9—5. Nine same as in No. 40, except Winsor, '80, h.

42. Harvard *vs*. Brown, at Providence. May 25, 1880. Harvard victorious, 5—3. Coolidge, '81, b.; Olmsted, '82, l.; Fessenden, '80, r.; Winsor, '80, h.; Shattuck, L. S., a.; Nichols, '83, m.; Alger, M. S., c.; Folsom, '81, p.; Richardson, '82, s.

43. Harvard *vs*. Dartmouth, on Jarvis Field. May 27, 1880. Dartmouth victorious, 4—2. Nine same as in No. 75, except Fessenden, '80; c.; Leavitt, '82, r., in place of Alger.

44. *Harvard* vs. *Yale, on Jarvis Field. May* 29, 1880. *Yale victorious*, 2—1. *Base hits: Harvard*, 8; *Yale*, 5. *Errors: Harvard*, 4; *Yale*, 5. *Nine same as in No.* 42, *except Holden*, '81, *in place of Alger.*

45. Harvard *vs*. Brown, on Jarvis Field. June 1, 1880. Brown victorious, 7—1. Nine same as in No. 44.

46. Harvard *vs*. Princeton, on Jarvis Field. June 4, 1880.

Princeton victorious, 7—6. Nine same as in No. 44, except Edwards, '83, in place of Richardson.

47. Harvard vs. Princeton, on Jarvis Field. June 5, 1880. Princeton victorious, 7—2. Coolidge, '81, b.; Olmsted, '82, l.; Fessenden, '80, r.; Winsor, '80, m.; Shattuck, L. S., p.; Jennison, '83, h.; Holden, '81, c.; Folsom, '81, a.; Richardson, '82, s.

48. Harvard vs. Beacon, on Jarvis Field. June 10, 1880. Harvard victorious, 4—2. Coolidge, '81, b.; Olmstead, '82, l.; Fessenden, '80, r.; Winsor, '80, m.; Shattuck, L. S., a.; Nichols, '83, h.; Holden, '81, c.; Folsom, '81, p.; Richardson, '82, s.

49. Harvard vs. Brockton, at Brockton. June 15, 1880. Harvard victorious, 4—2. Nine same as in No. 48, except Edwards, '83, in place of Fessenden.

50. Harvard vs. Stoneham, at Stoneham. June 19, 1880. Harvard victorious, 28—7. Nine same as in No. 47.

51. Harvard vs. Natick, on Jarvis Field. June 21, 1880. Natick victorious, 5—4. Nine same as in No. 47, except Winsor and Nichols interchanged and Edwards. '83, in Richardson's place.

52. Harvard vs. Beacon, on Jarvis Field. June 22, 1880. Harvard victorious, 3—0. Coolidge, '81, b.; Olmsted, '82, l.; Edwards, '83, s.; Winsor, '80, r; Shattuck, L. S., p.; Nichols, '83, m.; Holden, '81, c.; Folsom, '81, a.; Jennison. '83, h.

53. Harvard vs. Harvard, '77, on Jarvis Field. June 24, 1880. Harvard victorious, 17—11. Nine same as in No. 47.

54. Harvard vs. Brockton, at Springfield. June 26, 1880. Brockton victorious, 17—2. Coolidge, '81, b.; Shattuck, L. S., p.; Edwards, '83, s.; Winsor, '80, r. and l.; Nichols, '83, m.; Holden, '81, c.; Folsom, '81, a.; Jennison, '83, h.

55. *Harvard* vs. *Yale, at New Haven, June* 28, 1880. *Harvard victorious, 3—1. Coolidge, '81, b.; Fessenden, '80, r.; Shattuck, L. S., a.; Winsor, '80, h.; Nichols, '83, m.; Holden, '81, c.; Olmsted, '82, l.; Folsom, '81, p.; Edwards, '83, s. Base hits: Harvard, 7; Yale, 2. Errors: Harvard,* 1, *Yale,* 3.

56. *Harvard* vs. *Yale, on Jarvis Field. June* 30, 1880. *Yale victorious,* 3—0. *Nine same as in No.* 55.

Games won, 12; games lost, 18.

Junior Year, 1880-81.

Officers H. B. B. Association.

President . . . Harold Ernst, '76 (resigned).
" . . . E. H. Pendleton, '82.
Captain . . . . W. H. Coolidge, '81.
Managers . . . Pendleton, '82, Harvey, '81.
Scorer . . . . Barton, '81.

57. Harvard vs. Boston, at Boston. April 9, 1881. Boston victorious, 19—1. Coolidge, '81, b.; Olmsted, '82, l.; Nichols, '83, m.; Baker, '84, s.; Cutts, M. S., a.; Edwards, '83, r.; Brown, M. S., h.; Folsom, '81, p.; Snow, '82, c.

58. Harvard vs. Boston, at Boston. April 16, 1881. Boston victorious, 9—2. Coolidge, '81, b.; Cutts, M. S., a.; Baker, '84, s.; Edwards, '83, r.; Perin, '82, m.; Snow, '82, c.; Edmands, S. S., l.; Bean, '84, p.; Hamlin, '84, h.

59. Picked Nine vs. Boston, at Boston. April 19, 1881. Boston victorious, 10—5. Nine same as in No. 57, except Bond, p. and Snyder, h.

60. Harvard vs. Beacon, at Cambridge. April 21, 1881. Beacon victorious, 11—2. Coolidge, '81, b.; Cutts, M. S., a.; Nichols, '83, h.; Baker, '84, s.; Olmsted, '82, l.; Edwards, '83, r.; Bean, '84, p.; Folsom, '81, m.; Snow, '82, c.

61. Harvard vs. Worcester, at Worcester. April 23, 1881. Worcester victorious, 19—4. Coolidge, '81, b.; Olmsted, '82, l.; Nichols, '83, m.; Baker, '84, s.; Edwards, '83, r.; Folsom, '81, a.; Bean, '84, p.; Hamlin, '84, h.; Snow, '82, c.

62. Harvard vs. Bowdoin, at Cambridge. May 2, 1881. Harvard victorious, 18—5. Coolidge, '81, b.; Cutts, M. S., a.; Nichols, '83, m.; Baker, '84, s.; Olmsted, '82, l.; Edwards, '83, r.; Folsom, '81, p.; Hall, '82, h.; Snow, '82, c.

63. Harvard vs. Amherst, at Cambridge. May 4, 1881. Harvard victorious, 15—0. Nine same as in No. 62.

64. Harvard vs. Dartmouth, at Hanover. May 7, 1881. Harvard victorious, 13—11. Nine same as in No. 62.

65. Harvard vs. Brown, at Cambridge. May 9, 1881. Harvard victorious, 10—6. Nine same as in No. 62, except Nichols and Hall interchanged.

66. Harvard vs. Dartmouth, at Cambridge. May 12, 1881. Harvard victorious, 10—4. Nine same as in No. 65.

67. *Harvard* vs. *Yale. at Cambridge. May* 14, 1881. Harvard victorious, 14—9. Nine same as in No. 65. Base hits: *Harvard*. 11 ; *Yale*, 11. Errors: *Harvard*, 8 ; *Yale*, 7.

68. Harvard *vs*. Princeton. at Princeton. May 20, 1881. Game stopped in the middle of the fifth innings, score standing 3—1 in Harvard's favor. Nine same as in No. 65, except Burt, '82, in place of Cutts.

69. Harvard *vs*. Princeton. at Princeton. May 21, 1881. Harvard victorious, 4—1. Nine same as in No. 68.

70. Harvard *vs*. Amherst, at Amherst. May 25, 1881. Amherst victorious, 7—2. Nine same as in No. 68.

71. *Harvard* vs. *Yale. at New Haven. May* 28, 1881. *Yale victorious,* 8—5. *Nine same as in No.* 65. *Base hits: Harvard*. 7 ; *Yale*. 8. *Errors: Harvard*. 5 ; *Yale*, 5.

72. Harvard *vs*. Bowdoin. at Portland. May 30, 1881. Game stopped in middle of fifth innings on account of rain, score standing 4—0 in Harvard's favor. Nine same as in No. 68.

73. Harvard *vs*. Beacons. at Cambridge. June 3, 1881. Harvard victorious, 10—7. Nine same as in No. 68, except Edmands, S. S., in Olmsted's place.

74. Harvard *vs*. Princeton, at Cambridge. June 6, 1881. Princeton victorious, 6—5. Ten innings. Nine same as in No. 68.

75. Harvard *vs*. Princeton. at Cambridge. June 7, 1881. Harvard victorious. 6—3. Coolidge, '81, b.; Olmsted, '82, l.; Baker, '84, s.; Edwards, '83, m.; Hall, '82, h.; Snow, '82, c.; Burt, '82, a.; Lovering, '84, r.; Bean, '84, p.

76. Harvard *vs*. Brown. at Providence. June 15, 1881. Brown victorious. 9—6. Nine same as in No. 68, except Lovering, '84, in place of Edwards.

77. Harvard *vs*. Beacon, at Cambridge. June 17, 1881. Harvard victorious, 10—5. Coolidge, '81, b.; Olmsted, '82, l.; Edwards, '83, m.; Nichols, '83, h.; Baker, '84, s.; Hall, '82, m. and h.; Burt, '82, a.; Snow, '82, c.; Bean, '84, p.; Lovering, '84, r.

78. Harvard *vs*. Beacon. at Cambridge. June 21, 1881. Harvard victorious. 11—4. Nine same as in No. 77, except Edwards, with Hall, h., and Nichols, m.

79. Harvard *vs*. Beacon. at Cambridge. June 23, 1881. Harvard victorious. 7—6. Nine same as in 78, except Hall and Nichols interchanged.

Games won, 14; games lost, 8. Total, 22.

SENIOR YEAR, 1881-82.
Officers of H. B. B. Association.
E. H. PENDLETON, JR., '82, *President.*
H. R. EDWARDS, '83, *Vice-President and Scorer.*
O. A. OLMSTED, '82, *Captain.*

80. Harvard *vs.* Metropolitan, at Polo Grounds, New York, April 5, 1882. Metropolitan victorious, 3—2. Coolidge, L. S., b.; Olmsted, '82, l.; Nichols, '83, h.; Le Moyne, '84, c.; Hall, '82, r.; Burt. '82, a.; Bean, '84, p.; Crocker, '85, m.; Lovering, '84, s.

81. Harvard *vs.* Metropolitan, at Polo Grounds, New York, April 6, 1882. Metropolitan victorious, 17—3. Nine same as in 80.

82. Harvard *vs.* Metropolitan, at Polo Grounds, New York, April 10, 1882, Metropolitan victorious, 10—2. Nine same as in 80, but Tucker, M. S., in place of Bean.

83. Harvard *vs.* Boston, at Boston, April 15, 1882. Boston victorious, 8—7. Nine same as in 80, but Hall and Crocker interchanged positions

84. Harvard *vs.* Boston, at Boston, April 18, 1882. Boston victorious, 4—2. Nine same as in 80.

85. Harvard *vs.* Worcester, at Worcester, April 22, 1882. Worcester victorious, 18—12. Nine same as in 83.

86. Harvard *vs.* Lowell, at Lowell, April 26, 1882. Harvard victorious, 12—6. Coolidge, L. S., b.; Olmsted, '82, l.; Le Moyne, '84, c.; Hall, '82, m.; Burt, '82, a.; Bean, '84, p.; Crocker, '85, h.; Baker, '84, r; Lovering, '84, s.

87. Harvard *vs.* Boston, at Boston, April 28th, 1882. Boston victorious, 24—1. Coolidge, L. S., b.; Olmsted, '82, l.; Nichols, '83, m.; Le Moyne, '84, c.; Hall, '82, r.; Burt, '82, a.; Tucker, M. S., p.; Crocker, '85, h.; Lovering, '84, s.

88. Harvard *vs.* Providence, at Providence, April 29, 1882. Providence victorious, 7—1. Coolidge, L. S., b.; Olmsted, '82, l.; Burt, '82, a.; Le Moyne, '84, c.; Hall, '82, h.; Bean, '84, p.; Crocker, '85, r.; Follansbee, '85, m.; Lovering, '84, s.

89. Harvard *vs.* Tufts, at Cambridge, May 2, 1882. Harvard victorious, 23—2. Coolidge, L. S., b.; Olmsted, '82, l.; Nichols, '83, m.; Le Moyne, '84, c.; Hall, '82, h.; Burt, '82, a.; Bean, '84, p.; Crocker, '85, r.; Lovering, '84, s.

90. Harvard vs. Brown, at Cambridge, May 6, 1882. Harvard victorious, 7—6. Coolidge, L. S., b.; Olmsted, '82, l.; Nichols, '83, h.; Le Moyne, '84, c.; Crocker, '85, r.; Burt, '82, a.; Bean, '84, p.; Hall, '82, m.; Lovering, '84, s.

91. Harvard vs. Stock Exchange, at Polo Grounds, New York, May 12, 1872. Harvard victorious, 20—1. Six innings. Coolidge, L. S., b.; Olmsted, '82, l.; Nichols, '83, h.; Le Moyne, '84, c.; Crocker, '85, r.; Baker, '84, s.; Burt, '82, a.; Hall, '82, p.; Lovering, '84, m.

92. Harvard vs. Dartmouth, at Cambridge, May 17, 1882. Dartmouth victorious, 11—8. Coolidge, L. S., b.; Olmsted, '82, l.; Nichols, '83, h.; Baker, '84, s.; Crocker, '85, r.; Burt, '82, a.; Hall, '82, m.; Bean, '84, p.; Le Moyne, '84, c.

93. Harvard vs. Princeton, at Princeton, May 19, 1882. Princeton victorious, 9—4. Olmsted, '82, l.; Coolidge, L. S., b.; Nichols, '83, m.; Baker, '84, s.; Crocker, '85, r.; Burt, '82, a.; Hall, '82, m.; Bean, '84, p.; Le Moyne, '84, c.

94. Harvard vs. Princeton, at Princeton, May 20, 1882. Harvard victorious, 14—13. Olmsted, '82, l.; Coolidge, L. S., b.; Nichols, '83, h.; Baker, '84, s.; Lovering, '84, a.; Burt, '82, r.; Hall, '82, p.; Bean, '84, m.; Le Moyne, '84, c.

95. *Harvard* vs. *Yale, at New Haven, May 27,* 1882. *Harvard victorious,* 10—7. *Base hits:* Harvard, 12—12; Yale, 12—14. *Errors:* Harvard, 5; Yale, 8. Coolidge, L. S., b.; Olmsted, '82, l.; Nichols, '83, m.; Baker, '84, s.; Crocker, '84, h.; Hall '82, r.; Lovering, '84, a.; Bean, '84, p.; Le Moyne, '84, c.

96. Harvard vs. Amherst, at Amherst, May 29th, 1882. Harvard victorious, 19—8. Nine as in 95.

97. Harvard vs. Metropolitan, at Polo Grounds, New York, May 30, 1882. Metropolitan victorious, 12—4. Nine as in 95, but Winslow, '85, in place of Bean.

98. Harvard vs. Stock Exchange, at Staten Island, May 30, 1882. Harvard victorious, 3—2. Nine as in 97. Burt, '82, took the place of Lovering in the 7th innings.

99. Harvard vs. Princeton, at Cambridge, June 3rd, 1882. Princeton victorious, 9—3. Nine as in 95, but Burt, '82, in place of Lovering.

100. Harvard vs. Princeton, at Cambridge, June 5, 1882. Harvard victorious, 9—5. Coolidge, L. S., b.; Crocker, '85, h.;

Nichols, '83, m.; Baker, '84, s.; Hall. '82, r.; Burt. '82. a.; Follansbee, '85, l.; Bean, '84, p.; Le Moyne, '84. c.

101. Harvard vs. Amherst, at Cambridge, June 9, 1882. Harvard victorious, 10—0. Coolidge. L. S., b.; Olmsted, '82. l.; Crocker, '85, r.; Nichols, '83, m.; Baker. '84. s.; Hall, '82. h.; Burt, '82, a.; Bean, '84, p.; Le Moyne, '84, c.

102. Harvard vs. Brown, at Providence, June 12, 1882. Harvard victorious, 17—13. Coolidge, L. S.. b.; Olmsted, '82, l.; Baker, '84, s.; Nichols, '83, m.; Crocker, '85, r.; Hall. '82, h.; Burt, '82, a.; Bean, '84, p.; Le Moyne, '84, c.

103. Harvard vs. Beacon, at Cambridge, June 14, 1882. Harvard victorious, 24—9. Coolidge. L. S., b.; Olmsted, '82. l.; Baker, '84, s.; Nichols, '83. m.; Hall, '82. h.; Burt. '82, a.; Bean, '84, p.; Follansbee, '85, r.; Le Moyne, '84, c.

104. *Harvard* vs. *Yale, at Cambridge, June 22, 1882. Yale victorious, 5—4. Base hits: Harvard. 9-11; Yale, 4-6. Errors: Harvard, 7; Yale, 7. Coolidge, L. S., b.; Olmsted. '82, l.; Nichols, '83, m.; Baker, '84, s.; Burt, '82, a.; Crocker, '85, r.; Hall, '82, h.; Bean, '84, p.; Le Moyne, '84. c.*

105. Harvard vs. University Nine of '77, at Cambridge. June 23, 1882. Harvard victorious, 18—0. Coolidge, L. S.. b.; Olmsted. '82, l.; Nichols, '83, h.; Baker, '84, s.; Crocker, '85, r.; Hall, '82, p.; Lovering, '84, a.; Bean, '84, m.; Le Moyne, '84, c.

106. Harvard vs. Dartmouth. at Hanover. June 26, 1882. Dartmouth victorious, 11—10. Coolidge, L. S., b.; Olmsted, '82, l.; Nichols, '83, m.; Baker, '84, s.; Crocker, '85. r.; Hall. '82, h.; Lovering, '84, a.; Bean, '84, p.; Le Moyne. '84, c.

107. Harvard vs. Metropolitan, at New York. July 5, 1882. Metropolitan victorious, 5—4. 10 innings. Coolidge, L. S., b.; Olmsted, '82, l.; Baker. '84. s.; Hall, '82. m.; Burt. '82. r.; Richardson, S. S., h.; Clarkson, S. S., p.; Lovering. '84, a.; Le Moyne, '84, c.

Games played, 28; won, 13; lost. 15.

FOOTBALL.

CLASS MATCHES.

Freshman Year, 1878-79.

M. S. Crehore, *Captain*.
Prescott Lawrence, *Secretary and Treasurer*.

1. '82 *vs.* '81, October 26, 1878, at Cambridge. '82 victorious; 1 goal, 3 touchdowns; '81, 0. *Rushers:* Crehore, Kane, Boyd, Warren, Manning, Thacher. *Half-backs:* Sedgwick, Perin, Eldridge. *Backs:* Leatherbee, Blodgett.

2. '82 *vs.* Adams Academy, November 5, 1878, at Quincy. Adams Academy victorious; 2 goals; '82, 1 goal, 2 touchdowns. Team same as in 1.

3. '82 *vs.* Phillips Academy, November 13, 1878, at Andover. '82 victorious; 2 goals, 4 touchdowns; Phillips Academy, 0. Perin being ill, his place was filled by Warren, and Warren's by Williams. Rest of the team as in 1.

Games played, 3. Won, 2; lost, 1.

UNIVERSITY MATCHES.

Freshman Year, 1878-79.

L. Cushing, '79, *Captain;* H. S. LeRoy, '79, *Treasurer*.

1. Harvard *vs.* Amherst, November 8, 1878, Boston. *Rushers:* Cowdin, '79, ; Holmes, '79 ; Swift, '79 ; Perry, '79 ; G. F. Morse, '81 ; Warren, '82 ; Cushing, M. S. *Half-backs:* Cushing, '79 ; Winsor, '80 ; Sedgwick, '82 ; Harrington, M. S. ; Clark, '80 ; *Backs:* Houston, '79 ; Bacon, '80 ; Leatherbee, '82. Harvard, three goals, three touchdowns. Amherst, 0. Harrington injured and De Windt, '81, substituted.

2. Harvard vs. Princeton, November 16, 1878, Boston. *Rushers:* Cushing, M. S.; Harrington. M. S.; Swift, '79; Holmes, '79; Perry, '79; Cowdin, '79; G. F. Morse, '81. *Half-backs:* Cushing, '79; Blanchard, M. S.; Thacher, '82; Warren, '82; Houston. '79. *Backs:* Sedgwick, '82; Wetherbee, S. S.; Bacon, '80. Princeton, one touchdown; Harvard, 0.

3. Harvard vs. Yale, November 23, 1878, Boston. Harvard, same as in 2.

Yale: *Rushers:* Fowle, '79; Fuller, '81; Hull, '82; Harding, '80; Lamb, '81; King, '80; Eaton, '82. *Half-backs:* Badger, '82; Peters, '80; Thompson, '79; Watson, S. S.; Camp, '80 (*capt.*). *Backs:* Nixon, '81; Wakeman, M. S.; Lyman, '82. Yale, one goal; Harvard, 0. Referee: Ballard, Princeton. Umpires, Whiting, '77, Harvard; Clark, Yale.

4. University vs. Graduates, December 7, 1878, Holmes Field. *Rushers:* Swift, '79; Nunn, '79; Perry, '79; Manning, '82; Warren, '82; Thacher, '82; Cowdin, '79; G. F. Morse, '81. *Half-backs:* Cushing, '79; Sedgwick, '82; Houston, '79; Winsor, '80. *Backs:* Eldridge, '82; Cabot, '80. Graduates: Whiting, '77 (*capt.*); Russell, '77; Rollins, '77; Lombard, '78; Grant, '79; H. Grant, '74; Blanchard, M. S.; Jordan, '80; Rives, '74; Hoar, '76; Curtis, '77; Tower, '77; Tiffany, '78. University, seven goals, several touchdowns; Graduates, 0. Umpire, Holmes, '79.

Games played, 4; won, 2; lost, 2.

SOPHOMORE YEAR, 1879–80.

R. BACON, '80, *Captain;* W. HOOPER, '80. *Treasurer.*

5. Harvard vs. Britannia, October 25, 1879, Boston Grounds. *Rushers:* Cushing, M. S.; Manning, '82; Cushing, L. S.; Brooks, L. S.; Warren, '82; Tebbets, '80; Howe, M. S.; Thacher, '82; Nickerson, '80. *Quarter-back:* Bacon, 80. *Half-backs:* Austin, L. S.; Winsor, '80. *Three-quarter back:* Cabot, '83. *Backs:* Shattuck, L. S.; Leatherbee, '82. Harvard, two goals, one touchdown; Britannia, 0.

6. Harvard vs. Britannia, November 1, 1879, Montreal. Harvard, one goal; Britannia, 0.

7. Harvard vs. McGill, November 3, 1879, Montreal. Harvard, one goal, one touchdown (1st inning). McGill, 0 (1st

inning). The game was then stopped owing to a snow-storm; and, by mutual consent, declared a draw.

8. Harvard vs. Yale, November 8, 1879, Hamilton Park, New Haven. *Rushers:* G. F. Morse, '81; Manning, '82; Cushing, L. S.; Brooks, L. S.; Warren, '82; Tebbets, '80; Thacher, '82; Nickerson, '80; Cushing, M. S. *Quarter-back:* Bacon, '80. *Half-backs:* Austin, L. S.; Winsor, '80. *Three-quarter-back:* Holden, '81. *Backs:* Shattuck, L. S.; Leatherbee, '82.

Yale. *Rushers:* Hull, Beck, Vernon, Lamb, Harding, Remington, Eaton, Morehead. *Half-backs:* Badger, Camp (*capt.*), Peters, Clark. *Three-quarter-back:* Bacon. *Backs:* Lyman, Nixon. Harvard, 0; Yale, 0. Referee: Ballard, Princeton. Umpires: Houston, L. S., Harvard; McHenry, '80, Yale. Holden was hurt at beginning of game, and gave way to E. T. Cabot, '83.

9. Harvard vs. Princeton, November 15, 1879, Hoboken, N. J. *Rushers:* Nickerson, '80; Cushing, L. S.; Cushing, M. S.; Thacher, '82; Manning, '82; Tebbets, '80; G. F. Morse, '81; Howe, M. S.; Warren, '82. *Quarter-back:* Bacon, '80. *Half-backs:* Winsor, '80; Austin, L. S. *Three-quarter-back:* E. T. Cabot, '83. *Backs:* Shattuck, L. S., Leatherbee, '82. Princeton, one goal; Harvard, 0.

Games played, 5; won, 2; lost, 1; draw, 2.

JUNIOR YEAR. 1880–81.

W. H. MANNING, '82, *Captain.*
E. W. ATKINSON, '81, *Acting Captain* after November 2.
H. R. HOYT, '82, *Treasurer.*

10. Harvard vs. Britannia, October 23, 1880, Boston. *Rushers:* Atkinson, '81; Boyd, '82; Kendall, '84; L. M. Clark, '81; Dabney, '82; Manning, '82; Morison, '83; Perin, '82; Thacher, '82. *Half-backs:* Wesselhoeft, '84; Kent, '83; Keith, '83. *Three-quarter-back:* Cabot, '83. *Backs:* Leatherbee, '82; Edmands, S. S. Harvard, two goals; Britannia, 0.

11. Harvard vs. Ottawa, November 1, 1880, Ottawa. *Rushers:* Boyd, '82, L. M. Clark, '81; Dabney, '82; Cabot, '83; Manning, '82; Morison, '83; Perin, '82; Thacher, '82. *Half-backs:* Keith, '83; Kent, '83; Wesselhoeft, '83. *Three-quarter-back:* Edmands, S. S. *Backs:* Leatherbee, '82; Hardwick, '84. Harvard, two goals; Ottawa, 0.

12. Harvard vs. Montreal, November 2, 1880, Montreal. Team same as in 11. Harvard, 0; Montreal, 0.

13. Harvard vs. Columbia, November 6, 1880, New York. *Rushers:* Atkinson, '81, L. M. Clark, '81; E. T. Cabot, '83; Perin, '82; Thacher, '82. *Quarter-back:* Boyd, '82. *Half-backs:* C. H. W. Foster, '81; Kent, '83; Keith, '83. *Backs:* Leatherbee, '82; Edmands, S. S. Harvard, three goals; Columbia, 0.

14. Harvard vs. Princeton, November 13, 1880, Hoboken, N. J. *Rushers:* Atkinson, '81; L. M. Clark, '81; E. T. Cabot, '83; Houston, L. S.; Perin, '82; Thacher, '82. *Quarter-back:* Boyd, '82. *Half-backs:* C. H. W. Foster, '81; Kent, '83; Keith, '83. *Back:* Edmands, S. S. Princeton, two goals; Harvard, one goal.

15. Harvard vs. Yale, November 20, 1880, Boston. Harvard: *Rushers:* Atkinson, '81; Houston, L. S.; E. T. Cabot, '83; L. M. Clark, '81; Perin, '82; Thacher, '82. *Quarter-back:* Manning, '82. *Half-backs:* C. H. W. Foster, '81; Kent, '83; Edmands, S. S. *Back:* Cutts, M. S.

Yale. *Rushers:* Fuller, Beck, Hull, Harding, Lamb, Storrs, Adams. *Quarter-back:* Badger. *Half-backs:* Watson (capt.), Camp. *Back:* Bacon. Yale, one goal, one touchdown; Harvard, 0. Referee: Loney, Princeton. Umpires: Winsor, '80, Harvard; Clark, Yale. Boyd, '82, took Manning's place, who was injured; and, being himself hurt, was replaced by Manning. Foster being hurt, Keith, '83, was substituted.

Games played, 6; won, 3; lost, 2; draw, 1.

SENIOR YEAR. 1881–82.

W. H. MANNING, '82, *Captain*.
H. G. LEAVITT, '82, *Manager*.
H. R. HOYT, '82, *Treasurer*.

16. Harvard vs. Montreal, October 20, 1881, Boston. *Rushers:* Appleton, '84; Boyd, '82; Cabot, '83; Fuller, '83; Manning, '82; Morison, '83; Thacher, '82. *Quarter-back:* Mason, '84. *Half-backs:* Henry, S. S.; Clark, '84. *Three-quarter-back:* Kent, '83. *Back:* Edmands, S. S. Harvard, 2 goals; Montreal, 0.

17. Harvard vs. Ottawa, October 22, 1881. Cambridge Team same as in 16 except Morison, Henry, and Clark did not play; Keith, '83, and Woodward, '84, in place of Henry and Clark. Harvard, 7 goals, 1 touchdown; Ottawa, 1 goal.

18. Harvard vs. Britannia, October 29, 1881, Montreal. *Rushers:* Atkinson, '84; Boyd, '82; Cabot, '83; Dabney, '82; Kendall, '84; Morison, '83; Thacher, '82. *Quarter-back:* Manning, '82. *Half-backs:* Keith, '83; Woodward, '84. *Three-quarter-back:* Kent, '83. *Back:* Edmands, S. S. Game a tie. Britannia, 1 safety touchdown; Harvard, 2 safety touchdowns.

19. Harvard vs. University of Michigan, October 31, 1881, Boston. *Rushers:* Cabot, '83; Fuller, '83; Houston, L. S,; Kendall, '84; Thacher, '82. *Quarter-back:* Manning, '82. *Half-backs:* Henry, S. S.; Woodward, '84. *Three-quarter-back:* Kent, '83. *Back:* Edmands, S. S. Harvard, 1 touchdown; University of Michigan, 0.

20. Harvard vs. University of Pennsylvania, November 2, 1881, New York. *Rushers:* Atkinson, '84; Boyd, '82; Cabot, '83; Fuller, '83; Kendall, '84; Morison, '83; others as in 19. Harvard, 2 goals, 2 touchdowns; University of Pennsylvania, 6 safety touchdowns.

21. Harvard vs. Columbia, November 5, 1881, Cambridge. *Rushers:* Boyd, '82; Cabot, '83; Fuller, '83; Houston, L. S.; Kendall, '84; Thacher, '82. *Quarter-back:* Mason, '84. *Half-backs:* Henry, S. S.; Manning, '82. *Three-quarter-back:* Keith, '83. *Back:* Edmands, S. S. Harvard, 1 goal, 3 touchdowns; Columbia, 9 safety touchdowns.

22. Harvard vs. Yale, November 12, 1881, New Haven. Harvard. *Rushers:* Manning, '82; Cabot, '83; Kendall, '84; Appleton, '84; Perin, '82; Houston, L. S.; Thacher, '82. *Quarter-back:* Mason, '84. *Half-backs:* Henry, S. S.; Keith, '83. *Back:* Edmands, S. S.

Yale. *Rushers:* Knapp, Thompkins, Storrs, Farwell, Hull, Beck, Lamb. *Quarter-back:* Badger. *Half-backs:* Richards, Camp. *Back:* Bacon, '82. Yale, 0; Harvard, 4 safety touchdowns. Perin was injured and his place was taken by Fuller, '83.

23. Harvard vs. Princeton, November 19, 1881, New York. *Rushers:* Manning, '82; Kendall, '84; Cabot, '83; Appleton, '84; Houston, L. S.; Boyd, '82; Thacher, '82. *Quarter-back:* Mason, '84. *Half-backs:* Keith, '83; Henry, S. S. *Back:* Edmands, S. S. Game a tie. Harvard, 1 safety touchdown; Princeton, 2 safety touchdowns.

Games played, 8; won, 5; lost, 1; draw, 2.

ATHLETICS.

FRESHMAN YEAR. 1878-79.

Officers H. A. A.

W. HOOPER, '80, *President.*
I. T. BURR, JR., '79, *Vice-President.*
S. HAMMOND, JR. '81, *Secretary.*
G. P. UPHAM, JR., '81, *Treasurer.*

Stewards.

'79, { W. G. TWOMBLY.
     { F. M. WARE.
'80, { T. ROOSEVELT.
     { R. TRIMBLE.
'81, { R. H. MCCURDY.
     { G. P. UPHAM, JR.
'82, { W. KANE.
     { F. WARREN.

MEETING ON JARVIS FIELD, *Nov. 2, 1878.*

Hundred Yards Dash. Cowdin, '79; Donaldson, '79; Trimble, '80; Warren, '82; E. J. Wendell, '82. Won by Wendell. Time. 10¼ s. Second, Trimble. Time, 10½ s.

Half-Mile Run. Gaston, '80; Crehore, '82. Won by Crehore. Time, 2 m. 21 s.

Mile Walk. Holder, '81; Sterling, E. T. S.; Thompson, '82. Won by Sterling. Time, 8 m. 25 s.

Bicycle Handicap. (*Mile heats, best two in three.*) Swan '81 (scratch); Parker, '80; (15 yards); R. C. Sturgis, '81 (50 yards). Won by Swan. 3 m. 49 s.

Mile Run. C. O. Brewster, '79; Brewster, '81; Thacher, 82; Manning, '82. Won by Thacher. Time, 5 m. 14 s.

Hundred and Twenty Yards Hurdles. Torrey, '82; Cowdin, '79; Warren, '82. Won by Cowdin. Time, 19¼ s.

Quarter-Mile Run. Bacon, '80; Torrey, '82. Won by Bacon. Time, 1 m. 5 s.

Two Hundred and Twenty Yards Dash. Donaldson, '79; Upham, 81; E. J. Wendell, '82. Won by Wendell. Time, 24 s. Second, Donaldson. Time 25½ s.

GYMNASIUM MEETING. *March 15, 1879.**

Horizontal Bar. R. W. Ellis, '79; Fowler, '80. Won by Ellis.
Indian Clubs. Brandegee, '81; J. T. Howe, '80. Won by Howe.
Vaulting (two hands.) W. Watson, '81; Sneathen, L. S.; Fowler, '80; Paine, '81; Foster, '81. Won by Watson. 6 ft. 5 in.
Middle-Weight Sparring. Guiteras, '82; C. Brigham, '80; Hawkins, '81; Gaston, '80; Burr, '79. Won by Gaston.

GYMNASIUM MEETING. *March 22, 1879.*

Standing High Jump.—Fowler, '80; Keene, '80; Hubbard, '82; Paine, '81. Won by Paine. 4 ft. 5 in.
Light-Weight Sparring. Hanks, '79; Thomsen, '80; W. W. Coolidge, '79; Roosevelt, '80; Cushing, '79; Spalding, '81. Won by Hanks.
Fencing. Guild, '81; C. A. Coolidge, '81; Benham, '81. Won by Guild.

INTER-COLLEGIATE MEETING AT MOTT HAVEN,†

May 9, 1879.

Hundred Yards Dash. Lee, '79, University of Penn.; Randolf, '80, Rutgers; Duncan, '80, Lehigh; Moore, Stevens; Wendell, '82, Harvard; Stewart, '80, C. C. N. Y.; Donaldson, '79, Harvard; Loney, '81, Princeton. Won by Lee. $10\frac{1}{4}$ s. Second, Randolf. Wendell pocketed.
Two Hundred and Twenty Yards Run. Lee, University of Penn.; Duncan, Lehigh; Wendell, '82, Harvard; Donaldson, '79, Harvard; Brereton, Columbia. Won by Wendell. Time, $24\frac{3}{4}$ s.
Hundred and Twenty Yards Hurdles. Lawson, '82, Columbia; Strong, '81, Lehigh; Withington, '80, Princeton; Cowdin, '79, Harvard; Landon, '81, Princeton; Heins. Won by Cowdin. Time, $19\frac{1}{4}$ s. Second, Lawson.
Mile Walk. Won by Sayre, Columbia. Time, 7 m. 49 s. Second, Emmerich, Lehigh. Time, 7 m. 56 s. Third, Huidekoper, '80, Harvard. Time, 7 m. $56\frac{1}{4}$ s.

---

* For the Heavy-Weight Sparring there were but two entries: Bacon, '80; and Guiteras, '82. Prize awarded to Bacon, as Guiteras did not appear on time.

† Only those events are given in which Harvard was represented.

Quarter-Mile Run. Won by Cogswell, Dartmouth. Time, $54\frac{4}{5}$ s. Second, Simmons, '81, Harvard.

Columbia first, with seven first prizes and five second. Princeton second. Harvard fourth, with two firsts and one second.

Meeting on Jarvis Field, *May 22, 1879.*

Mile Walk. Huidekoper, '80; Pendleton, '82; Learned, '80; Baldwin, '82; Holder, '81. Won by Huidekoper. Time, 7 m. $59\frac{1}{2}$ s.

Hundred Yards Dash. Freeland '81; Warren '82; Donaldson, '79; Wendell, '82. Won by Wendell. Time, $10\frac{1}{2}$ s. Second, Donaldson. Time, $10\frac{4}{5}$ s.

Quarter-Mile Run. Freeland, '81; Butler, L. S.; Donaldson, '79; Simmons, '81. Won by Simmons. Time, $55\frac{1}{5}$ s. Second, Butler. Time $56\frac{1}{5}$ s.

Running Long Jump. Thompson, '82; Paine, '81: Freeland, '81. Won by Thompson. 18 ft. 1 in.

Mile Run. Brewster, '81; James, '80; Bell, '81; W. G. Taylor, '80; G. F. Morse, '81; Rolfe, '81. Won by Bell. Time, 4 m. 56 s. Second, Taylor. 4 m. $56\frac{1}{2}$ s.

Throwing the Hammer (16 pounds). Otis, '81; Brandegee, '81. Won by Brandegee. 59 ft. 8 in.

One Hundred and Twenty Yards Hurdle Race. Cowdin, '79; Lamson, '80; Brooks, '81. Won by Cowdin. Time $18\frac{1}{5}$ s. Second, Lamson. Time, $20\frac{1}{5}$ s.

Two Hundred and Twenty Yards Dash. Donaldson, '79; Wendell, '82. Won by Wendell. Time, $25\frac{3}{5}$ s. Second, Donaldson. Time, $25\frac{4}{5}$ s.

Three Mile Run. James, '80; Gardiner, '80. Won by James. Time, 18 m. 53 s.

Meeting on Jarvis Field, *May 23, 1879.*

Bicycle Handicap (mile heats, best 2 in 3). Abbe, '81 (75 yards); J. D. Sturgis, '81 (scratch): Swan, '81 (scratch); Creesy, '82 (100 yards); J. A. C. Wright, '81 (50 yards); Homer, '79 (scratch). Won by Swan. Time in final heat, 3 m. 30 s. Second, Wright. Time in final heat, 3 m. $31\frac{1}{2}$ s.

One Hundred Yards Dash (open to Union A. C.). Brackett. U. A. C.; Edmands, U. A. C.; Lathrop, U. A. C.; Donaldson, '79; Wendell, '82. Won by Wendell. Time, 10½ s. Second, Brackett, by 7 ft.

Putting the Shot (16 pounds). Bacon, '80; Cruger, '82. Won by Cruger. 33 ft. 10 in.

Hurdle Race. (One-fifth mile, 15 hurdles 2½ feet high.) Cowdin, '79; Butler, L. S.; Twombley, '79; Urquhart, '79; Story, '79; Won by Cowdin. Time, 52 s. Second, Twombley. Time, 53½ s.

Hop, Step, and Jump. Taft, '81; Thompson, '82; Fowler, '80; Paine, '81; Otis, '81; Hubbard, '82; R. Sturgis, '81. Won by Thompson. 38 ft. 11 in. Second, Taft. 37 ft. 7 in.

Half-Mile Run. Dennie, U.A.C.; Crehore, '82; Allen, U.A.C.; Simmons, '81; Riley, U. A. C.; Williams, U. A. C.; Greenough, U. A. C.; Won by Simmons. Time, 2 m. 8 s. Second, Greenough. Time, 2 m. 12 s.

Running High Jump. R. Sturgis, '81; Hubbard, '82. Won by Hubbard. 4 ft. 11 in.

Mile Walk. (Open.) Merrill, U. A. C.; Green, U. A. C.; Rodee, U. A. C.; Shedd, U. A. C. Won by Merrill. Time, 7 m. 5 s.

Pole Vaulting. Fowler, '80; Paine, '81. Won by Fowler. 7 ft.

Steeple Chase. (About 1½ miles.) 10 volunteer entries. Won by Cowdin, '79. Time, 9 m. 10 s.

SOPHOMORE YEAR, 1879-80.

Officers H. A. A.

W. Hooper, '80, *President.*
S. Hammond, Jr., '81, *Vice-President.*
G. P. Upham, Jr., '81, *Treasurer.*
F. Warren, Jr., '82, *Secretary.*

Stewards.

'80 { C. Morgan.
     { H. R. Shaw.
'81 { C. R. Sanger.
     { W. R. Thayer.
'82 { M. S. Crehore.
     { W. Kane.
'83 { R. D. Sears.

MEETING ON JARVIS FIELD, *Nov. 1, 1879.*

Mile Walk. Wentworth, '82; Huidekoper, '80. Won by Wentworth. Time, 8 m. 36 s. Huidekoper, 8 m. 42½ s.

Running High Jump. Denniston, '83; R. Sturgis, '81. Won by Denniston. 5 ft. 2 in. Sturgis, 5 ft.

Hundred Yards Dash. Wendell, '82; Stetson, '81; Field, '80; Kent, '82. Won by Wendell. Time, 10⅗ s.

Quarter-Mile Run. Simmons, '81; Underwood, '82; Buell, '82. Won by Simmons. Time, 54¾ s.

Running Broad Jump. Denniston, '83; Thompson, '82; Curtis, '83. Won by Denniston. 18 ft. 8 in. Second, Thompson. 18 ft. 3 in.

Two Hundred and Twenty Yards Dash, Wendell, '82; Stetson, '81; Kent, '82. Won by Wendell. Time, 24½ s.

Half-Mile Run. Simmons, '80; Norman, '82; Buell, '82. Won by Simmons. Time, 3 m. 2 s.

One Hundred and Twenty Yards Hurdles. Denniston, '83; Lamson, '80. Won by Denniston. Time, 21 s.

Mile Run. A. L. Hall, '80; Oxnard '82: Won by Hall. Time, 5 m. 25¼ s.

Hop, Step, and Jump. Thompson, '82; Taft, '81. Won by Thompson. 38 ft. 10 in. Taft, 37 ft. 11 in.

One-fifth Mile Hurdles. Wendell, '82; Elliott, L. S. S. Won by Wendell. Time, 57 s.

HEMENWAY GYMNASIUM, *March 13, 1880.**

Ladies' Day.

Standing High Jump. S. Coolidge, '83; C. H. W. Foster, '81; Keene, '80. Won by Coolidge. 4 ft. 9 in. Second Keene, 4 ft. 8 in.

Middle-Weight Sparring. C. Brigham, '80; Gaston, '80; Bullard, L. S. Won by Brigham.

Light-Weight Sparring (First bout.) Thomsen, '80; Heilbron, '83. Won by Heilbron.

(Second bout.) Sharon, '81; Plummer, L. S. S. Won by Sharon. The third bout, between Spalding, 81, and Heilbron, was postponed until the next meeting.

---

* This meeting was the first held in the Hemenway Gymnasium.

Club Swinging. (*Juggling.*) Howe, '60. No one entered against Mr. Howe. He performed a number of exercises, however, and was then presented with a cup, as a mark of esteem from the H. A. A.

Horizontal Bar. Keene, '80; Freeland, '81. Won by Freeland.

Tug of War. '82—Chalfant, Lawrence, Jennings, Perin, Warren. '83—Curtis, E. T. Cabot, Morison, Kip, C. M. Hammond. Won by '82.

HEMENWAY GYMNASIUM, March 20, 1880.

Vaulting (two hands). Keene, '80; C. H. W. Foster, '81. Won by Foster. 6 ft. 9 in.

Heavy Weight Sparring. (*First bout.*) Kane, '82; Burr, L.S. Won by Burr. The next bout, between Burr and Bacon, '80, was postponed until the next meeting.

Fencing. Guild, '80; Guild, '81. Won by Guild, '81.

Feather-Weight Sparring. Plummer L.S.S.; R. B. Fuller, '83. Won by Fuller.

Light-Weight Sparring. (*Third bout*). Spalding, '81; Heilbron, '83. Won by Heilbron.

Parallel Bars. Keene, '80; Mueller, '81; Rolfe, '81. Won by Mueller.

HEMENWAY GYMNASIUM, March 27, 1880.

Vaulting (one hand). Keene, '80; J. L. Paine, '81. Won by Paine. 5 ft. 4 in. Keene, 5 ft. 3 in.

Light-Weight Sparring. (*Final bout*). Sharon, '81; Heilbron, '83. Won by Sharon.

Club Swinging (*Legitimate*). Rolfe, '81; Howe, '80; Luce, '82; Brandegee, 81. Winners: Howe and Brandegee.

Heavy-Weight Sparring. (*Final bout.*) Burr, L. S.; Bacon, '80. Won by Bacon.

Running High Jump. R. Sturgis, '81; Morison, '83. Won by Morison. 5 ft. 2 in.

At the close of this meeting Keene, '80, was presented by the H. A. A., with a cup for general excellence.

JUNIOR CLASS MEETING, JARVIS FIELD, *May 19. 1880.*

Throwing the Hammer. Freeland, W. Watson. Won by Freeland. 62 ft. 1 in. Watson, 56 ft. 8 in.
Quarter-Mile Run. (*First heat.*) Elliott, C. H. W. Foster, F. S. Williams, Brewer, Mueller. Won by Elliott in $57\frac{3}{4}$ s. Foster, second, in $61\frac{1}{8}$ s.
Running High Jump. R. Sturgis, Paine. Won by Sturgis. 5 ft. $\frac{1}{2}$ in. Paine, 4 ft. $11\frac{1}{2}$ in.
Hundred Yards Dash. Stetson, Evarts, Taft. Won by Stetson. Time, $10\frac{7}{8}$ s. Second, Evarts, 11 s.
Quarter-Mile Run. (*Second heat.*) R. Sturgis, Swinburne, Hemenway, A. S. Thayer. Won by Sturgis, $61\frac{1}{2}$ s.
Mile Run. Thorndike, Bell. Both ran a dead heat in 4 m. $50\frac{1}{8}$ s.
Quarter-Mile. (*Final heat.*) Elliott, Sturgis, Foster, Swinburne. Won by Elliott. Time, $56\frac{1}{8}$ s. Second, Sturgis, $57\frac{3}{8}$ s.

CHAMPIONSHIP MEETING, JARVIS FIELD, *May 22. 1880.*

Hundred Yards Dash. (*First heat.*) Wendell, '82; Evarts. '81; Keene, '80; Haupt. '82. Won by Wendell. Time, $10\frac{3}{8}$ s. Second, Evarts. Time $10\frac{1}{2}$ s.
Running High Jump. Denniston, '83; R. Sturgis. '81; Morison, '83; Keene. '80. Won by Denniston. 5 ft. 4 in. Second, Sturgis. 5 ft. 3 in.
Hundred Yards Dash. (*Second heat.*) Stetson. '81; Butler. '83; Perin, '82. Won by Stetson. Time, $10\frac{3}{8}$ s.
Putting the Shot. Kip, '83; Thompson, '82; Keene, '80; Freeland, '81. Won by Kip. 33 ft. 1 in. Second, Thompson. 32 ft. 4 in.
Quarter-mile Run. Wendell, '82; Elliott, L. S. S.; Beals, '83; Hawes, '80; R. Sturgis, '81; Coolidge, '83. Won by Wendell. Time, $53\frac{1}{2}$ s. Second, Elliott. 56 s.
Broad Jump. Thompson, '82; Denniston, '83; J. L. Paine, '81. Won by Thompson. 20 ft. $1\frac{1}{4}$ in. Second, Denniston, 17 ft. 9 in.
Mile Run. A. L. Hall, '80; Ellis, '80; Bell. '81; Thorndike. '81; Morison, '83. Won by Bell. Time, 4 m. $44\frac{3}{8}$ s. Second, Thorndike. Time, 4 m. $44\frac{7}{8}$ s.

Mile Walk. Huidekoper, '80; Herrick, '82. Won by Herrick. Time, 7 m. $48\frac{3}{8}$ s.

Throwing the Hammer. Keene, '80; Freeland, '81; Thompson, '82; Denniston, '83. Won by Thompson. 72 ft. 7 in. Second, Freeland, 71 ft. 8 in.

Hundred Yards Dash. (*Final heat.*) Wendell, '82: Evarts, '81; Stetson, '81: Butler, '83. Won by Wendell. Time, $10\frac{1}{2}$ s. Second, Evarts. Time, $10\frac{5}{8}$ s. Stetson fouled Evarts; consequently Evarts took second place.

Hundred and Twenty Yards Hurdles. Denniston, '83: Keene, '80; Haupt, '82. Won by Denniston. Time, 20 s. Second, Keene. Time, $20\frac{3}{4}$ s.

Two Hundred and Twenty Yards Dash. (*Open.*) Wendell, '82: Stetson, '81. Won by Wendell. Time, 26 s.

Half-Mile Run. (*Open.*) H. Lunt, U. A. C.; C. M. Ward, U. A. C.; E. L. Estabrook, U. A. C.; J. K. Simpson, U. A. C. Won by Lunt. Time, 2 m. $13\frac{1}{8}$ s. Second, Ward. Time, 2 m. 19 s.

Inter-Collegiate Meeting, at Mott Haven.

May 29, 1880.

Hundred Yards Dash. Moore, '82, Stevens Institute; Wendell, '82, Harvard; Brown, '83, Columbia; Brereton, '83, Columbia; Bissel, '80, Columbia. Won by Wendell, Harvard. Time, $10\frac{4}{5}$ s. Second, Brown, Columbia. Third, Moore, Stevens Institute.

Mile Walk. Sayre, '81, Columbia: Herrick, '82, Harvard: Emmerich, '83, Lehigh. Won by Sayre, Columbia. Time, 7 m. $54\frac{2}{5}$ s. Second, Herrick, Harvard.

Standing High Jump. Soren, '83, Harvard: Keene, '80, Harvard; Moore, '82, Stevens Institute. Won by Soren, Harvard. 5 ft. $1\frac{1}{4}$ in. Second, Keene, Harvard. 4 ft. $11\frac{1}{4}$ in. Moore, 4 ft. 6 in.

Mile Run. Cuyler, '82, Yale; Thorndike, '81, Harvard; Bell, '81, Harvard; Coe, '83, Stevens; Wilcox, Univ. of Penn; Newborough, '80, Columbia: Parker, '82, Dartmouth. Won by Cuyler, Yale. Time, 4 m. $37\frac{3}{5}$ s. Second, Thorndike, Harvard. Time, 4 m. $42\frac{2}{5}$ s. Third, Bell, Harvard. Time, 4 m. $43\frac{3}{5}$ s.

Throwing the Hammer. Bush, '80, Columbia; Irons, '81. Brown; Moore, '82, Stevens. Won by Bush, Columbia. 84 ft. 3 in. Second, Irons, Brown. 75 ft. 10½ in.

Two Hundred and Twenty Yards Dash. Wendell, '82, Harvard; Flint, '80, Dartmouth; Bissell, '80, Columbia; Brown, '83, Columbia; Brereton, '83, Columbia. Won by Wendell, Harvard. Time, 24 ⅖ sec. Second, Flint, Dartmouth, by six feet.

Running High Jump. Denniston, '83, Harvard; Lawson, '82, Columbia; Sayre, '81, Columbia; Taylor, '81, Columbia. Won by Denniston, Harvard. 5 ft. 1¼ in. Second, Lawson, Columbia. 4 ft. 11¾ in.

Putting the Shot. Moore, '82, Stevens; Irons, '81, Brown; Thompson, '82, Harvard; Bush, '80, Columbia; Wilson, '83, Lehigh; Haxall, '83, Princeton. Won by Moore, Stevens. 35 ft. 1¼ in. Second, Irons, Brown. 33 ft. 1¼ in. Third, Thompson, Harvard. 32 ft. 9¼ in.

Half-Mile Run. Ballard, '81, Univ. of Penn.; Taylor, '81, Columbia; Parker, '82, Dartmouth; Donohue, '82, Lehigh. Won by Ballard, Univ. of Penn. Time, 2 m. 9¼ s. Second, Taylor, Columbia, by seven yards.

Pole-Leaping. Tewksbury, '80, Princeton; Keene, '80, Harvard. Won by Tewksbury, Princeton. 9 ft. 4 in.

Running Broad Jump. Thayer, '81, Univ. of Penn.; Thomson, '82, Harvard; Irons, '81, Brown. Won by Thayer, Univ. of Penn. 20 ft. 2 in. Second, Thompson, Harvard. 19 ft. 10¼ in.

Hundred and Twenty Yards Hurdles. Strong, '81, Lehigh; Jones, '83, Yale; Morrow, '82, Lehigh. Won by Strong, Lehigh. Time, 19½ s. Second, Jones, Yale.

Standing Broad Jump. Soren, '83, Harvard; Irons, '81, Brown; Rutherford, '82, Columbia. Won by Soren, Harvard. 10 ft. 1¼ in. Second, Irons, Brown. 9 ft. 9¼ in.

Quarter-Mile Run. Wendell, '82, Harvard; Combes, '82, Columbia; Hyslop, '81, Stevens. Won by Wendell, Harvard. Time, 55¼ s. Second, Combes, Columbia.

Bicycle Race. (*Two Miles.*) Field, '83, Princeton; Wurts, '80, Yale; Snyder, '80, Columbia; Taylor, '81, Columbia. Won by Field, Princeton. Time, 7 m. 57 s. Second, Wurts, Yale.

Harvard first, with six first prizes and five seconds. Columbia second, with three firsts and six seconds.

JUNIOR YEAR. 1880-81.

Officers H. A. A.

E. W. ATKINSON, '81, *President.*
F. WARREN, JR., '82, *Vice-President.*
M. S. CREHORE, '82, *Treasurer.*
G. E. LOWELL, '83, *Secretary (resigned).*
G. B. MORISON, '83, *Secretary.*

Stewards.

'81 { C. R. SANGER. W. R. THAYER.

'82 { W. KANE. E. J. WENDELL.

'83 { R. D. SEARS. G. B. MORISON. G. E. LOWELL.

'84 { W. F. WESSELHOEFT. W. M. BURR.

JARVIS FIELD, *Nov. 10, 1880.*

Five-Mile Run. Lummis, '81; Herrick, '82; Agassiz, '84; Tevis, '84. Won by Tevis. Time, 29 m. 29 s.

FIRST WINTER MEETING, HEMENWAY GYMNASIUM.

March 12, 1881.

Middle-Weight Wrestling. Mills, '81; Perin, '82. Won by Mills.

Heavy-Weight Sparring. Otis, '81; Kip, '83. Won by Kip.

Standing High Jump. S. Coolidge '83; Morison, '83; Batchelder, '83; Denniston, '83; Edmands, S. S.; Fay, '83. Won by Edmands. Height, 4 ft. 6½ in. Second, Fay. 4 ft. 6 in.

One-Hand Vault. Paine, '81; Bachelder, '83; Luce, '82; Morison, '83; Denniston, '83. Won by Paine. Height, 5 ft. 3¾ in. Second, Bachelder and Luce. 5 ft. 1¾ in.

Middle-Weight Sparring. Kane, '82; Richmond, '83; Brigham, L. S. Won by Richmond.

Light-Weight Wrestling. Lummis, '81; Cabot, '82. Won by Cabot.

Tug of War. '83 — Easton, Getchell, Baxter, Kip, Hubbard; '84 — Woodward, Mumford, Wesselhoeft, Clarke, Harrington. Won by '83.

SECOND WINTER MEETING, HEMENWAY GYMNASIUM.

March 19, 1881. Ladies' Day.

Fencing. (*First bout.*) Leavitt, S. S.; Underwood, '84. Won by Leavitt.

Light-Weight Sparring. (*First bout.*) Heilbron, '83; W. H. Page, '83. Won by Heilbron. (*Second bout.*) Spalding, '82; Turner, '84. Won by Turner. Final bout won by Heilbron.

Fencing. (*Second bout.*) Ordway, L. S.; Leavitt, S. S. Bout and match won by Leavitt.

Two-Hand Vault. Field, '84; Morison, '83; C. H. W. Foster, '81; Bachelder, '83; Mandell, '84; Denniston, '83; Woodward, '84. Won by Morison, 6 ft. 8 in. Second, Woodward, 6 ft. 7 in. Third, Foster.

Feather-Weight Sparring. Heilbron, '83; Lowman, '84. Won by Heilbron.

Tug of War. '81 — Mills, Crehore, Otis, Stephens, Studley; '82 — Jennings, Lawrence, Delaney, Hubbard, Warren. Won by '81.

THIRD WINTER MEETING, HEMENWAY GYMNASIUM.

March 26, 1881. Exhibition under direction of Dr. D. A. Sargent, and Ladies' day.

The events marked thus (*) are those in which a prize was given, and the men whose names are printed in italics in those events did not compete for the prize.

* *Running High Jump.* Denniston, '83; Morison, '83; Edmands, S. S.; Bachelder, '83. Won by Denniston, 5 ft. 7¾ in.; Morison, 5 ft. 1 in.; Edmands, 5 ft.; Bachelder, 4 ft. 11 in.

* *Horizontal Bar.* Dabney, '82; Bachelder, '83; Morison, '83; Denniston, '83; Fay, '83; *Mueller*, '81; *Freeland*, '81; *Dr. Sargent*. Prize awarded to Dabney.

Double Trapeze. Spalding, '81; Squibb, '81.

* *Parallel Bars.* Squibb, '81; De Windt, '81; Morison, '83; Bachelder, '83; Denniston, '83; *Mueller*, '81; Prize awarded to Squibb.

Balancing Trapeze. Dr. Sargent.

Tumbling. Davis, '84; Freeland. '81; Elliott, L. S. S.; Morison, '83; Dabney, '82; Fox, '83; Denniston, '83; Mueller, '81; Kendall, '84; Spalding, '81; Fay, '83; Dr. Sargent.

Flying Rings. Squibb, '81; Morison, '83; Dabney, '82; Fox. '83; Bachelder, '83; Woodward, '84.

* *Rope Climbing (50 feet).* A. S. Thayer, '81; Hemenway, '81; De Windt, '81; Rolfe, '81. Won by Thayer in $25\frac{3}{4}$ s. Hemenway, second, in $33\frac{1}{2}$ s.

Triple-Barred Echelle. Dr. Sargent; Freeland, '81; Davis, '84.

Tug of War. '83 vs. '81. Teams same as in previous meetings. Won by '83.

The medal for general athletic excellence in these three meetings was competed for by Morison, '83; Denniston, '83; and Bachelder, '83. Won by Morison with 28 points out of a possible 36; the others being tied at $24\frac{1}{2}$ points.

This exhibition was repeated on the evening of March 28, 1881.

SENIOR CLASS MEETING, JARVIS FIELD.
May 20, 1881.

Hundred Yards. Witherbee, Freeland. Elliott, S. S., Jackson. Won by Witherbee. Time, $10\frac{3}{4}$ s. Elliott and Freeland tied for second place, which being run off was won by Elliott in $10\frac{7}{8}$ s.

Running High Jump. R. Sturgis. 4 ft. $11\frac{1}{4}$ in.; Paine, 4 ft. $10\frac{1}{4}$ in.

Quarter-Mile Run. Witherbee. Simmons. Won by Witherbee. Time. $53\frac{3}{8}$ s. Simmons, $54\frac{3}{4}$ s.

CHAMPIONSHIP MEETING, JARVIS FIELD.
May 24, 1881.

Hundred Yards. Wendell. '82; Witherbee, '81; Mandell, '84; Mitchell, '83. Won by Wendell. Time, 10 s. Witherbee, $10\frac{1}{4}$ s.

* *Half-Mile Run.* Coolidge, '84; Simmons, '81. Won by Coolidge. Time, 2 m. $6\frac{1}{8}$ s. Simmons, 2 m. $10\frac{1}{4}$ s.

Running High Jump. Soren, '83; Denniston, '83; Edmands, S. S.; R. Sturgis, '81; Haupt, '82. Won by Soren. 5 ft. $6\frac{1}{2}$ in. Denniston, and Edmands tied at 5 ft. $4\frac{1}{2}$ in.

Mile Walk. Herrick. '82; Blodgett, '84. Won by Herrick by half a lap. Time, 9 m.

Throwing the Hammer (16 lbs.). Kip. '83, 73 ft. 6 in.; Freeland, '81, 70 ft. 6 in.

Quarter-mile Run. Goodwin, '84; Wendell, '82; Witherbee, '81. Won by Goodwin. Time, 50¾ s. Wendell, second.

Running Broad Jump. Soren, 83; Field, '84; Paine. '81. Won by Soren. 20 ft. Field, 18 ft. 5½ in.

Putting the Shot (16 lbs.). Kip. '83; Bonsal, '84. Won by Kip, 34 ft. Bonsal, 31 ft. 7 in.

Two Hundred and Twenty Yards (Open). Witherbee, '81; Brackett (B. A. C.), Simpson (B. A. C.), Williams (B. A. C.), Jackson, '81. Won by Witherbee. Time, 23¾ s. Brackett, 24¼ s.

Mile Run. Thorndike, '81; Bush. '82. Won by Thorndike. Time, 4 m. 55 s. Bush, 5 m. 26½ s.

Hundred and Twenty Yards Hurdles. Mandell, '84; Haupt, '82; Mitchell, '83. Won by Mandell. Time, 20 s. Haupt, 21⅝ s.

Pole Vault. Mandell. '84'; Soren. '83. Won by Mandell. 8 ft. 2 in.

INTERCOLLEGIATE MEETING, AT MOTT HAVEN.
May 28, 1881.

Hundred Yards. (*First heat.*) Wendell, '82. Harvard; McIntosh, '84, Lafayette. Walk over for Wendell. (*Second heat.*) Jenkins, '84, Columbia, 10¼ s. Davison, '84, Columbia, 2; Wilson, '83, Princeton, 3; Peters, '83, Rutgers. 4. (*Final heat.*) Wendell, 10¼ s. Jenkins, 2; Davison, 3.

Running High Jump. Soren, '83, Harvard, 5 ft. 2¾ in.; Sayre, '81, Columbia, 5 ft. ¾ in.

Mile Run. Cuyler, '82, Yale, 4 m. 40⅞ s. Thorndike, '81, Harvard, 2.

Pole Vault. Dalrymple. '83, Lehigh, 8 ft. 9 in. Harriman, '83, Princeton, Goodnow, '83. Lehigh, tied at 8 ft. 6 in. Jumping off, Harriman cleared 8 ft. 9 in; Soren, '83, Harvard, 8 ft.

Quarter-mile Run. Ballard, '81. Univ. Penn., 53¼ s. Wilson, '83, Princeton, 2.

Standing High Jump. Soren, '83, Harvard, 4 ft. 6¾ in. and 4 ft. 9¾ in.; Jenkins, '84, Columbia, 4 ft. 4¾ in.; Harriman, '83, Princeton, 4 ft. 2¾ in.; Moore, '82, Stevens. 4 ft. 2¾ in.; Fell, '84, Princeton, 4 ft. 2¾ in.

Mile Walk. Sayre, '81, Columbia, 7 m. 36½ s. Herrick. '82, Harvard, 2.

Throwing the Hammer. Montgomery, '81, Columbia, 76 ft. 9½ in.; Porter, '83, Columbia. 76 ft. 9 in.; Briggs, '81, Yale, 74 ft. 1½ in.; Wilson, '83, Lehigh, 72 ft. 11 in.; Harrison, '81, Lafayette, 71 ft. ¼ in.; Kip, '83, Harvard, 66 ft. 9½ in.

Hundred and Twenty Yards Hurdles. (*First heat.*) Thayer, '81, Univ. Penn.; Jenkins, '84, Columbia. Walk over for Thayer. (*Second heat.*) Trowbridge, S. S. S., Yale, 18⅞ s. Morrow, '81. Lehigh, 2; Mitchell, '83, Harvard, 3; How, '81, Rutgers. 4. (*Final heat.*) Morrow, 18⅞ s. Trowbridge, 2; Thayer, 3.

Two Hundred and Twenty Yards. (*First heat.*) Jenkins, '84, Columbia, 24 s. Wendell, '82, Harvard, 2; Davison, '84, Columbia, 3; Baker, '83, Dartmouth, 4. (*Second heat.*) McIntosh, '84, Lafayette; Ballard, Univ. Penn. Walk over. (*Final heat.*) Wendell, 23¼ s. Jenkins, 2.

Half-mile Run. Coolidge, '84, Harvard, 2 m. 7⅞ s. Parker, '82, Dartmouth, 2; Hyde, '83, Columbia, 3; Donahoe, '82, Lehigh, 4.

Putting the Shot. Moore, '82, Stevens, 34 ft. 11 in.; Wilson, '83, Lehigh, 34 ft. 4½ in.; Briggs, '81, Yale, 31 ft. ½ in.; Kip, '83, Harvard, 31 ft.; Fitzgerald, '84, 5; Bond, '83, Lafayette, 6; Hunter, '82, Univ. Penn., 7.

Running Long Jump. Jenkins, '84, Columbia, 20 ft. 9¼ in.; Thayer, '81, Univ. Penn., 19 ft. 2¾ in.; Soren, '83, Harvard, 18 ft. 11 in.; Moore, '82, Stevens, 18 ft. 5½ in.; Harriman, '83, Princeton, 17 ft. 3 in.

Two-Mile Bicycle Race. Reed, '83, Columbia, 6 m. 51 s.; Williston, '82, Harvard, 6 m. 54⅞ s. Billings, '82, Yale, 3; Taylor, '81, Columbia, 4.

The tug of war between Princeton and Columbia, teams of four limited to 600 lbs., 10 minutes time, was won by Princeton.

Harvard first, with five first prizes and three seconds.

Columbia second, with four firsts and five seconds.

SENIOR YEAR, 1881–82.

Officers H. A. A.

E. J. WENDELL, '82, *President.*
M. S. CREHORE, '82, *Vice-President.*
G. B. MORISON, '83, *Treasurer.*
H. R. WOODWARD, '84, *Secretary.*

Stewards.

'82 { W. G. Fellows.
     H. G. Leavitt.

'83 { G. E. Lowell.
     R. D. Sears.

'84 { F. Wesselhoeft.
     W. M. Burr.

'85 { C. H. Atkinson.
     J. E. Thayer.

Fall Meeting. Jarvis Field, *October 26, 1881.*

Mile Run. Bradley, '82 ; Herrick, '82 : Smith, '82 : Macready, S. S. Won by Bradley in 5 m. 17¾ s.

Hundred Yards Dash. (*For those who had never beaten 11 seconds.*) (*First heat.*) 1. Snow, '82, 11¾ s. 2. Norton, '85. (*Second heat.*) 1. Cary, '83, 11¾ s. 2. Kallock, S. S. 3. Glover, '84. (*Third heat.*) 1. Kemp, '84, 11¾ s. 2. Williston, '82. 3. Jack, '83. (*Fourth heat.*) 1. Edmands. S. S., 11½ s. 2. Darling, '84.

The final heat and the event were won by Edmands in 11 s.

Hurdle Race (*120 yards, 10 hurdles, 3½ feet high*) 1. Agassiz, '84, 19¼ s. 2. Mandell, '84. 3. Cowdin, '85. 4. Haupt, '82.

Hundred Yards Dash. (*For members of the Foot-Ball Teams*). Won by Edmands, S. S. in 11¼ s.

Half-Mile Run. 1. Goodwin, '84, 2 m. 3¾ s.* 2. T. J. Coolidge.

Pole Leaping. 1. Mandell, '84, 7 ft. 6 in. 2. Denniston, '83. 7 ft. 3 in.

Two Hundred and Twenty Yards Dash. (*Open to all colleges*). 1. Wendell, '82, 24½ s. 2. Yates (Williams Coll.)

Quarter-Mile Run. (*For those who had never beaten 55 s.*) 1. Agassiz, '84, 56½ s. 2. Biddle, '84. 3. Page, '83. 4. Duryea, '85.

Running Broad Jump. 1. Mandell, '84. 17 ft. 8 in. 2. Page, '83. 3. Denniston, '83.

Quarter-Mile Run. (*For members of the Foot-Ball Teams.*) Won by Edmands, S. S. in 58½ s.

Hurdle Race (*One-fifth mile, 10 hurdles. 2½ ft. high*). 1. Yates. Williams Coll.) 57¾ s. 2. Page, '83. 3. Haupt, '82.

* Beating the best college record.

First Winter Meeting, Hemenway Gymnasium.
March 11, 1882.

Parallel Bars. Bachelder, '83; Morison, '83; Denniston, '83. Won by Bachelder.

Middle-Weight Wrestling. Atwood, L. S.; Crane, '84; Bangs, S. S. (*First bout.*) Atwood, Crane. Won by Crane. (*Final bout.*) Crane, Bangs. Won by Crane.

Middle Weight Sparring. Page, '83; Cobb, '84; Biddle, '84; Lee, '83; Pendleton, '84. (*First bout.*) Page, Cobb. Won by Page. (*Second bout.*) Biddle, Lee. Won by Lee. (*Second Drawing. First bout.*) Page, Pendleton. Won by Page. (*Second bout.*) Page, Lee. Postponed till next meeting and won by Lee, who was declared winner of the event.

Feather-Weight Wrestling. J. E. Davis, '83; Goodspeed, '84; Carnochan, '85. (*First bout.*) Davis, Goodspeed. Won by Davis. (*Final bout.*) Davis, Carnochan. Won by Carnochan.

Heavy-Weight Wrestling. Atkinson, '84; Winthrop, '83. Won by Atkinson.

Heavy-Weight Sparring. Appleton, '84; Bonsal, '84. Won by Appleton.

Putting the Shot. 1. Kip, '83, 83 ft. 9 in. 2. Mirkland, D.S.

Light Weight Wrestling. Page, '83; Bangs, '84. Won by Page.

Tug of War. (*6 minutes on cleats.*) '84—Walker, Bryant, Le Moyne, Kemp (*anchor*). '85—Clark, Homans, Baldwin, Bradford (*anchor*). Won by '84.

Second Winter Meeting, Hemenway Gymnasium.
March 18, 1882. Ladies' Day.

Two-Hand Vault. Bachelder, '83; Soren, '83; Field, '84; Stone, '85; Atkinson, '85; Howard, '85; Woodward, '84; Morison, '83; Denniston, '83. Soren and Atkinson tied at 6 ft. 11¾ in., but Soren was declared winner on account of superior style.

Fencing. Henry, S. S.; Ordway, L. S.; Underwood, '84; R. H. McDonald, '82; Leavitt, S. S. (*First bout.*) Henry, Ordway. Won by Ordway, 7-3. (*Second bout.*) Underwood, McDonald. Won by Underwood, 7-4. (*Third bout.*) Leavitt, Underwood. Won by Leavitt, 7-5. (*Final bout.*) Leavitt, Ordway. Won by Ordway, 7-4.

Light-Weight Sparring. Spalding, '82 ; Smith, '83 ; Dorr, '83 ; Butler, '83. (*First bout.*) Spalding, Smith. Won by Spalding. (*Second bout.*) Dorr, Butler. Won by Butler. (*Final bout.*) Butler, Spalding. Won by Spalding.

Club Swinging (legitimate). A. Hamlin, '84 ; Barnes, '85 ; Luce, '82 ; Kent, '82. Won by Barnes.

Standing High Jump. Bachelder, '83 ; Soren, '83 ; Edmands, S. S. ; Morison, '83 ; Denniston, '83. Won by Soren, 4 ft. 11¾ in.

Feather-Weight Sparring. Lowman, '84 ; Heilbron, '83. Won by Heilbron.

Tug of War. '82—McArthur, Smith, Manning, Delaney (*anchor*). '83—Bachelder, Page, Mitchell, Codman (*anchor*). Won by '82. Besides the contests the University crew gave an exhibition of rowing on the weights.

Third Winter Meeting, Hemenway Gymnasium.

March 25, 1882. Ladies' Day.

Running High Jump. Denniston, '83 ; Morison, '83 ; Soren, '83 ; Edmands, S. S. Won by Denniston at 5 ft. 5¾ in.

Horizontal Bar. Bachelder, '83 ; Dabney, '82 ; Denniston, '83 ; Morison, '83 ; Fay, '83 ; Bishop, '82 ; Ripley, L. S. The prize was awarded to Bishop.

Rope Climbing. Kaan, '83 ; Crane, '84 ; Dean, S. S. ; Woodward, '84. (*First bout.*) Kaan, Crane. A tie at 33½ s. (*Second bout.*) Neither contestant reached the top of the hall. The tie between Kaan and Crane was postponed to March 27, and won by Crane in 26 s. Distance, 44½ ft.

Pole Vault. Mandell, '84 ; Chase, '83 ; Field, '84. Won by Mandell, 9 ft. ¾ in.

Running High Kick. Soren, '83 ; Edmands, S. S. ; S. Coolidge, '83 ; Fox, '83 ; Ripley, L. S. Won by Soren, 8 ft. 4 in. (This does not stand as a record as the kicking was done from a mattress.)

Flying Rings. Bachelder, '83 ; Dabney, '82 ; Denniston, '83 ; Morison, '83 ; Bishop, '82 ; Ripley, L. S. Won by Bachelder.

Tumbling. Dabney, '82 ; Fox, '83 ; Denniston, '83 ; Kendall, '84 ; Belshaw, '83 ; Wells '82. Won by Kendall.

Tug of War. (*6 minutes on cleats. Final heat.*) '82—McArthur, Smith, Manning, Delaney (*anchor*). '84.—Walker, Bryant, Le Moyne, Kemp (*anchor*). Won by '82.

An exhibition in Grotesque Tumbling was given by Mr. Swinscoe, '85, and Mr. Langdon. Messrs. Bachelder, '83 and Davis, '84, gave an exhibition on the Double Trapeze. The University crew gave an exhibition of rowing on the weights, and the Zuni Indians, who were present, performed several dances.

CLASS MEETINGS.

JUNIOR AND FRESHMAN, JARVIS FIELD, *May 15, 1881.*

Junior Contests.

Hundred Yards Dash. 1. S. Mitchell, $10\frac{3}{5}$ s. 2. Soren.
Half-Mile Run. 1. Page, 2 m. 28 s. 2. Mackie.
Two Hundred and Twenty Yards Dash. 1. Soren, $24\frac{1}{2}$ s. 2. Cary. 3. Moulton.
Quarter-Mile Run. 1. Cary, $56\frac{1}{4}$ s. 2. Soren.
The other events were walk overs.

Freshman Contests.

Hundred Yards Dash. 1. Johnson. 11 s. 2. Billings. 3. Bradford. 4. Codman. 5. Morris.
Quarter-Mile Run. 1. Atkinson. $59\frac{1}{4}$ s. 2. Livingston. 3. Carnochan.
Two Hundred and Twenty Yards Dash. 1. Bradford, $24\frac{3}{4}$ s. 2. Codman.
Half-Mile Run. 1. Taylor, 2 m. $20\frac{1}{4}$ s. 2. Simes. 3. Wilkshire.
The other events were walk overs.

SENIOR AND SOPHOMORE, *May 16, 1882.*

None of the events in the Senior meeting were contested.

Sophomore Contests.

Two Hundred and Twenty Yards Dash. 1. Edmands, $24\frac{1}{4}$ s. 2. Sturgis.
Running Broad Jump. 1. Mandell, 18 ft. $\frac{1}{2}$ in. 2. Field, 17 ft. 7 in.

SPRING CHAMPIONSHIP MEETING. JARVIS FIELD, *May 20, 1882.*

Mile Walk. 1. Herrick,' '82. 7 m. 52¾ s. 2. Baxter, '83. 9 m. 19 s. 3. Mills, '85.

Throwing the Hammer. 1. Kip, '83, 84 ft. 2. Biddle, '84.

Hundred Yards Dash. Soren, '83; Billings, '85; Wendell, '82; Johnson, '85; Edmands, S. S. (*First heat.*) Soren, Billings. A dead heat, 11¾ s. (*Second heat.*) 1. Wendell, 10¼ s. 2. Johnson. 3. Edmands. (*Final heat.*) 1. Wendell, 10¾ s. 2. Johnson. 3. Billings, '85. 4. Soren, '83.

Half-Mile Run. 1. Goodwin, '84. 2 m. 5¼ s. 2. Taylor, '85. 3. Page, '83.

Discus Throwing. Denniston, '83; Kip, '83; Page, '83; Paulin, '83; Follensbee, '85; Leavitt, '82; Cumming, '82. Won by Kip, 82 ft.

Quarter-Mile Run. 1. Goodwin, '84, 55¼ s. 2. Cary, '83. 3. Atkinson, '85.

Mile Run. 1. Morison, '83, 4 m. 39 s. 2. Trask, '85. 3. Penrose, '84.

Running Broad Jump. 1. Soren, '83, 19 ft. 8 in. 2. Mandell, '84. 3. Denniston, '83.

Hundred and Twenty Yards Hurdles. 1. Mitchell, '83, 17¾ s.* 2. Haupt, '82.

Two Hundred and Twenty Yards Dash. 1. Wendell, '82, 24 s. 2. Soren, '83. 3. Edmands. S. S. 4. Bradford, '84.

Putting the Shot. 1. Kip, '83, 35 ft. 5½ in. 2. Biddle, '84. 3. Follansbee, '85.

Running High Jump. 1. Soren, '83. Denniston, '83, 5 ft. 5½ in. 2. Edmands, S. S.

Bicycle Race. 1. Codman, '83, 7 m. 52 s. 2. Norton, '85. 3. French, '85.

INTER-COLLEGIATE ATHLETIC ASSOCIATION. SEVENTH ANNUAL MEETING, MANHATTAN POLO GROUNDS, NEW YORK.

Hundred Yards Dash. (*First heat.*) 1. Brooks, Yale, '85, 10⅜ s. 2. Derrickson, Columbia, '85. (*Second heat.*) 1. Wendell, Harvard, '82, 10⅜ s. 2. McIntosh, Lafayette, '84. (*Final heat.*) 1. Brooks, Yale, '85, 10¼ s. 2. Derrickson, Columbia, '85.

* Beating the best college record.

Running High Jump. 1. Soren, Harvard, '83. 5 ft. 6 in. 2. Edmands, Harvard, S. S. 5 ft. 5 in.

Mile Run. 1. Morison. Harvard, '83. 4 m. 40¾ s. 2. Bryan, Princeton. '82.

Mile Walk. 1. Biddle, Univ. of Penn. '85. 7 m. 44⅕ s. 2. Miller. Rutgers, '83.

Bicycle Race. (2 Miles.) 1. Norton. Harvard, '83, 6 m. 52⅖ s. 2. Rood, Columbia, '84. 3. Reed, Columbia, '84.

Hundred and Twenty Yards Hurdles. (First heat) Walk over for Jenkins, Columbia, '84. *(Second heat.)* 1. McIntosh, Lafayette, '84, 21 s. 2. S. Mitchell, Harvard, '83. *(Final heat.)* 1. Jenkins, Columbia, '84, 17⅘ s. 2. McIntosh, Lafayette, '84.

Quarter-mile Run. 1. Goodwin, Harvard, '84, 58 s. 2. Cary, Harvard, S. S. 3. F. C. Perot, Univ. of Penn. '82.

Throwing the Hammer. 1. Porter. Columbia, '83. 87 ft. 3½ in. 2. Kip, Harvard, '83. 79 ft. 9½ in.

Tug of War. Won by Columbia. Bodleson, '84 ; Banks. '83 ; Henry, '82 ; Morgan, '84 *(anchor).*

Two Hundred and Twenty Yards Dash. (First heat.) 1. Brooks, Yale, '85, 23¼ s. 2. Edmands, Harvard, S. S. *(Second heat.)* Won by Derrickson, Columbia, '85, 23¾ s. *(Final heat.)* 1. Brooks, Yale, '85, 22⅖ s. 2. Derrickson.

Putting the Shot. 1. Moore, Columbia, '84, 36 ft. 3 in. 2. Kip, Harvard, '83, 35 ft. 11 in.

Running Broad Jump. 1. Jenkins. Columbia. '84, 21 ft. 3 in. 2. Soren, Harvard. '83, 20 ft. 10 in.

Half-Mile Run. 1. Goodwin, Harvard, '84. 2 m. 2⅖ s. 2. Trask, Harvard, '85, 2 m. 4⅖ s.

Pole Vault. 1. Soren. Harvard. '83. 9 ft. 6 in. 2. Harriman. Princeton, '83, 9 ft.

Harvard first with six first and six second prizes. Columbia second with four first and three second prizes and the tug of war.

TEMPORARY MEMBERS.

An asterisk is used to denote deceased members.

HERBERT AUSTIN.

Entered the wholesale metal business with his uncle. For further information consult the Sec'y of 1881.

CHARLES SIDNEY AVERILL.

Left college at the close of Freshman year on account of illness, intending to return. After spending a year and a half in seeking health gave up a college education, and in the spring of 1881 began to teach and has continued doing so with quite good success.

RENÉ BACHE.

Is employed upon the New York Sun.

CHARLES HAMMATT BARTLETT.

Has been reading law in the office of Wilson and Woodard, at Bangor, Maine.

GEORGE EDWIN BACHELDER.

See '81's Report.

CHARLES WESLEY BIRTWELL.

Left college early in Senior year and has been living since in Cambridge, a part of the time employed by Moses King in the publishing business. Will join the class of 1883 next year.

FRANK TAYLOR BROWN.

Left college in the spring of 1880 and in June started for Wyoming Territory where he spent a year in learning the business of sheep-raising. "In the course of a few weeks (Dec. 1881) he will be in business for himself, as he is just completing negotiations for the purchase of a ranch and a band of sheep."

WILLIAM CHALFANT, Jr.
Joined the class of 1883.

STEPHEN CUTLER CLARK.
Has not been heard from.

JAMES PENDLETON CRUGER.
See '81's report.

JOHN POMEROY DABNEY.
For about a year was engaged at Chicago in a branch office of the Taunton Tack company, and then went to Taunton, Mass., into the main office of the company, where he is at present.

HIRAM IRVING DILLENBACK.
For some time after leaving college was connected with various papers as regular and special correspondent. From October, 1881, to March, 1882, was associate editor of the East Boston Argus, and then accepted the position of managing editor of the (Boston) Saturday Evening Express. This position he has given up and is now a reporter, for what paper I do not know.

JAMES JOSEPH DOOLING.
Joined the class of 1884.

HILAND HULBURD DUNLEVY.
Joined the class of 1883.

CHARLES HAMLIN DUNTON.
Has not been heard from.

CLINTON JOHNSON EDGERLY.
Since leaving college has been reading law in Boston.

FREDERICK LARNAC ELDRIDGE.
Since leaving college at the beginning of Sophomore year has been in business in New York, the first year as clerk with Fred'k G. Eldridge & Co., commission merchants (his father's firm). Since his father's retirement a little more than a year ago, has been with H. B. Hollins & Co., stock brokers.

DANIEL BUTLER FEARING.

"After leaving college I had a try at farm-life on Deerfoot Farm, Southboro, for a few months, and am now settled down quietly in New York with a position in Mr. W. D. Morgan's office, the Great Western S. S. Co."

EDWIN THAYER FEARING.

Is with A. L. Fearing & Co., agents of New Bedford Cordage Co., etc., Boston.

EDWARD ASHLEY FERGUSON.

Has not been heard from.

JOHN QUINCY ADAMS GRIFFIN.

Left college at the end of Sophomore year and began the study of law in the Boston University Law School, where he remained a year. Then went into the law office of his brother F. W. Griffin in Charlestown, where he now is.

ALMON WHITING GRISWOLD.

Joined the class of 1881.

RAMON BENJAMIN GUITERAS.

"After leaving college at the end of my Freshman year, I spent about a year and a half travelling in Europe and Africa, and returning, entered the class of 1883 in the Harvard Medical School, where I am still studying."

PERCIVAL SMITH HILL.

Has not been heard from.

FRANCIS MARION HOLDEN.

See '80's Report.

CHARLES HARVEY HOLMAN.

Left college near the end of Senior year and has been living in Boston.

FRANK WHITEHOUSE HOWE.

Left college on account of illness and travelled in California and the west to gain health. Returning, entered the lumber business and now has an interest in his father's lumber firm at Lowell, Mass.

WILLIAM ADDISON HOWE.

See '81's Report.

WOODBURY KANE.

Joined the class of 1883.

*GEORGE CLARK KENNETT.

A sketch of his life will be published in the triennial. It would have appeared here had not the gentleman who promised to write it neglected to do so.

WILLIAM AMOS LAMPREY.

Left college in October, 1879, on account of a sudden hemorrhage from the lungs. In the summer of 1880 began to gain rapidly and spent a few months among the mountains of New Hampshire gaining strength. About a year ago began studying medicine with a physician and now intends to enter the Harvard Medical School in October, 1882.

COURTNEY LANGDON.

Has been teaching modern languages at the Episcopal Academy, Cheavie, Conn.

PRESCOTT LAWRENCE.

After leaving college went abroad and travelled, mostly in England. Returned to Boston in the autumn of 1881, and in February, 1882, sailed for Paris. Returned to Boston in May and is now living there. Returns to England in July, 1882.

*CLINTON HILL LORD.

The son of Dr. F. D. Lord, he was born at Casco, Maine, June 5, 1859. With his parents he moved to Newton, Mass., in June 1860, and lived there till his death. In June, 1877, he graduated from the Newton High School, and in September, 1878, joined our class. His life in college was exemplary, and he was not only a general favorite but he won the respect and esteem of those who did not know him personally. To his strict adherence to the right is to be added marked ability, for he attained high rank in his studies and was early elected a member of the board of Editors of the Advocate. Few men have been in college for whom one could predict a more successful life than one could for him; and his early death was the cause of great sorrow on the part of his many friends and of sincere regret on the part of those who respected him although unacquainted with him.

January 30, 1880, he died after a short but painful illness, at his home in Newton, but the class will always feel that in him, it lost one of its soundest and most able members.

CHARLES WASHINGTON LUCK.

Has been tutoring private pupils in Boston.

EDGAR WILLIAM McCOLL.

Neither the Sec'y of '81, of which class he was once a member, nor the Sec'y of '82 has been able to hear anything from him.

CHARLES HERBERT McFEE.

Left college in the spring of 1881, to take charge of Washington Academy at Wickford, R. I. After one term was elected principal of the Consolidated Grammar Schools at Woonsocket, R. I. Will return there next fall, but does not intend to make teaching his profession.

CHARLES HENRY MAHON.

Has not been heard from, but is living in Lynn, Mass.

ERNEST HOMER MARIETT.

Left the class to enter the Harvard Divinity School at which he was a student for two years. Then entered the Episcopal Theological School at Cambridge, where he will remain a year.

CHARLES ANDREWS MITCHELL.

Entered the class of 1881.

JOHN KEARSLEY MITCHELL.

Entered the Medical School of the University of Pennsylvania. For further information consult the Secretary of 1881.

SOLLACE MITCHELL.

Joined the class of 1883.

HENRY WHITING MUNROE.

Entered the banking house of Munroe & Co., Paris, France.

HUGH KINSLEY NORMAN.

Has been living in Boston and travelling.

RICHARD CHAPPELL PARSONS.

Has spent most of the time since leaving college in travelling in the west.

WILLIAM HERBERT PRESCOTT.

Entered the Harvard Medical School.

FREDERICK HENRY PRINCE.

Soon after leaving college entered the banking house of C. E. Fuller & Co., Boston, with which firm he now is.

HAZEN KIMBALL RICHARDSON.

Left college on account of illness and has been at home in Middleton, Mass., most of the time at work for his father. Health has returned and he hopes soon to return to study.

HERBERT ST. PIERRE RUFFIN.

Has been studying law in Boston. For further information consult the Secretary of 1881.

EDWARD DAVID SCOTT.

Since leaving college has been occupied in various ways trying to earn a livelihood and pay debts contracted in getting an education. In this he has been successful, and since the autumn of 1881 has been teaching school in Virginia. He has married, since he left the class, a Miss Molyneaux of Cambridge.

HENRY DWIGHT SEDGWICK.

Has been reading law in Boston.

ARCHIBALD LOWERY SESSIONS.

Joined the class of 1883.

*HENRY SHIPPEN.

The son of Rev. Rush R. Shippen and Zoe Rodman Shippen. Henry Shippen was born in Worcester, Mass., December 22, 1859. From September, 1872, to April, 1877, he was a student at the Roxbury Latin School, Boston, where he prepared for college, entering Cornell University as a Freshman in September, 1877. In September, 1878, he entered our class and passed through Freshman year with us. After one week's illness he died of typhoid pneumonia at Jamaica Plain, Mass., July 28, 1879.

"At college he soon attracted friends by all the amiable qualities of good-fellowship. In the intimacy of friendship he disclosed the higher qualities which command respect. His sincerity and conscientiousness were most marked. Those who knew him, remember him with affection, and cherish above all, the memory of the virtues, the possession of which made his a strong and manly spirit. S.

DENISON ROGERS SLADE.

Since leaving college has been in business in Boston. For further information consult the Secretary of 1881.

CHARLES INCHES STURGIS.

"Left college at end of Sophomore year. In October obtained a position on the C. B. & Q. R. R'y in Chicago, and left that city in the following June to fill a position in the joint office of the C. B. & Q. and Han. & St. Joe R. R'ys in Denver, Colorado.

WILLIAM ELDRIDGE THAYER.

Met with a severe accident at the Hemenway Gymnasium, Dec. 17, 1880, which made it necessary to give up study for the remainder of the year. "Knowing finally that the results of my accident were likely to render me incapable of study for some years, I reluctantly gave up any idea of trying to finish my college course." For the present is associated with the firm of H. F. Thayer and Co., manufacturing chemists, Boston.

FRANK HARRISON THOMPSON.

Has not been heard from.

EDWARD JAMES TILTON.

Has not been heard from.

CHARLES EVERETT TORREY.

Has not been heard from but is living in Boston.

GEORGE MACBETH TRENHOLM.

See '81's report.

*GEORGE CHRYSTIE VAN BENTHUYSEN.

"Was born in Spencer. Van Buren County, May 23, 1858, and died in Boston, June 24, 1882. He graduated from the Boston Public Latin School, the first scholar of the class of 1878. For so young a man, he had taken an unusually prominent part in public life, and had held a number of important political offices. He was a valued member of the Democratic City Committee of Boston, and was connected among other societies with the Independent Order of Foresters, the Bostonian Society and the inter-collegiate Greek letter society of Beta Theta Pi, in the revival of the Harvard Chapter of which he was largely instrumental."

H.

CHARLES MICHAEL VAN BUREN.

Left college on account of ill health, went to Europe and entered the University at Heidelberg. For further particulars consult the Sec'y of 1881.

MARS EDWARD WAGAR.

Entered the class of 1881.

WILLIAM BERNARD WARING.

Is instructor at St. John's College, Shanghai, China.

GORDON WENDELL.

Left college on account of an injury received at football. After travelling in the west returned to New York with improved health and entered the commission business.

ALFRED JEROME WESTON.

Joined the class of 1883.

HENRY WHITE.

Has not been heard from.

GEORGE WALTON WILLIAMS.

Left college on account of impaired health. "As I did not improve as rapidly as I thought I ought — in October '79 I sailed for England — went to Bonn in Germany where I matriculated as a student. I attended lectures very regularly, heard some very eminent men — made an extended tour of Europe — completely regaining my health. At present I am engaged in the iron business. Am. at the head of an Iron Foundry and Machine Shops from which I am glad to say I receive a good profit as the fruit of my labors. I am also a partner of my father's in the banking business." (Charleston, S. C.)

FRANK HERBERT YOUNG.

"I left college in Feb. '79 and have been and am now engaged in the 'Clothiers' & Tailors' Trimmings' business, on Summer St., Boston. Am doing well, better than I anticipated.

ADDRESSES.

ADDRESSES.

A list of addresses will be distributed annually. Those who have sent me no addresses are requested to do so immediately, and it will be the cause of much inconvenience to me and to you if I am not promptly notified of all mistakes and changes in address.

ALLEN, A. M., Glendale, Hamilton Co., Ohio.
ANDERSON, L. S., Quincy, Mass.
ANDREWS, C. W., 110 James St., Syracuse, N. Y.
AUSTIN, HERBERT, 9 Arlington St., Boston, Mass.
AVERILL, A. PRESTON, Middleton, Mass.
AVERILL, C. S., Middleton, Mass.
BABCOCK, J. W., Chester, South Carolina.
BABSON, R. T., care of William Babson, Gloucester, Mass.
BACHE, RENE, New York Sun, New York, N. Y.
BACHELDER, G. E., Salem, Mass.
BACON, CHARLES F., Lock Box 19, Newton, Mass.
BACON, JAMES H., Wilmington. N. C.
BAIRD, CHAMBERS, JR., 20 Holyoke St., Cambridge, Mass.
BAKER, EDWARD W., Brookline, Mass.
BALDWIN, C. A., 560 Fifth Ave., New York, N. Y.
BANCROFT, CLARENCE, Hopedale, Mass.
BARLOW, GEO. F., 405 Clermont Ave., Brooklyn, N. Y.
BARTLETT, C. H., Bangor, Maine.
BEALE, J. H., JR., Train St., Dorchester, Mass.
BIRTWELL, CHAS. W., 30 Stoughton, Cambridge, Mass.
BISHOP, JOHN R., till Sept., 1882, New Brunswick. N. J.; then St. Paul's School, Concord, N. H.
BLAIR, W. A., High Point, Guilford Co., N. C.
BLODGETT, W. A., 397 Beacon St., Boston, Mass.
BOWEN, JAMES W., Commonwealth Ave., Boston, Mass.
BOYD, ALEX. JR., Care James Boyd & Sons, Boston, Mass.
BOYNTON, C. E., 29 White St., Haverhill, Mass.
BRADLEY, R. M., 122 Commonwealth Ave., Boston, Mass.
BROWN, CHAS. J., 100 Mulberry St., Worcester, Mass.
BROWN, F. T., Carbon, Carbon Co., Wyoming Ter.
BRYANT, JOHN S., 236 Niagara St., Buffalo, N. Y.

BUELL, G. C., JR., Rochester, N. Y.
BULLARD, JOHN ELIOT, 149 Beacon St., Boston, Mass.
BURNHAM, WM. H., Dunbarton, N. H.
BURT, CHARLES D., 40 Somerset Ave., Taunton, Mass.
BURTON, F. R., Malden, Mass.
BUSH, WALTER N., Fall River, Mass., P. O. Box 528.
CABOT, G. L., 11 Park Sq., Boston, Mass.
CHALFANT, W.. JR.. West Chester, Chester Co., Penn.
CHAPIN, H. G.. 290 State St., Springfield, Mass.
CHASE, H. LINCOLN, JR., Brookline, Mass.
CHASE, WALTER G., Brookline, Mass., P. O. Box 579.
CHENEY, EDWARDS, Lowell, Mass., P. O. Box 218.
CLARK, J. P., 385 Marlborough St., Boston, Mass.
CLARK, S. C., Tewkesbury, Mass.
CLEMENT, H., 131 Newbury St., Boston, Mass.
COCHRANE, JOHN M., 14 State St., Cambridgeport, Mass.
CODMAN, ROBERT, JR., 27 Kilby St., Boston, Mass.
COLE, F. N., Marlboro', Mass.
COMEY, ARTHUR M., 4 Granite St., Somerville, Mass.
COOK, FRANK G., Warsaw, Wyoming Co., N. Y.
COOLIDGE, J. A., Coolidge Ave., Cambridge, Mass.
COPELAND, C. T., Calais, Maine.
CREESY, FRANK L., Brookline, Mass.
CREHORE, M. S., care Henry W. Daniels, P. O. Box 1283, Boston, Mass.
CROCKETT, MONTGOMERY A., Medford, Mass.
CUMMING, ROBERT, Care of the Secretary.
CUNNINGHAM, H. W., 31 St. James Ave., Boston, Mass.
CUNNINGHAM, W. de L., care J. W. Cunningham & Bro., 11 Wall St., New York, N. Y.
CUTLER, CHARLES F., 89 Broad St., Boston, Mass.
DABNEY, JOHN P., Taunton Tack Works, Taunton, Mass.
DABNEY, R. P., Care Mr. John E. May, 67 Commercial Wharf, Boston. Mass.
DAKIN, FRANKLIN A., Natick, Mass.
DANFORTH, W. H.. Plymouth, Mass., Lock Box 370.
DAVIS. WENDELL P.. Florence, Mass.
DEAN, C. R., Box 3, Taunton, Mass.
DELANEY, RICHARD, Woodville, Mass.
DICKERMAN, GEORGE W., Randolph, Mass., Box 473.

DICKEY, CHARLES D., Care of the Secretary.
DILLENBACK, H. I., Sat. Eve. Express. 247 Washington St., Boston, Mass.
DOOLING, J. J., 1490 Washington St., Boston, Mass.
DUNBAR, GEO. B., Care of Prof. C. F. Dunbar, Cambridge, Mass.
DUNBAR, W. H.,   "   "   "   "   "   "
DUNLEVY, HULBURD, 1812 Indiana Ave., Chicago, Ill.
EATON, G. H., 52 Weld, Cambridge, Mass.
EDGERLY, CLINTON J., 40 Water St., Rooms 52, 53, 54, Boston, Mass.
ELDRIDGE, FRED'K L., Care H. B. Hollins & Co., 74 Broadway, New York, N. Y.
ELIOT, CHARLES, Care C. W. Eliot, Cambridge, Mass.
ELLIOT, ALBERT DANNER, Market St., York, Penn.
EMERSON, F. W., Care of the Secretary.
FEARING, D. B., Care W. D. Morgan, 70 South St., New York, N. Y.
FEARING, E. T., Care H. L. Fearing & Co., 91 & 93 Commercial St., Boston, Mass.
FELLOWS, GORDON, 584 Fifth Ave., New York, N. Y.
FERGUSON, EDWARD A., 521 Jefferson Ave., Detroit, Mich.
FERNALD, F. A., Boston, Mass., Care H. W. Fernald, Post Office.
FIRMAN, B. M., Wakefield, Mass.
FISKE, WILLIAM B., 9 Clinton St., Cambridgeport, Mass.
FLAGG, JOSHUA G., 23 East 24th St., New York, N. Y.
FOSTER, J. M., Bangor, Maine.
FRANCIS, GEO. H., Brookline, Mass.
FRENCH, H. C., Centre St., Jamaica Plain, Mass.
FULLER, F. E., West Newton, Mass.
GAGE, HOMER, Worcester, Mass.
GARDNER, J. P., 152 Beacon St., Boston, Mass.
GARRETT, DAVID CLAIBORNE, Burlington, Iowa.
GILLESPIE, JOHN, Malden, Mass.
GILMAN, HENRY H., Haverhill, Mass.
GODDARD, F. NORTON, Care J. W. Goddard & Son, 516 Broadway, New York, N. Y.
GOLDTHWAITE, C. H., Holbrook, Mass.
GOODNOUGH, X. H., Brookline, Mass.
GORDON, L., Lowell, Mass., P. O. Box 66.
GREENOUGH, JAS. JAY, Cambridge, Mass.

GRIFFIN, J. Q. A., 25 City Sq., Charlestown District, Boston. Mass.
GRISWOLD, ALMON W., JR., 21 Courtland St., New York, N. Y.
GUITÉRAS, RAMON, Bristol. R. I.
HALL, ASAPH, JR., 18 Gay St., Georgetown, D. C.
HALL, F. S., Winthrop St., Taunton, Mass.
HARDON, H. W., 8 Hollis, Cambridge, Mass.
HARLOW, H. W., Care Dr. H. M. Harlow, Augusta, Maine.
HARTSHORN, GEO. T., Care Chas. W. Hartshorn, Esq., Taunton, Mass.
HAUPT, F. S., Care Gen. H. Haupt, Nor. Pac. R. R. Office, St. Paul, Minn.
HERRICK, W. H., Care W. A. Herrick, Esq., 3 Niles Block, 33 School St., Boston, Mass.
HEYWOOD, FRANK E., Worcester, Mass., P. O. Box 923.
HOAR, SHERMAN, Concord, Mass.
HOLDEN, FRANCIS M., Care A. R. Holden, 77 Poplar St., Boston, Mass.
HOLMAN, C. H., Cambridge, Mass.
HOPKINS, JAMES H., Barnstable, Mass.
HOWARD, A. A. Care of the Secretary.
HOWE, F. W., Care Howes & Burnham, Lowell, Mass.
HOWE, W. A., Bolton, Mass.
HOYT, HENRY R., Care Alfred M. Hoyt, Esq., 15 State, St., New York, N. Y.
HUBBARD, H. M., 387 La Salle Ave., Chicago, Ill.
HUNT, FREDERICK T., Weymouth, Mass.
JENNINGS, C. G. R., Bennington Centre, Vt.
JONES, WILLIAM, Wollaston, Mass.
KANE, WOODBURY, Care H. S. Ely, 22 Pine St., New York, N. Y.
KEEP, C. H., Till Oct., 1882, Lockport, N. Y.; then Harvard College, Cambridge, Mass.
KENT, W. W., 274 Delaware Ave., Buffalo, N. Y.
KINGSBURY, A. B., JR., Quincy, Ill.
KITTREDGE, B. R., Peekskill, N. Y.
KITTREDGE, G. L., 245 Longwood Ave., Roxbury, Mass.
KNOWLES, C. F. S., Yarmouth Port, Mass.
LANE, A. F., St. Albans, Vt.
LAMPREY, WILLIAM A., 33 Mt. Pleasant St., Somerville, Mass.
COURTNEY, LANGDON, Episcopal Academy, Cheavie, Conn.

Lawrence, Prescott, 38 Beacon St., Boston, Mass.
Leatherbee, Geo. H., 122 East Dedham St., Boston, Mass.
Leavitt, Heyward G., 1 East 40th St., New York, N. Y.
Lothrop, A. P., Care T. J. Lothrop, Esq., Taunton, Mass.
Luce, Robert, Care E. T. Luce, Waltham, Mass.
Luck, Charles W., Marion, Mass.
Ludlow, T. W., 14 East 16th St., New York, N. Y.
Lyons, John P., Montrose, Penn.
McArthur, A. F., 275 Ashland Ave., Chicago, Ill.
McCoy, W. I., 10 Washington Place, Troy, N. Y.
McDonald, E. V., Fall River, Mass.
McDonald, R. H., Jr., Care Pacific Bank, San Francisco, Cal.
McFee, Chas. H., P. O. Box 433, Woonsocket, R. I.
McKendry, W. H., Canton, Mass.
McKone, Wm. T., North Andover Depot, Mass.
Manning, W. H., Care W. W. Manning, 139 Merrimack St., Lowell, Mass.
Mariett, E. H., St. Armand, Quebec.
Mason, Charles F., Medfield, Norfolk Co., Mass.
Mason, John W., Brookline, Mass.
Matthews, Albert, 145 Beacon St., Boston, Mass.
Mayberry, G. L., Weston, Mass.
Merritt, E. P., 94 Pearl St., Boston, Mass.
Miles, A. E., Care Jonas M. Miles, 23 Court St., Boston, Mass.
Mitchell, John K., Care Dr. S. Weir Mitchell, Philadelphia, Penn.
Mitchell, Sollace, Cor. Forsyth & Julia Sts., Jacksonville, Fla.
Morrill, Sam Henry, 58 Mt. Auburn St., Cambridge, Mass.
Munroe, H. W., Care Munroe & Co., 9 Rue Scribe, Paris, France.
Nagle, G. E., 58 North Ave, Cambridge, Mass.
Norman, H. K., Care Mr. Geo. H. Norman, Newport, R. I.
Olmsted, O. A., Le Roy, N. Y.
Oxnard, Henry T., 278 Henry St., Brooklyn, N. Y.
Page, W. E., P. O. Box 31, Peabody, Mass.
Paine, Robert T., 46 Mt. Vernon St., Boston, Mass.
Panin, I. N., Care Gen. R. S. Oliver (Rathbone, Sard & Co.), Albany, N. Y.
Parsons, R. C., Jr., Cleveland, Ohio.
Pendleton, Elliott H., Jr., 100 East 4th St., Cincinnati, Ohio.
Perin, E. S., 168 West 7th St., Cincinnati, Ohio.

PERKINS, GEO. W., Topsfield, Essex Co., Mass., P. O. Box 220.
PERKINS. J. W., Hyde Park, Mass.
PERRIN, E. N., 20 East 43rd St., New York, N. Y.
PICKERING, M. J., 13 Exchange Place, Boston, Mass.
POTTER, WHIPPLE N., JR., 26 Waverly St., Roxbury Station, Mass.
PRESCOTT, W. H., Concord, Mass.
PRESTON, JOHN, New Ipswich, N. H.
PRINCE, F. H., C. E. Fuller & Co., 2 State St., Boston, Mass.
PUTNAM, W. L., Care George Putnam, Esq., 35 Court St., Boston, Mass.
RHINELANDER, F. W., JR., Redwood St., Newport, R. I.
RICE, C. M., Care W. W. Rice, Worcester, Mass.
RICHARDSON, G. M., Care F. J. Stimson, 209 Washington St., Boston, Mass.
RICHARDSON, H. A., South Framingham, Mass.
RICHARDSON, H. K., Middleton, Mass.
ROBINSON, LUCIEN MOORE, Maplewood Farm. East Sumner, Maine.
ROGERS, W. A., Box 613, Decatur, Ill.
RUFFIN, H. St. P., 13 Court Sq., Boston, Mass.
RUSSELL, JOHN, Plymouth, Mass.
RUSHMORE, W. J., 22 Mt. Auburn St., Cambridge, Mass.
SCOTT, EDWARD D., 311 College St., Richmond, Va.
SEDGWICK, H. D., 31 Pemberton Sq., Boston, Mass.
SESSIONS, A. L., 81 Hicks St., Brooklyn, N. Y.
SEWALL, H. M., Bath, Maine.
SHERWOOD, H. H., Care Rob't Sherwood, Esq., 309 California St., San Francisco, Cal.
SLADE, DENISON R., Chestnut Hill, Mass.
SMITH, H. E., 270 North West St., Indianapolis, Ind.
SNOW, CHAS. A., 41 Rutherford Sq., Boston, Mass.
SPALDING, GEO. F., 86 Worcester St., Boston, Mass.
STETSON, ELIOT D., New Bedford, Mass.
STEVENS, C. H., 308 Harvard St., Cambridge, Mass.
STEVENS, E. K., Newport, R. I., P. O. Box 79.
STONE, F. M., Cottage St., New Bedford, Mass.
STONE, W. E., Care Mr. Walter C. Robbins, 83 Chester Sq., Boston, Mass.
STORER, JOHN H., 182 Boylston St, Boston, Mass.
STURGIS, C. I., Han. & St. Joe & C. B. & Q. R. R.'s, Denver, Col.

THACHER, T. C., 16 Pearl St., Boston, Mass.
THAXTER, ROLAND, Kittery Pt., Maine.
THAYER, W. E., Savin Hill Ave., Savin Hill, Dorchester, Mass.
TORREY, C. E., Care Bowker, Torrey & Co., Chardon St., Boston, Mass.
TOWNE, G. W., Topsfield, Mass.
TOWNSEND, S. V. R., 21 Elk St., Albany, N. Y.
TRENHOLM, GEO. M., Charleston, S. C.
TUCKERMAN, GUSTAVUS. Till Sept. 1882, Care Francis Skinner, Esq., Newport, R. I.; then General Theological Seminary, West 20th St., New York, N. Y.
UNDERWOOD, EDWARD L., 55 E. Newton St., Boston, Mass.
VAN BUREN, C. M., Care T. S. Mandell, Newton, Mass.
WAGAR, MARS EDWARD, East Rockport (Near Cleveland) Ohio.
WAIT, WM. C., 400 Warren Ave., Chicago, Ill.
WARING, GUY, Newport, R. I.
WARING, W. B., St. Johns College, Shanghai, China.
WARNER, HENRY E., Care C. H. Warner, Esq., Nat'l Bank of Commerce, Boston, Mass.
WARREN, F., JR., Care Geo. Warren & Co., Alexandra Building, Liverpool, England.
WASHBURN, F. L., Care of the Secretary.
WASHBURN, P. M., 36 Elm St., Worcester, Mass.
WEBB, JOHN S., 1918 F. St., Washington, D. C.
WELD, J. E. Orchard Ave., Forest Hills, Boston, Mass.
WELLS, EDWARD F., Marietta, Ohio.
WENDELL, EVERT J., 8 East 38th St., New York, N. Y.
WENDELL, GORDON, "   "   "   "   "   "
WENTWORTH, ELMER, Care J. F. Wentworth, Chelsea, Mass.
WESTON, A. J., Yonkers, N. Y.
WHITING, ISAAC S., Wilton, N. H.
WHITMAN, RUSSELL, Plymouth, Mass.
WILLIAMS, GEO. W., JR., Charleston, S. C.
WILLISTON, S., N. T. Survey, Box 752, Newport, R. I.
WISTER, OWEN, Care of the Secretary.
WOODBURY, FRED'K C., 60 Buckingham St., Cambridge, Mass.
WOODWORTH, H. G., 31 Central St., Boston, Mass.
WORCESTER, JOSEPH R., Waltham, Mass.
YOUNG, FRANK HERBERT, 760 Tremont St., Boston, Mass.

Harvard College.

Secretary's Report.

Class of 1882.
II.

June, 1885.

Wheeler, Printer, 416 Harvard St., Cambridge.

CLASS COMMITTEE.

RUSSELL WHITMAN.
ARTHUR PRESCOTT LOTHROP.
FRANKLIN ARTHUR DAKIN.

Class Secretary.
ALFRED EUGENE MILES.

INTRODUCTION.

CLASSMATES:

The information contained in this report was given in reply to the following questions:

1. Have you married? Please state time and place of marriage, with the full name of your wife, and those of her parents, and dates of birth and full names of your children, if any have been born.

2. Please give an account of any journeys you have made, if you have travelled either in America or abroad, and tell what you have seen or visited, and have been interested in.

3. If you have been admitted to practice in either of the professions, or have studied to prepare for either, or have been in business, please state when and where you have studied or practised, when admitted to practice or to membership in your firm, and where you propose to settle and pursue your profession or business.

4. Please give the exact titles and dates of publication of any essays, books, pamphlets, music, or sketches you have written, also the names of any scientific, social or literary clubs of which you have become a member.

Where it has been possible I have given your own accounts in your own words and most of the sketches are therefore reliable. For many I have had to depend on what I could find out from the friends of those who neglected to answer my requests for information. If I have made any mistakes I shall be obliged to any who will inform me of them. There are no new features in the report, unless it is the detailed statement of finances.

If my time had not been almost fully occupied with other matters which I could not postpone or neglect I should have taken great pleasure in the work, and could have prepared, perhaps, a more satisfactory report, but I have been extremely busy and a great many of you have neglected to answer my requests without repeated circulars and letters. I hope, however, that those who have replied to my letters will feel satisfied with what I am able to give.

Hereafter, reports will be made every five years unless you request them oftener. Please remember that I can do very little unless you keep me informed of your addresses, and believe me,

     Yours sincerely,

          ALFRED E. MILES.

CLASS OF 1882.

(An asterisk (*) is used to denote deceased members.)

Alfred Marston Allen
Luther Stetson Anderson
Charles Walker Andrews
Andrew Preston Averill
James Woods Babcock
Robert Tillinghast Babson
Charles Franklin Bacon
James Hayward Bacon
Chambers Baird
Edward Wild Baker
Charles Adolphe Baldwin
Clarence Bancroft
George Francis Barlow
Joseph Henry Beale
John Remsen Bishop
William Allen Blair
William Ashley Blodgett
James William Bowen
Alexander Boyd
Charles Edgar Boynton
Richards Merry Bradley
Charles Jerome Brown
John Sweeney Bryant
George Clifford Buell
John Eliot Bullard
William Henry Burnham
Charles Dean Burt
Frederick Russell Burton
Walter Nelson Bush

Godfrey Lowell Cabot
Henry Gardner Chapin
Heman Lincoln Chase
Walter Greenough Crase
Edwards Cheney
Joseph Payson Clark
Hazen Clement
John McGregor Cochrane
Robert Codman
Frank Nelson Cole
Arthur Messinger Comey
Frank Gaylord Cook
Joseph Austin Coolidge
Charles Townsend Copeland
Frank Leonard Creesy
Morton Stimson Crehore
Montgomery Adams Crockett
Robert Cumming
Henry Winchester Cunningham
William de Lancey Cunningham
Charles Francis Cutler
Ralph Pomeroy Dabney
Franklin Arthur Dakin
William Henry Danforth
Wendell Phillips Davis
Clarence Randall Dean
Richard Delaney
George Washington Dickerman
Charles Denston Dickey

The first list is of those who received degrees as members of 1882. You will be pleased to see that the list is larger than it was at our Commencement Day.

George Bradford Dunbar
William Harrison Dunbar
George Herbert Eaton
Charles Eliot
Albert Danner Elliot
Frederick Ware Emerson
William Gordon Fellows
Frederic Atherton Fernald
Burton Monroe Firman
William Boyd Fiske
Joshua Gardner Flagg
John McGaw Foster
George Hills Francis
Harry Cormerais French
Frank Edward Fuller
Homer Gage
Joseph Peabody Gardner
David Claiborne Garrett
John Gillespie
Henry Hale Gilman
Frederick Norton Goddard
Charles Henry Goldthwaite
Xanthus Henry Goodnough
Lysson Gordon
James Jay Greenough
Asaph Hall
Frederick Stanley Hall
Henry Winthrop Hardon
Henry Williams Harlow
George Trumbull Hartshorn
Frank Spangler Haupt
William Hale Herrick
Frank Everett Heywood
Sherman Hoar
James Hughes Hopkins
Albert Andrew Howard
Henry Reese Hoyt
Harry Mascarene Hubbard
Frederick Thayer Hunt
Charles Green Rockwood Jennings
William Jones
Charles Hallam Keep
William Winthrop Kent
Albert Benjamin Kingsbury
Benjamin Rufus Kittredge
George Lyman Kittredge
Charles Francis Swift Knowles

Albert French Lane
George Henry Leatherbee
Heyward Gibbons Leavitt
Arthur Prescott Lothrop
Robert Luce
Thomas William Ludlow
John Plumer Lyons
Arthur Fred McArthur
Walter Irving McCoy
Edward Valentine McDonald
Richard Hayes McDonald
William Henry McKendry
William Thomas McKone
William Hobbs Manning
Charles Frank Mason
John Whiting Mason
Albert Matthews
George Lowell Mayberry
Edward Percival Merritt
Alfred Eugene Miles
Sam Henry Morrill
Garrett Edward Nagle
Oliver Allen Olmsted
Henry Thomas Oxnard
William Enoch Page
Robert Treat Paine
Ivan Nikolayevitsh Panin
Elliott Hunt Pendleton
*Edmund Sehon Perin   *1882
George William Perkins
John Walter Perkins
Ernest Perrin
McLaurin Jameson Pickering
Whipple Nahum Potter
John Preston
William Lowell Putnam
Frederic William Rhinelander
Charles Moen Rice
George Morey Richardson
Herbert Augustus Richardson
Lucien Moore Robinson
William Armstrong Rogers
William Joseph Rushmore
John Russell
Harold Marsh Sewall
Henry Hamilton Sherwood
Horace Emmet Smith

Charles Armstrong Snow
George Frederick Spalding
Eliot Dawes Stetson
Charles Herbert Stevens
Edward Knights Stevens
Frederic Mather Stone
William Enos Stone
John Humphreys Storer
Thomas Chandler Thacher
Roland Thaxter
George Warren Towne
Stephen Van Rensselaer Townsend
Gustavus Tuckerman
Edward Livingston Underwood
William Cushing Wait
Guy Waring

Henry Eldridge Warner
Frederic Warren
Frederic Leonard Washburn
Philip Moen Washburn
John Sydney Webb
J. Edward Weld
Evert Jansen Wendell
Elmer Ellsworth Wentworth
Isaac Spalding Whiting
Russell Whitman
Samuel Williston
Owen Wister
Frederick Clinton Woodbury
Herbert Grafton Woodworth
Joseph Ruggles Worcester

—183

Herbert Austin
Charles Sidney Averill
René Bache
Charles Hammatt Bartlett
George Edwin Bachelder
Charles Wesley Birtwell
Frank Taylor Brown
William Chalfant
Stephen Cutter Clark
James Pendleton Cruger
John Pomeroy Dabney
Hiram Irving Dillenback
James Joseph Dooling
Hiland Hulburd Dunlevy
Charles Hamlin Dunton
Clinton Johnson Edgerly
Frederick Larnac Eldridge
Daniel Butler Fearing
Edwin Thayer Fearing
Edward Ashley Ferguson
John Quincy Adams Griffin
Almon Whiting Griswold
Ramon Benjamin Guiteras
Percival Smith Hill
Francis Marion Holden
Charles Harvey Holman
Frank Whitehouse Howe
William Addison Howe

Woodbury Kane
George Clark Kennett   *1879*
William Amos Lamprey   *1882*
Courtney Langdon
Prescott Lawrence
Clinton Hill Lord   *1880*
Charles Washington Luck
George William McColl
Charles Herbert McFee
Charles Henry Mahon
Ernest Homer Mariett
Charles Andrews Mitchell
John Kearsley Mitchell
Sollace Mitchell
Henry Whiting Munroe
Hugh Kinsley Norman
Richard Chappell Parsons
William Herbert Prescott
Frederick Henry Prince
Hazen Kimball Richardson
Hubert St. Pierre Ruffin
Edward David Scott
Henry Dwight Sedgwick
Archibald Lowery Sessions
Henry Shippen   *1879*
Denison Rogers Slade
Charles Inches Sturgis
William Eldredge Thayer

Frank Harrison Thompson
Edward James Tilton
Charles Everett Torrey
George Macbeth Trenholm
*George Chrystie Van Benthuysen
1882*
Charles Michael Van Buren
Mars Edward Wagar

William Bernard Waring
Edward Freeman Wells
Gordon Wendell
Alfred Jerome Weston
Henry White
George Walton Williams
Frank Herbert Young

—70 = 253

RECORD OF THE CLASS.

July 1882—July 1885.

ALFRED MARSTON ALLEN.

"My life since graduation has been an uneventful one. In September, 1882, I began the study of law in the offices of King, Thompson and Maxwell, in Cincinnati, and in October entered the Law School of the Cincinnati College, where I graduated in May, 1884. I was admitted to the bar by the Supreme Court of Ohio about the first of June and at once began the practice of law in this city (Cincinnati), not doing much, however, till last fall (1884). I reside at my old home at Glendale, one of the suburbs of Cincinnati, and expect to pursue my profession in this city. I was married to Hannah C. Smith, daughter of Erastus M. and Mary McAlpin Smith of this city, on Thursday, March 26, 1885."

LUTHER STETSON ANDERSON.

"After the usual summer vacation I entered the General Freight Department of the Old Colony Railroad and have since remained in the employ of that Corporation, learning the business in all its branches. Very naturally, owing to the soulless nature of Railroad Corporations, the vacations, and consequently the travels, have been rather few and far between. It is quite probable that at no distant day I shall be called upon to abandon New England for the West, a change which, although pleasant in some respects, will not be particularly fascinating to a dyed-in-the-wool Yankee."

CHARLES WALKER ANDREWS.

"Am not married. The fall after graduation I returned to the Harvard Law School where I remained but two years. Since last July (1884) I have been in the law office of Knapp, Nottingham and Andrews (Syracuse, N. Y.) studying. I hope to pass the bar examination next June (1885) but whether or not after that I will practise law in Syracuse is wholly uncertain."

ANDREW PRESTON AVERILL.

"I was married in New York City to Miss Clara Ada McKay, December 25, 1882, daughter of Rodney R. and Adelina McKay. We have one son, Charles Peabody Averill, born March 17, 1884. I began to teach in September, 1882, and have taught ever since. I am now Principal of the Houghton High School, Bolton, Mass."

JAMES WOODS BABCOCK.

Has been pursuing the regular three years' course at the Harvard Medical School in Boston, and will probably take his degree in June, 1885. Was appointed Assistant at the Tewkesbury (State) Almshouse and spent a part of the time in 1883 attending to his work there. Is now one of the house officers at the McLean Asylum, Somerville.

ROBERT TILLINGHAST BABSON.

Has been studying law all the time since graduation in the Boston University Law School, and has been living at home at Gloucester, Mass. Expects to take his degree in June, 1885.

CHARLES FRANKLIN BACON.

"A few months after leaving college I went abroad in company with Dr. Blodgett of Smith College and Professor Platt of Hartford, and spent a portion of the year in Europe, visiting England, Scotland, Wales, France, Holland, Belgium, Germany, Austria, Switzerland and Italy, and derived great good from the various adventures and experiences which I had. I was particularly pleased with Scotland and old England, where I visited the homes of many famous men, and North Italy where I saw so much relating to the Classic ages. I attended the "Parsifal" at Bayreuth, also performances by various noted artists in the several capitals of Europe, and having decided to study music on my return to America I made many researches in the system of musical education abroad, particularly in Germany where I saw the famous conservatories in operation. Since my return I have been studying music in Boston. I belong to the Newton Art and Musical Club, a social and literary organization—and am also secretary of the Eliot Literary Union."

JAMES HAYWARD BACON.

"In July, 1882, I received employment as 'Rodman' upon the 'Improvement of the Cape Fear River' below Wilmington, N. C. I held this position till August, 1884, when I received an appointment as Assistant Engineer from Major Ernst, Officer in charge of the 'Improvement of the Mississippi River' between the Illinois and Ohio Rivers. In March, 1885, owing to the failure of Congress to make an appropriation for rivers and harbors, nearly half of the assistants were discharged, myself among the number. Shortly after I was offered and accepted a subordinate position (U. S. Engineer's Office, Custom House, St. Louis), which I am now holding."

CHAMBERS BAIRD, JR.

After graduation entered the Harvard Law School, taking the first year course during the college year 1882-83. The next year entered the Senior Class of the Cincinnati Law School, in which were also numbered Allen and Pendleton, Harvard, '82. Graduated May 28, 1884, and on the following day at Columbus, O., was admitted to the bar of the State. In September, 1884, returned to Cincinnati, but about October 1, removed to Denver, Col., where he became associated with the firm of Tilford, Gilmore and Rhodes, and was admitted to the Colorado bar. Is still in Denver, has dissolved his connection with the above firm, and has opened an office of his own. Is a member of the Glenarm Literary Club and of a law club.

During 1882-83, while at the Harvard Law School, contributed the following verse to college papers: to the *Crimson*, "Far O'er the Western Seas"; to the *Lampoon*, "Identity," "By Degrees," and "His Crazy-bone." Has also contributed poems since graduation to the *Youth's Companion* and *Evening Transcript* of Boston; to the former, "Sunset on the Ohio" (March 29 1883), "The Light-house," and "On the Heights"; to the latter, "Wild

Roses of Cape Ann" (July 27, 1882), "Love and Music" "Regret," "Without and Within" (January 24, 1883), "Heine," (February 8, 1883), and some others. During attendance at the Cincinnati Law School, 1883-84, was Managing Editor of the *Beta Theta Pi*, a monthly, during the college year, the organ of the college fraternity of that name. Besides editorial work and writing, also contributed prose articles and verse as follows: "Out of the World," January, 1884, "Wooghlin on Chautauqua," February, 1884, and "Through Annisquam River," March, 1884, prose; "Heine" (new version) November, 1883, "Two Chords in a Minor Key," December, 1883, "Unconsoled," February, 1884, "The Maid of the Mist" and Memorials," March, 1884, "Ohio Reunion Poem," May, 1884, and "Recompense," May, 1884, verse. Is still an associate editor of the *Beta Theta Pi* during 1884-85, and has contributed the following verse: "To Rose" and "To Juno," November, 1884, and "Roses" and "On the Veranda," January, 1885. Contributed an article on "College Journalism" to the Chicago *Current* of November 22, 1884. Has also contributed verse, "Left and Bereft" (December 6, 1884) and "Denver" (December 20, 1884), to the Denver *Opinion* and has written other matter in prose and verse for Denver publications and other papers. Has at different times and places been a regular correspondent for various papers, and has also written some short stories and sketches.

Was a delegate from the Harvard Chapter to the 43d Annual Convention of the Beta Theta Pi Fraternity, held at Cincinnati about September 1, 1882; was also delegate to and second vice-president of the 45th Annual Convention, held at Lake Chautauqua, N. Y., in 1884, and was elected alternate Poet for the convention of 1885, to be held at St. Louis, Mo. Was Poet at the Ohio Reunion of Betas held at Columbus, O., in May, 1884. Is a member of the Beta Theta Pi Alumni Club, a private stock company, which owns a place of twenty acres and a large club house called "Wooglin," on Lake Chautauqua, N. Y., opposite Mayville.

Time since graduation has been spent uneventfully and busily, chiefly in the study of law and literature. Summers have mainly been passed at home in Ripley, Brown Co., O., and in general recreation. In summer of 1882 visited Cape Ann, Mass., Saratoga, and Lake Chautauqua, N. Y. In summer of 1883 made

a yachting trip along the "North Shore" and the coast of Maine, concluding with a visit of nearly a week on Minot's Ledge Light, off Cohasset, Mass. (For description and impressions see "Out of the World" and "Through Annisquam River" in *Beta Theta Pi*.)
Is in good health and unmarried.

EDWARD WILD BAKER.

"In the fall of 1882 I entered the service of the Mexican Central Railway, with which I am still connected. At present, I am holding a position as clerk and stenographer in the Boston Offices of the Company."

CHARLES ADOLPHE BALDWIN.

Soon after Commencement entered the employ of Messrs. C. Adolphe Low and Co., San Francisco, in the business of preparing and canning fruits, etc., for shipment, and though he has not been directly heard from your Secretary believes he is still with the above firm. This information was given by Mr. H. M. Gillig, also in the same firm, who was socially a member of 1882, and will be remembered by many of the class.

CLARENCE BANCROFT.

"I sailed for Europe in July, 1882. I spent a year in the Polytechnikum at Zurich, where I continued my study of Chemistry. My attention was given to the science of Chemistry in its application to manufactures, more particularly to the subject of dyes, both in the preparation and in the application of the same. I was fortunate enough to visit some of the large chemical works, dye-works and print works in Germany and in Switzerland. I spent a portion of my spare time during vacations in travel through Germany, Switzerland and Italy. I made some extended foot-tours in the mountains of Switzerland. I spent some time in Italy where I made a foot-tour of several hundred miles. I returned to America late in the fall of 1883, and took the position of Chemist for the Manchester Mills. I have introduced many German and French methods of dyeing and finishing cloth into the mills, and thus improved the goods and reduced the expense about one-fourth. I devote most of my time at present to conducting experiments with a view to improving woolen and mixed goods in the process of dyeing and finishing. I have opportunity for obtaining a practical knowledge of the manufacture of a variety of goods in one of the largest works in the country, and am well satisfied with the progress that I have made."

GEORGE FRANCIS BARLOW.

"I have not married, nor has any fair one a mortgage on my affections. *Sequentur* my wife, children and mother-in-law are still like one of our philosophical electives, a matter of speculation. After the summer of 1882, having recovered from the dire effects of the years of study and importunities of creditors, I entered the office of Gen. T. C. Barlow, 206 Broadway, New York, as a student, and the class of 1884 at the Columbia Law School. I worked all day in an office taking the two years in one at the Law School the last hours in the afternoon. On December 10, 1883, I was admitted to practice as an attorney and counsellor. I then hung out my shingle and began practising. In May, 1884, I took a degree of LL.B. at the Columbia Law School. The same month I formed a copartnership under the style of Barlow & Rockwell, and took offices at 62 Temple Court, New York City, where I still continue to do a general law business. In the spring of 1883 I sailed for Europe, travelled through England, then to Paris, and *did* the Continent from Amsterdam to Naples and as far east as Vienna. Returned in September, 1883. My impressions? Give me America with her republican ideas— free schools—free press—free church—America prolific of opportunities, rich in natural resources, and progressive almost to a fault. I am not an Anglo-maniac."

JOSEPH HENRY BEALE.

Spent the year of 1882-83 at Concord, N. H., as a master at St. Paul's School, under Dr. Coit. In the fall of 1883 returned to Cambridge and devoted the ensuing year to study in the graduate department of Harvard College, taking courses in Classics and History. Decided upon law as a profession in the summer of 1884 and has since been a student in the Harvard Law School.

JOHN REMSEN BISHOP.

"After graduation I taught in St. Paul's School, Concord, N. H., for one year. Abandoning the occupation of teaching, I then entered the office of the Bureau of Statistics of Labor, of the State of New Jersey, as assistant. Being driven out of this office by pressure brought to bear by labor demagogues, I turned to my first love, teaching. Recommended by Dr. Coit of St. Paul's School to see Dr. McCosh of Princeton, I was induced by Dr. McCosh to purchase, with the aid of friends, the Princeton Preparatory School, of which institution I am now proprietor and Head Master."

WILLIAM ALLEN BLAIR.

"1. Have not.

"2. Have travelled considerably among the mountains in western North Carolina, for pleasure and minerals.

"3. Have taken my Master's degree, been elected State Professor of English in the Normal, and am Principal of a large private school at this place." (High Point, N. C.)

WILLIAM ASHLEY BLODGETT.

Shortly after leaving college went into the employ of Messrs. Clark, Adams & Clark (wholesale and retail Crockery), Boston, and has been with them ever since. Was married at Fitchburg, Mass., October 9, 1882, to Miss Emma S. Garfield of Fitchburg. A daughter, Emily Louise Blodgett, was born July 6, 1883.

JAMES WILLIAMS BOWEN.

Travelled in Europe about a year for pleasure and for the study of the German and French languages, and then entered the employ of F. S. Mosely, Note Broker, Boston.

ALEXANDER BOYD.

"After graduating I spent the summer in having a good time. About the first of the following October I entered the employ of the American Rubber Co. of Boston, where I have since been."

CHARLES EDGAR BOYNTON.

Has been teaching and is at present in the High School, Spencer, Mass.

RICHARDS MERRY BRADLEY.

"From October, 1882, to August, 1883, I was a student in the Law Office of Messrs. Ropes, Gray and Loring, Boston. In October, 1883, I entered the Harvard Law School and remained there till March, 1884. Then went into the office of J. T. Eldredge & Co., Real Estate Agents, Boston. Since August, 1884, I have been engaged in the real estate business with my classmate, John H. Storer, under the firm name of Bradley and Storer, at No. 40 State St., Boston."

CHARLES JEROME BROWN.

"After graduation I spent my time at home for the most part aiding my father, and in the following winter had a school in a town near by. In June following I passed the first set of Civil Service examinations held in Boston, receiving a percentage of 80.6. I have not, however, secured a position therefrom. The fall found me in Ohio, in a kind of mixed school, embracing scholars from the letters to the High School branches. Success as a teacher has not seemed to follow me, and since done with my second attempt I have been engaged in several pursuits, both in Chicago and Worcester. At present I am here in New Haven, working in a carriage factory. I am looking forward to a participation in the New England School of Hebrew, which meets here in July next, as a preparation to further study if so it may be."

JOHN SWEENEY BRYANT.

"I am not married nor do I anticipate entering that blissful state for some time to come. After graduation I was for a period of perhaps six months without any definite aim, when finally I decided to study law; having made so weighty a decision, I thought it necessary for my health to visit the "sunny South" so on the first of January, 1883, I with the remainder of my family departed for Florida. I spent a couple of weeks in

Washington. I then left for Charleston. Charleston is a decayed reminder of former greatness, and I can say truthfully that when one goes below Washington he enters a district where energy seems unknown and where a semi-civilization reigns supremely. At Jacksonville I found summer in earnest. I spent two months in Florida, at the several places of general resort, Palatka, Glen Cove Springs and Enterprise—arriving in Buffalo about the middle of April. I then entered on my law studies with earnestness, and was admitted to practice in the Courts of New York State in January, 1885, at Buffalo, where I shall try to work up a practice. Beyond a law club and a French class, I have become the member of no society; as for essays, etc., I have not the inclination to indulge if I had the time. I keep up my Latin, French, German and Greek, and think that these, with the legal profession and casual reading, ought to keep my mind from becoming torpid."

GEORGE CLIFFORD BUELL.

After leaving college went into business and has been in business since except when prevented by illness, notably by a very severe attack of typhoid fever in the spring of 1884. Has been and is now with Messrs. Geo. C. Buell & Co. (his father's firm), wholesale grocers, Rochester, N. Y.

JOHN ELIOT BULLARD.

Immediately after graduation entered the employ of Messrs. Henry W. Peabody & Co., Australian Shippers. Remained in their offices in Boston and New York for two years. Sailed for Melbourne, December 7, 1884.

WILLIAM HENRY BURNHAM.

"The first year after graduation I spent as teacher in the Preparatory Department of Wittenburg College, Springfield, Ohio. In November, 1883, I began work in my present position in the State Normal School, Potsdam, N. Y. The first year I taught Latin; this year I teach Latin and Rhetoric. My work as a teacher has been pleasant, and whatever has been its effect on my pupils, I think it has been beneficial to me. I have furnished nothing for publication except a few contributions to college papers in Springfield, Ohio."

CHARLES DEAN BURT.

"Since we graduated I have been living at my home in Taunton and have been at work in a tack manufactory. I am not married nor have I made any journeys worth recording. I have become a member of the Sportsman's Club, a social club—and another devoted mostly to theatricals, called 'The Social Club.'"

FREDERICK RUSSELL BURTON.

"The summer immediately following our Commencement Day I passed in vocal and theoretical study with a view to making the teaching of music my business. In the autumn I hung my sign in a Tremont Street doorway and sat down inside to receive my patrons. The door was not besieged by regiments of aspiring students and those who came, generally were talented but penniless. On the first of January, therefore, I departed as dignified and stately as possible from the musical profession, and soon after found my way into the newspaper business, where I still remain. My first regular position was on the Boston Globe, as reporter. After various changes in the character of my work, I was finally made night City Editor in February, 1884. In June following I accepted an offer to go to Troy, N. Y., to write editorials for the Daily Telegram. I was made City Editor soon after my arrival and gradually dropped editorial writing. Some time during August I received an offer of the editorship of the Fall River Daily Herald. I began work on that paper about September 1, and continued the same until the first of October, when the business management and myself suddenly parted company. I turned my eyes toward New York City and was about to set out for the Metropolis, when I heard that the Boston Post was without a City Editor. I presented myself, was accepted, and here I am.

"My musical publications, I regret to say, have been few and far between. I need not explain, I suppose, that publishers look askance at young composers, and that money with them is more eloquent than art. I have made little effort to force my work on the market, content to wait until my circumstances shall permit me to devote myself wholly to music. Outside of a few quartettes and one or two trifles my only publications are the following songs: 'Kitty Bhan,' 'My Cigarette,' 'The Engineer,' 'Sea-weed' (for bass voice), 'I Think of Thee.' Was married February 14, 1885, to Miss Winnifred N. Baxter, of Malden, Mass."

WALTER NELSON BUSH.

"I am still loyal to Mr. Malthus, have published nothing, and am not ungrateful to that kind, mysterious power that has guided and guarded me.

"After graduating and recovering from the midnight exercises of Commencement, I left the home of the Poco for Peoria. Here I tarried during the year 1882-83, teaching Mathematics and the Sciences in the High School; but I had set my face westward and at the close of that year came to California, sojourning on the way in Chicago, as bookkeeper for Sprague, Warner & Co., for about two months. Upon my arrival in Oakland I took up a course in mathematics and chemistry at the State University, spending my afternoons in the laboratory and mornings and evenings as instructor at Hopkins Academy. February, 1884, I was elected to take charge of the High School —a position I still occupy; happy, and for the time being, contented.

"As soon as circumstances are favorable I shall invest with relatives here in cattle and fruit ranching—and so plant the germs of a class scholarship (sic itur).

"I am a member of the San Francisco Harvard Club, the only member from '82, also of the Gamma Eta Kappa Fraternity, a High School organization confined to this coast, and of a literary society, composed mainly of the alumni of the State University."

GODFREY LOWELL CABOT.

"I worked the first year in the employ of my brother, Samuel Cabot, Jr., 70 Kilby Street, Boston. June 30, 1883, I sailed for England, got back last November 10th (1884). While abroad I studied Chemistry at Zürich for one year, and travelled in England, Scotland, Ireland, Austria, Hungary, Italy, Sicily, Belgium and Switzerland. I have worked two months for my brother since returning, and have at present no fixed employment."

HENRY GARDNER CHAPIN.

Since graduation has been in the paper manufacturing business in Springfield, Mass., and is now a member of the Springfield firm of Chapin and Gould, note paper manufacturers.

HEMAN LINCOLN CHASE.

"Am pursuing the studies of the third year at the Harvard Medical School."

WALTER GREENOUGH CHASE.

"July 5, 1884, as special correspondent of the Boston Daily Globe, went to Madison, Wisconsin, and stayed there until July 18, reporting the National Educational Association Meeting. Thence to Portland, Oregon, Puget Sound, Vancouvers Island, and by steamer to Sitka, Alaska. Stopped in Sitka ten days and came down to San Francisco on man-of-war Adams. Leaving San Francisco, September 20, visited Puget Sound again and returned via Northern Pacific R. R. in November. Left Journalism for business in December, 1884, having become interested in certain patents relative to steam pumping machinery, and am at present Treasurer of the Mason Regulator Co., an incorporated company having offices in Boston, New York, and Philadelphia. I shall still retain my interest in the Mason Regulator Co. and may in the near future travel as correspondent. Have written a series of articles on Alaska for the Boston Herald during the summer and fall of 1884."

EDWARDS CHENEY.

Upon graduation took the position of bookkeeper for his father's firm, Parker and Cheney, Lowell, Mass., manufacturers of bobbins, spools, etc., and is still in their employ.

JOSEPH PAYSON CLARK.

"My history since graduation is very briefly told. This is my third year in the Harvard Medical School. As to where I propose to settle after I have finished my studies, I am as yet unable to say. I have become a member of the Boylston Medical Society and of the Puritan Club."

HAZEN CLEMENT.

Went abroad for a short trip, and returning went into the office of a shipping firm in Boston where he remained till about October 1, 1884, when he started on another European tour and has not yet returned.

JOHN McGREGOR COCHRANE.

"In reply to your request for an account of what I have been doing since June, 1882, I would state that immediately after graduating I made a trip through the British Provinces, returning in time to enter in September the Medical School of Harvard University, where I have attended lectures up to the present time. During the summer of '83, I made a tour through Europe, and most of last summer I passed on the New England roads in the saddle of a bicycle. I am as yet a bachelor and have not as yet decided where I shall practise my profession."

ROBERT CODMAN.

Entered the Harvard Law School in 1882, and remained there till March 1, 1885, and then entered the Law office of R. D. Smith, Esq. Boston.

FRANK NELSON COLE.

"After graduating I applied for a Fellowship and was appointed to one in October of 1882. Until July, 1883, I stayed at Harvard University studying under Professor Peirce :—then I started for Leipsic via Gibralter, Marseilles and Geneva. I have been here for the last two years, nearly all the time at work on German mathematics in Professor Klein's Seminar. Last summer I made a rapid trip in South Germany and Austria, visiting Vienna and Munich.

"In August I shall probably return to America but am as yet quite uncertain as to my future course.

"In May, 1884, I published a small mathematical affair entitled 'The Potential of a Shell, bounded by Confocal Ellipsoidal Surfaces.' It appeared in the Proceedings of the American Academy, pp. 226-231."

ARTHUR MESSINGER COMEY.

"Since Commencement I have been pursuing principally the study of chemistry. The year 1882-83 I had a position as assistant in Chemistry at Tufts College, and while there did some original work with Professor Michael, which was published in the American Journal of Chemistry. I was assistant in the summer course of chemistry at Harvard College the summer of 1883, and in August the same year I sailed for Europe, and went to Zurich, Switzerland, where I worked in the Polytechnikum with Professor S. Meyer and published a paper in the 'Berichte der Deutschen Chemischen Gesellschaft' of which society I was a member Unfortunately, I was taken sick with pneumonia at Zurich and was obliged to give up my work and go South, and I spent the winter in Nice. In the spring I travelled through Italy, as far south as Naples, taking in the usual sights. Then I went to Heidelberg where I spent two summers with Professor Bunsen, and took my examination and obtained the degree of Ph.D. in February, 1885. During the time I was in Europe I travelled over the greater part of the country.

"I have been chosen Professor of Chemistry *pro tem*, at the University of Vermont, and State Chemist of Vermont during the absence of Professor Sabin on business."

FRANK GAYLORD COOK.

"1. I am not married.

"2. November 1, 1882, I went, as tutor to two young men in a private family, to Florida, and remained there into the following May; meanwhile, besides doing the tutoring, seeing more or less of the country, and working up privately the first year's work of the Harvard Law School. August and September, 1884, I spent at York Harbor, Maine, as private tutor.

"3. Entered the Harvard Law School in September, 1883, and I expect to be graduated this June, 1885. I expect to take the Boston Bar Examination in December, 1885, and practice law in that city."

JOSEPH AUSTIN COOLIDGE.

"I have been teaching in an Academy in Mount Pleasant, Pa. for two years, but may change next year. My work has been in fitting students for college in Greek and Sciences. I am getting along nicely and as far as I know now intend to continue teaching."

CHARLES TOWNSEND COPELAND.

"During the year after we left college I was assistant in a Boy's School at Englewood, New Jersey; last year I spent at the law school, and this year I have been reading law in an office here (Calais, Maine), and writing a good many book reviews for the Boston *Daily Advertiser*."

FRANK LEONARD CREESY.

"In the autumn of 1882 I entered the Law School at Cambridge. I studied during the next two years at the Law School. For the last year I have been studying law in the office of Morse and Allen, in Boston. I shall take the examination this spring. I intend to settle in Boston."

MORTON STIMSON CREHORE.

Shortly after graduation entered the employ of Messrs. Lawson, Douglas & Co., Stock Brokers, Boston, and remained there till the autumn of 1884. Gave up his position there to enter the coal business in Boston, with H. G. Jordan and Co. in which firm he is a partner.

Was married September 6th, 1883, to Miss Alicia V. Robson, daughter of Mr. and Mrs. Stuart Robson.

MONTGOMERY ADAMS CROCKETT.

"Immediately after Commencement sailed for Europe with a classmate Mr. F. C. Woodbury. Spent the summer in making a walking tour in the Tyrol and Switzerland, and in visiting Venice, Geneva, Milan, Paris and several cities of Germany. Returned to America in time for the opening of the Harvard Medical School, and studied there for two years. In September, 1884, went to New York in order to spend my third year at the Bellevue Hospital Medical School, where I am at present."

ROBERT CUMMING.

"On leaving college I went to New York for a time, leaving there on August 26 by the S. S. 'Baltic' for Liverpool, where I arrived on September 3. I was in London for some three or four weeks and then went to Scotland for a time, returning to London in November. I was for six months in London in an engineer's office. I also blew the trombone in an amateur orchestra. Leaving London in May, 1883, I came to Glasgow, where I commenced an apprenticeship in a marine engineer's yard, but my health giving way in the summer of 1884, I was obliged to give up my apprenticeship in October, 1884. Since then I have been engaged mostly musically, having received an appointment as choir-master in one of the churches in this neighborhood. I am also conducting a small orchestra in Glasgow, and giving music lessons. I have been elected a member of the Glasgow Society of Musicians, and have published a nocturne for piano, violin and 'cello, and have other compositions on their way towards being published."

HENRY WINCHESTER CUNNINGHAM.

Travelled in Europe for pleasure for about three months immediately following graduation, and on his return to Boston, entered the office and employ of the Continental Sugar Refinery, and has remained in Boston except during a short time in the early part of 1885, when he took a trip to the West Indies.

WILLIAM DE LANCEY CUNNINGHAM.

Entered the Banking House of J. W. Cunningham & Bro., 11 Wall Street, New York, and has continued in business there.

CHARLES FRANCIS CUTLER.

Has been since graduation with Cutler Bros. & Co., Wholesale Druggists, Boston.

RALPH POMEROY DABNEY.

Entered the office of Charles W. Dabney & Sons, Fayal, Azores.

FRANKLIN ARTHUR DAKIN.

"Since September, 1882, I have been teaching in St. Johnsbury Academy, St. Johnsbury, Vt. The school has a corps of fourteen teachers, numbers three hundred pupils, with a graduating class last year of seventy-three. It is generously endowed, its founders and trustees being members of the Fairbanks Scale Co. My work has been entirely in the Classical course, at present preparatory Latin for College. I expect to continue teaching as a profession. My marriage took place at Natick, Mass., January 17, 1884. My wife's maiden name was Estella True, daughter of Joseph O. and Sarah True."

WILLIAM HENRY DANFORTH.

"Since graduation I have studied medicine one year under a physician, and two years in the Harvard Medical School. I shall graduate in June, 1885, and intend to settle in the West, probably in Minnesota."

WENDELL PHILLIPS DAVIS.

After leaving college he taught one year in Belvidere Seminary, N. J. Has since been in California teaching for a while as private tutor in a family at Los Angeles, since then in a private Seminary in Oakland.

CLARENCE RANDALL DEAN.

"For three months after graduation, I was surveying on the Island of Campobello, and since then have been working in a cotton mill in Fall River learning the practical part of the business."

RICHARD DELANEY.

Was a private tutor at Cambridge for a year, and then entered the Harvard Medical School, from which he expects to graduate in June, 1886.

GEORGE WASHINGTON DICKERMAN.

"Soon after our graduation I secured a position as master in the Berkeley School, a boys' preparatory school in New York City. I have spent three very pleasant years hunting for "innate ideas" of mathematics; although I have not found any, I don't propose to give it up."

CHARLES DENSTON DICKEY.

Travelled in Europe for a year and then returned to New York to enter the Banking House of Brown Bros. & Co., where he has been ever since.

GEORGE BRADFORD DUNBAR.

"For the past year I have been employed in the office of the Wisconsin Central R. R. in St. Paul, Minn., and previous to that I was working in the office of an Iron Mining Co. at Metropolitan, Michigan."

WILLIAM HARRISON DUNBAR.

"On July 1, 1882, I sailed for Europe with some of the members of my family. While gone I spent a large part of the time in Italy, passing the winter in Florence and returned to America in the summer of 1883 by way of Portugal and Fayal. In the fall of 1883 I entered the Harvard Law School and have been pursuing the full course of study there ever since."

GEORGE HERBERT EATON.

"From July 1, till early in November, 1882, I travelled through the countries of Western Europe, following in the main the beaten track of the tourist. I do not know that my experiences differed materially from those of a goodly number of other nomadic '82 men whom I was constantly encountering everywhere, from the Heart of Midlothian to the Forum of Rome. My course took me to the larger cities and more important places of interest in Scotland, England, Belgium, Germany, Switzerland, Italy and France. I spent the lion's share of my time in England and Italy.

"On my return to this country I entered the Harvard Law School at once and spent two years there. On leaving the school last June (1884) I returned to my native place, Lawrence, Mass., where I have managed to secure a tolerably remunerative practice while prosecuting my studies. In January, 1885, I passed successfully the examination for admission to the Massachusetts Bar in the county of Essex. For the immediate present I think to remain in Lawrence, but before the close of the year I purpose opening an office in Boston and there I hope to secure a permanent settlement. Of quill-driving I have done some little in the way of newspaper special articles, but as yet my pen has not given birth to anything of so sustained a character as a book or an essay."

CHARLES ELIOT.

"The winter after graduation I took a course in Horticulture, Surveying, etc., at the Bussey Institution. On May 1, 1883, I became a draughtsman and assistant in the office of Mr. Frederick Law Olmsted, Landscape Architect, formerly of New York, but now of Brookline, Mass. Besides studying and draughting plans for the arrangement and planting of a great variety of private places, I have had to do with plans for certain public works— namely, the Back Bay Improvement and Dorchester Point, Wood Island and West Roxbury Parks, at Boston, Belle Isle Park at Detroit, Beardsley Park at Bridgeport, Conn., and the Capitol Grounds at Washington.

"A trip with Mr. Olmsted to Detroit and Buffalo, and occasional visits to works in progress at Baltimore, Washington, Philadelphia, New York, Bridgeport, Newport, Portland, and Mt. Desert, have broken up the office work very agreeably.

"As to the future my intention is to give at least another year to travel and study, first in this country and then abroad, particularly in England, before setting up as a Landscape Gardiner on my own account. I am a member of the Puritan Club of Boston, and it is in Boston that I hope to be able to settle and pursue my profession."

ALBERT DANNER ELLIOT.

Has not been heard from since September, 1884.

Was married at Washington, D. C., September 9, 1884, to the youngest daughter of Senator Pugh of Alabama.

FREDERICK WARE EMERSON.

During the first year after graduation travelled in the Azores, Madeira, and Europe. Second year was at home in Newton, Mass., and entered the Boston University Law School in the third year. Is studying law in Boston.

WILLIAM GORDON FELLOWS.

Has been living in Europe and travelling most of the time since graduation, but spent the summer of 1884 in this country, a part of the time in a yachting trip along the New England coast. Returned to Europe in the fall of 1884, and is there at time of writing.

FREDERICK ATHERTON FERNALD.

"I graduated intending to follow the profession of chemistry, and during the term of the Summer School of Chemistry in 1882 was an assistant in the college laboratory. The next three months I spent at Everett, Mass., and early in December came to New York to be the secretary of Prof. E. L. Youmans, editor of the *Popular Science Monthly*. I assisted him on hiz private literary work and on the *Monthly* until March 1, 1884, when I was transferred to the office of the Magazine, in the publishing house of Messrs. D. Appleton & Co. I staid there the rest of the year, and this year hav bin librarian of the Union Club in New York. My only articles in the Monthly which need be mentioned are 'Constructive Elements of the East River Bridge,' July, 1883, and 'German Testimony on the Classics Question,' November, 1884. I wrote the article on spelling Reform in the *Annual Clyclopaedia* for 1884, and hav contributed to various New York periodicals letters and short articles on popular scientific subjects, science, and the classics at Harvard, international copyright, spelling, etc.; I hav also published under a pen-name a small paper-covered book of humorous selections. Either editorial or library work will probably be my permanent vocation, and I hope to return to New England. Sins November, 1883, I hav bin a member of the Harvard Club of this siti. In March, 1885, I was elected Secretary of the newly organized New York Branch of the Spelling Reform Association. On the subjects of marriage and travelz I hav nothing to report."

BURTON MONROE FIRMAN.

" On the 12th of August following graduation I began work on the Springfield *Republican* as a local reporter. Four months later I was sent to Boston to '*do*' the Legislature for that paper during the exciting 'Butler Year.' At the close of the session the latter part of July, I returned to Springfield, but the reassembling of the legislature in January, 1884, found me again at the State House. At the end of this session I again returned to Springfield, but resigned my position on the *Republican* September 1 to accept another on the Boston *Daily Advertiser*, with which I am now connected.

WILLIAM BOYD FISKE.

"I entered the Harvard Medical School immediately after leaving college, and have remained there ever since. I expect to complete my course this spring (1885). When and where I shall begin to practise are as yet undecided. At present I am one of the Home Officers at the Childrens' Hospital."

JOSHUA GARDNER FLAGG.

"Your appeal" (for information) "would affect me sensibly provided I had anything in the shape of a history to relate,— but unfortunately my life during these few years has been mostly made up of negatives, so that in answer to the various questions you submit, viz., marriage, business, profession, etc., I only have to answer 'No.' I have entered into neither social nor other contracts. Am simply engaged at present in taking care of my health, which, just at present, does not thrive over much."

JOHN McGAW FOSTER.

"Immediately after Commencement I sailed for Europe, where I spent three months in travel, visiting points in England, France, Italy and Germany, and spending several weeks in Switzerland. In the autumn, I went to Göttingen, Germany, where I entered the University and attended some lectures, but devoted my time to the study of the languages. I spent a month in Berlin and Dresden, and returned to America in February,

1883. I immediately began a course of Theological Study in Bangor (Maine), and in August, 1883, entered the middle class at Andover Theological Seminary, where I expect to complete the course in June of this year. In April, 1885, I asked to become a candidate for Orders in the Protestant Episcopal Church, and hope to be ordained in the autumn. In the spring of 1884 I wrote a short play called 'Black and White,' for private performance. A small number of copies of this were issued for private circulation. My only other published writing is a short article in the 'Christian Union' for February 26, 1885."

GEORGE HILLS FRANCIS.

Since graduation has been studying medicine, taking the regular course at the Harvard Medical School, and will graduate in June 1885.

HARRY CORMERAIS FRENCH.

" In September, 1882, I went into the employ of the American Rubber Co. of Boston, to learn the business. Remained there till the middle of January, 1883, when an opportunity was offered me of going to the factory of the Pairpoint Manufacturing Co. (manufacturers of silver-plated ware) at New Bedford, to learn the process of manufacture, etc., preparatory to coming to Chicago, in the employ of French, Potter & Wilson (importers and jobbers of crockery, china, glassware, lamp-goods, etc.), who held the western agency for the above mentioned Pairpoint Manufacturing Co. I came to Chicago in March, 1883, and immediately started out on the road as a travelling man. This migratory life I pursued with varying results, until November, 1884, and I find the experience gained worth much more to me than the time expended was. February 1, 1885, the firm of French, Potter & Wilson, in whose employ I had been, was incorporated under the laws of this state and became the corporation of 'French, Potter & Wilson.'"

Became Treasurer of the Corporation and says, "I am, therefore, settled in Chicago, probably for good. I am living a comfortable life of celibacy at 'Kenwood,' one of our most attractive and convenient suburbs and am most happily and contentedly located."

FRANK EDWARD FULLER.

"After graduation I remained at Cambridge for the greater part of one year, pursuing graduate courses in English and in History. I had intended to take an examination for the degree of A. M., but illness prevented that. In the following fall I entered the office of the *Daily Advertiser* (November, 1883), to take charge of the railroad column. In the following spring I was transferred to editorial work, which I continue to do—writing, besides, occasional book reviews and assisting at the dramatic criticisms. I propose to follow the journalistic profession. I shall live in or near Boston, permanently, I hope."

HOMER GAGE.

"Since graduating I have been studying medicine at the Harvard Medical School, Boston. I do not expect to take my degree for a year or two and have not decided where to settle. I have joined the Cobden Club of London, the New York Free Trade Club, and am a member of the Boylston Medical Society."

JOSEPH PEABODY GARDNER.

Went abroad soon after graduation and travelled for six months. On his return went into farming at Hamilton, Mass., and entered the Bussey Institution and the school of Veterinary Medicine. Expects to receive degree in June, 1885, from the Bussey Institution, and in June, 1886, from the School of Veterinary Medicine.

DAVID CLAIBORNE GARRETT.

"1. Married September 1, 1883, at the Church of the Messiah, Boston, to Miss Lily Selmes, daughter of the late Tilden R. Selmes (of Quincy, Ill.), and Sarah B. Selmes.

"3. Finished my theological course (which was begun before my one year at Harvard) at the Theological School of Griswold College, Davenport. Ordained to the Priesthood of Protestant Episcopal Church at Christ Church, Burlington, Iowa, May 20, 1883. Called first to the Rectorship of Christ Church, Davenport, and later (June 1883), to Trinity Church, Davenport. I am now Rector of the United Parishes in Davenport. A series of sermons were printed in the 'Davenport Democrat,' November, 1883, on what is termed the 'New Theology.'

"4. I am a member of the 'Davenport Academy of Music.'"

JOHN GILLESPIE.

"On graduating from college I entered the Harvard Medical School, where I have continued studying ever since. I hope to take my degree in medicine in the coming June (1885), and mean to continue my studies abroad for the next two years."

HENRY HALE GILMAN.

"1. As yet I am neither married nor have I any immediate prospect of being.

"2. In the spring following the completion of my college course, I went South for a trip of six weeks. I visited all the chief cities in that section of our country and for two weeks was in Florida. In the autumn of 1884, I went to England. My time, two months, was so limited that I spent the whole of it in that country, Scotland and Ireland, thinking that on my trip the coming season, it would be of greater interest to me to go elsewhere. Both of these have been pleasure trips and with my time at my own disposal, going wherever I chose, if they have not been a success it is my own fault.

"3. Directly after leaving college I gave my attention to the manufacture of wool hats, and at present am associated with my brother in that business. We have a small mill at Bradford, Massachusetts, with a daily capacity of 100 dozen hats, which we sell direct from the factory. As well as everything else, this branch of business has its outs, but after a fair trial of three years, I like it well enough to continue.

"4. To your fourth suggestion I must give a negative answer to each head for I am not a literary genius."

FREDERICK NORTON GODDARD.

Since leaving Cambridge has been in business in New York with J. W. Goddard & Son, 516 Broadway.

CHARLES HENRY GOLDTHWAITE.

"After the vacation following graduation, I came to St. Albans, Vt., as Principal of the High School. I have to give instruction in the Classics and such other subjects as I may select, and superintend the schools of the lower grades. There are some eleven hundred children and twenty teachers, and the combined duties of instructor and superintendent make the place anything but a sinecure."

Made a flying trip to England in 1883, for the purpose chiefly of studying English country towns and notably the country about Stratford-on-Avon. After the completion of his fourth year at St. Albans, expects to spend a year in Germany.

XANTHUS HENRY GOODNOUGH.

Went to Chicago shortly after graduation and remained there, employed in a railroad office, until early in 1885, when he returned to Boston, and is now engaged with the Massachusetts Drainage Commission in Boston.

LYSSON GORDON.

Writes "I shall not reply to questions 1, 2, and 4, because I have nothing whatever to say, and if I had I scarcely think it would interest or concern my classmates.

"For three months after graduation I was employed in the Old Lowell National Bank at Lowell. On the 10th of October, 1882, I was elected Assistant City Clerk of Lowell, and received two re-elections, serving until January 5, 1885, when I was suppressed, for political reasons, by the victorious Republicans. Since that time I have been connected with the Mercantile Agency of Edward Russell & Co. in Boston."

JAMES JAY GREENOUGH.

"In September, 1882, I went to Media, Pa., as instructor in mathematics in Shortlidge's Media Academy, a boarding school for boys, accommodating about one hundred and thirty. Spent my summer in Shelburne, N. H., in the White Mountains.

"In September, 1883, I returned to Media and took charge of the school work—teaching only about two hours a week as I had to arrange and take the responsibility of the school work during school hours. During my whole connection with the school I had my rooms outside, but took my meals with the boys in the school dining room. In July I acted as Proctor at the Harvard Entrance Examinations at Andover, Mass. Spent the summer at Shelburne, N. H.

"In October, 1884, I returned to Cambridge as I had accepted a position as tutor in Mr. Hopkinson's Private Classical School, 20 Boylston Place, Boston, where I now am. My work is largely Mathematics and Physics."

ASAPH HALL.

"Since graduation I have been employed as assistant in the Naval Observatory at Washington. Have been studying Mathematics and Astronomy and intend for my future occupation to continue this study."

FREDERICK STANLEY HALL.

Has been studying law at the Boston Law School since graduation. "Graduate in June, 1885, the Gods and the Faculty willing." Was admitted to the Bristol County Bar in March, 1885, and expects to practise in Taunton, Mass.

In the summer of 1884, spent between four and five months abroad, travelling in Great Britain and Ireland, and was a member of the "Beacons" of Boston, during one season.

HENRY WINTHROP HARDON.

"I sailed on the Gallia from New York June 14, 1882; reached Liverpool in due time, and made a hundred days' trip from there. My course in outline was London, Paris, three weeks in Switzerland and one in the Dauphine, the Italian lakes, Rome, Venice, Munich, Heidelberg, the Rhine, Brussels, Amsterdam, England again. I entered the Law School in October, 1882, and continued there till February 10, 1885, since which date I have been with

Evarts, Choate and Beaman (New York) in the capacity of law clerk. I shall return to Cambridge in time for the examinations for the law degree, and July 1 I shall resume my labors in the New York office. In the summer of 1883 with Paine, Sewall and Storer, I sailed along the Maine coast from Portland to Bar Harbor and nearly back again. Our mast gave way under stress of weather and we had to abandon the craft at the nearest harbor. For the fullest kind of history of this voyage I refer to Paine's 'Diary.' Governor Robinson has been pleased to appoint me a J. P. and in January, 1883, I was admitted to the Suffolk Bar. At the Law School I was a member of the Ames Pleading Club. This fills the list of my honors and offices."

HENRY WILLIAMS HARLOW.

"I have been devoting myself to the study of medicine and expect to be admitted to practice in June, 1885. I am not married."

Has been studying at home at Augusta, Maine, and at Portland.

GEORGE TRUMBULL HARTSHORN.

"I have remained in Cambridge since graduation, continuing the study of chemistry with especial reference to organic work. In 1883 I received the degree of A. M. In the college year of 1883-84 I received the appointment of Assistant in Chemistry and during the absence of Professor Jackson took charge of the recitations and laboratory work in Chemistry 1. During the present year I have been working in Professor Jackson's laboratory as his private assistant. In the fall of 1883 I entered my name for the degree of Ph.D., and at present am a graduate student. I have published the following papers:

"1. With Professor Jackson. 'Certain Parabrombenzyl Compounds.'—Proceedings of the American Academy, April, 1883.

"2. With Professor Hill. 'Ueber einige Furfuranderivate.'—Berichte der Deutschen Chemischen Gesellschaft, No. 5, 1884.

"It is my intention to continue the study of chemistry, take my degree in 1886, and make chemistry my profession."

FRANK SPANGLER HAUPT.

Has travelled extensively in the northwest, and visited the Indians, Yellowstone Park, etc. Is at present engaged in the lumber business in St. Paul, Minn., with the firm of Haupt & Co.

WILLIAM HALE HERRICK.

"One month after I graduated I accepted a position as clerk in the office of a Sugar Refinery in Boston. I was fortunate enough not to have to undergo the experience of cleaning inkstands for $2.50 a week. But the dull routine of a clerk's duties, after the freedom of college life, proved unendurable, and as there was no prospect of advancement in the concern and little money to be made in business in Boston, I left in February. In March I was sent by Dr. Sargent to take charge of the new gymnasium of Lehigh University, where I have remained since. My intention is to return to the Harvard Medical School, and take the course there which has always interested me."

FRANK EVERETT HEYWOOD.

"Shortly after our Commencement I began work for S. R. Heywood and Co. of Worcester, Mass. (of which firm my father was the senior partner), who were engaged in the manufacture of boots and shoes. January 1, 1883, I was admitted to membership in the firm. For two years I was engaged partly at Worcester, and partly in travelling through the West. At present am at home the greater part of the time. December 1, 1884, the firm of S. R. Heywood and Co. was succeeded by the Heywood Boot and Shoe Co. of which Corporation I am at present Vice-President and Clerk. December 18, 1884, was married, at East Orange, N. J., to Miss Hattie D. Jennings, the eldest daughter of Horace N. and Myra D. Jennings of that place."

SHERMAN HOAR.

Has spent the time since graduation, except when prevented by illness, in studying law. Took two years at the Harvard Law School, and then went into his father's office in Boston, where he had also been at work in the law a part of the time while a student at the Law School. Took an active interest in the Presidential Campaign and made a number of speeches against Mr. Blaine. In January, 1885, owing to ill health, gave up the law for the time being, at least, and went to Alabama. Has been studying the iron industry and may go into it, but will return to the law if his health permits.

Returned to Boston in May, 1885, and his health having improved, returned at once to the study of law.

JAMES HUGHES HOPKINS.

Continued at Barnstable, Mass., the study of law begun in previous vacations. December 1, 1882, to February 28, 1883, was principal of the grammar school at North Eastham, Mass. August 20, 1883, till February 1, 1884, was principal of the grammar school at West Barnstable, Mass. October, 1883, was admitted to practice. February 1, began the practice of law in New Bedford, Mass., but moved to Provincetown, Mass., in June, 1884, and is now practising law at Provincetown. Is one of the Trustees of the Provincetown Public Library, and March 11, 1885, was appointed by Governor Robinson "Trial Justice" for County of Barnstable.

ALBERT ANDREW HOWARD.

"I sailed July 24, 1882, for Europe, spent a year in study at Leipzig, and several months in travel, visiting chief cities of Germany, France and Italy. Returned to America in 1883, late in the year, and became a candidate for the degree of Ph.D. at Harvard. Married, July 1, 1884, Anna Hellrigl, the daughter of Franz and Anna Hellrigl of Meran, Tyrol. I shall again visit Europe this summer (1885), and expect to remain there a year at Leipzig."

HENRY REESE HOYT.

Has not been heard from.

Studied law at the Columbia Law School, was admitted to the bar and began practice with the firm of Leavitt, Torrey & Hoyt. The firm was dissolved after eight months. At time of writing is travelling in Europe.

HARRY MASCARENE HUBBARD.

"I am neither married nor engaged to be.

"During the summer of 1882, I made a trip of about two months to California, choosing that rather than spending about the same length of time in Europe. I made one of a party of about twelve, making the journey both ways in a car of our own. Most of the time was spent in Southern California, where I was very much interested in the fruit culture and wheat raising. I was very strongly tempted to invest something in the former, but concluded not to. Up to the time of my return to Chicago I fully intended studying law, but at the advice of a friend, resolved to go into business for a year, at least. I studied bookkeeping for one month and then entered the employment of the Erie and Western Transportation Co. and Lake Anchor Line. I was with them about seven months when I left to take a position with Crane Bros. Manufacturing Co. After about seven months' stay with the latter firm I left to take my present position with the Adams and Westlake Manufacturing Co. My special duty is to ascertain the cost of the articles which we manufacture. I have now no expectation of ever studying any profession. I purpose to make Chicago my home as it always has been. I have neither written nor published any essay, book or pamphlet. I am not a member of any purely social club. I belong to the Chicago Congregational Club, and The Young Republican Club, and in the latter have taken an active interest, as I am the Secretary for my own ward."

FREDERICK THAYER HUNT.

"1. In answer I can say I have not married.

"2. Nothing very startling as to travels. Abroad last summer and fall (1884), six months. Headquarters there with my brother (artist), in London. Saw most everything of interest in England possible in the time, also somewhat of the Continent, chiefly Belgium, Holland and France. Interested mainly, in the different schools of art (I ought to have been an artist rather than a lawyer?) and antiquities.

"3. Have read law in Boston in office of Hon. Chas. T. Gallagher since beginning of 1883, also at Boston University Law School (grinding now for May Examination, Suffolk Bar). Probably hang out (shingle) in Boston.

"4. Done nothing in literature, nothing in a social line, excepting a few minor societies in Weymouth, including Weymouth Historical Society.

"Wish I could puff myself better, but as I said before fame is prospective."

CHARLES GREEN ROCKWOOD JENNINGS.

"After graduating I studied medicine at the College of Physicians and Surgeons, Twenty-third St., New York, also during three months at Bennington, Vermont. I took a degree from the latter place this last summer, 1884, and in May next I expect to take a degree at New York. I received a very flattering offer to go into partnership with the foremost physician in this part of the State, and I begun in the firm of Rockwood and Jennings, Bennington, last August (1884.) Am pleasantly located here, hard at work, plenty of practice already. Am making some investigations with the microscope, and everything is propitious. I shall probably remain here."

WILLIAM JONES.

"In February, 1883, I accepted a position as private tutor in Tampa, Florida, and remained there until the first of July, 1884. In the meantime, I had been appointed Assistant Master at Yates Institute in Lancaster, Pa., and began my work there on the first of September. This is my present position. I am still unmarried."

CHARLES HALLAM KEEP.

"For two years I attended the Harvard Law School. In September, 1884, I entered the Law office of Bissell, Sicard & Goodyear, at Buffalo, where I have been ever since in the capacity of clerk. The firm was formerly Cleveland, Bissell & Sicard, Mr. Cleveland retiring on his election to the Governorship of New York. I have written no books, and held no office, save one, without either honor or profit viz., Notary Public, in and for Erie County, New York. I am not married nor engaged."

WILLIAM WINTHROP KENT.

Entered an architect's office in Buffalo, and remained there one year, and then went into the office of his father's firm, Flint and Kent, wholesale and retail dry goods, Buffalo. In February, 1884, entered the office of H. H. Richardson, Brookline, Mass., and has been there since, studying architecture, which he proposes to make his profession.

ALBERT BENJAMIN KINGSBURY.

"You may condense into a line the account of my pilgrimage since I left Cambridge. Shortly after graduation I became Secretary of an agricultural implement manufacturing company in Quincy, Ill., and remained in that position for two years. After that I was placed on the editorial staff of the Chicago Daily News, and am now Foreign Editor of that paper."

BENJAMIN RUFUS KITTREDGE.

"Replying to your circular letter of February 1, I passed some time in Europe after graduation: at present I am living part of the time in New York and part of the time at Peekskill, N. Y."

GEORGE LYMAN KITTREDGE.

Has been and now is teaching at Exeter, N. H. He writes, "My position is that of Professor of Latin in the Academy."

CHARLES FRANCIS SWIFT KNOWLES.

"Since I graduated I have been teaching school and studying law. I am at present studying law at Boston University Law School. I expect to be admitted to the Suffolk bar next June (1885). I cannot at this early date tell where I shall locate, but probably in Massachusetts. Have taken a deep interest in American politics; have written some articles for the papers on Free Trade and Reduction of our Tariff, some of which have been accepted, and during the late campaign I did what my humble position allowed towards reducing the Republican majority on Cape Cod."

ALBERT FRENCH LANE.

Entered the Harvard Law School in October, 1882, and remained there for two years; then entered the office of Gaston and Whitney, Boston, where I have continued ever since. Was admitted to the Suffolk Bar January 20, 1885. Expect to practice in Boston.

GEORGE HENRY LEATHERBEE.

Sailed for Europe in July, 1882, in company with Miles and remained there until November. On my return to Boston, entered the employ of my father's firm, Messrs. Wm. H. Leatherbee & Son, Lumber Dealers, and have been with them ever since, a few months in the Boston office and later in the west where I am now in general charge of their western business with headquarters at Parkersburg, West Virginia.

HEYWARD GIBBONS LEAVITT.

Went to Europe immediately after graduation and spent five months in travelling in Scotland, England, and on the Continent, and has since travelled considerably in the United States east of the Mississippi.

Studied at the Columbia Law School during the seasons of 1882-83 and 1883-84, and was admitted to the New York Bar in May, 1884, receiving the degree of LL. B. at the Columbia Law School at the same time, and began the practice of law at once as a member of the firm of Leavitt, Torrey & Hoyt ('82). Gave up practice and dissolved the firm after eight months to go into the business of building gas works, under a new process for making water gas. Promoted a company, the United Coal and Oil Gas Company, which bought up the patents. Is now Vice-President and General Manager of the Company.

Is a member of the Calumet Club and of the City Reform Club of New York.

ARTHUR PRESCOTT LOTHROP.

Soon after graduation went abroad. Spent one semester in Jena, Germany, studying certain topics connected with the history of law, and then travelled five months in England and on the Continent. In September, 1883, entered the Harvard Law School and is now in the second year of his course. Is a member of the Pow-Wow Law Club.

ROBERT LUCE.

"1. I have not married.

"2. I have made no journeys of any consequence.

"3. In the first year after graduation I studied for the degree of A. M., receiving it in June, 1883. During part of the time and for some months afterwards I worked in that branch of the Census of 1880 pertaining to the "Social Statistics of Cities," under Col. G. E. Waring of Newport, R. I. My work consisted of sketches of various cities, and; if the Census ever gets money enough, may be published some time in the ages to come. Also, in the same year, I taught the High School at Lexington, Mass., for a brief period. Then, from October, 1883, to July, 1884, I was sub-master of the High School in Waltham, Mass., doing considerable newspaper work at the same time. On the first of August, 1884, I went on the editorial staff of the Boston Globe, where I have since remained. I intend to remain in journalism, hoping some time to get a paper of my own. For the last year I have been one of the Directors of the Tropical Products Company, office 95 Milk St., Boston, plantations in Guatemala, near Livingston.

"4. I wrote an essay for the Bay State Monthly, May, 1884, entitled 'Town and City Histories'; also an essay for Van Rostraud's Engineering Magazine, February, 1883, entitled 'The Transmission of Power by Electricity.'"

THOMAS WILLIAM LUDLOW.

I get the following from the Triennial report of the class of '80, to which Mr. Ludlow referred me.

"Was married at Grace Church in New York City, on January 16, 1879, to Miss Harriet Frances Putnam Carnochan. Has three children, as follows; Julia Elektra Livington, born October 29, 1879, in Athens, Greece; Thomas William, born April 15, 1881, in New York City; and Henry Gouverneur Corbett, born November 7, 1882, at Yonkers, N. Y."

Has not been engaged in any particular occupation except in carrying on studies begun in Cambridge.

Is a member of the following societies:
Archeological Institute of America.
Society for the Promotion of Hellenic Studies, of London.
Association pour l'Encouragement des Etudes Grecques, of Paris.
Société Français d'Archéologie pour la Conservation des Monuments Historiques.
Archeological Society of Athens.
Dante Society, of Cambridge, Mass.
Harvard Club, of New York City.
Managing Committee of the American School of Classical Studies at Athens. Has been the Secretary of the Committee since its definitive organization in April, 1882.

The following are the chief articles written:

'The Archeological Society of Athens.'—Nation, September 16, 1880: January 11, 1883.

'The Site of Homeric Troy.'—Nation, December 8, 1881.

'The American Duty on Foreign Publications.'—N. Y. Times. February 6, September 4, October 13, 1882; Nation February 1, 1883.

'Les Explorations de l'Institut Archéologique d'Amérique en Mexique et á Assos.'—Revue Archéologique, of Paris, for December, 1881.

'Review of the First Assos Report.'—New York Times, July 17.

'The Theatre of Epidauros.'—Nation, September, 28, 1882.

'The Athenian Naval Arsenal of Philon.'—American Journal of Philology, No. II (October, 1882).

'Note on a Terra-Cotta Figurine of a Centaur from Cyprus, in the Metropolitan Museum of Art, New York.'—Bulletin of the Archeological Institute of America, No. 1, January, 1883.

'Notices of the work of the Archeological Institute, one of the American Schools at Athens, in the New York Critic, Times, Post, and Nation, the London Athenaeum, etc., and minor communications upon various subjects.

Writes, "I have only to add (as far as I am aware), that in June, 1884, I received the degree of A. M. from Columbia College, and that I am now attached to the editorial staff of the New-York Evening Telegram. Also that I have another little boy, Lewis Walton Morris Ludlow, born May 17, 1884."

JOHN PLUMER LYONS.

"1. I am not married.

"2. My travels since graduation have been limited to one winter passed in different parts of Florida and Georgia, and a brief trip West.

"The first winter after graduating I studied law. Last winter I taught and tutored in New York and Brooklyn, and this winter I have passed in the Naval Office Department of the New York Custom House."

ARTHUR FRED McARTHUR.

"About the middle of July, 1882, I entered Bryant & Stratton's Commercial School in Chicago, and took courses in Bookkeeping and Commercial Law. I remained at this Institution until November 1, when I accepted a position as foreman with McArthur Bros., Contractors for Railroads and Public Improvements. I served in this capacity with the firm during their construction of the Lock in the Illinois and Michigan Canal at Chicago. On May 1, 1883, I accepted the position of chief clerk in the office of W. and A. McArthur, Wholesale Lumber Dealers and Manufacturers, in Chicago, where I remained until June 1 1884, when I was admitted to membership in the contracting firm of McArthur Bros. and transferred to a large piece of work here in St. Paul, which the firm had under contract. Will remain here until our work is finished about June 1."

WALTER IRVING McCOY.

"Travelled in Europe a few months after graduation, returning at Christmas time, 1882. In September, 1883, entered the Law School, Cambridge, where I still am, and expect to remain for one more year."

EDWARD VALENTINE McDONALD.

"The only information about myself worth noting is that I have been since graduation in the Medical School of the University, whence I expect to graduate this coming June, 1885. I am very misty at present about my future plans, intended location, further study, etc."

RICHARD HAYES McDONALD.

"After graduating from college I went to New York City Saratoga, Lake Champlain; up into Canada, down the St. Lawrence to Niagara, along the Lakes to Duluth, Minn. Thence down the Mississippi to St. Louis, westward to Colorado, where I remained over a month, visiting Denver, Leadville, Maniton, Colorado Springs and other places. After my sojourn there, I left by the 'Atchison, Topeka and Santa Fe' for Los Angeles, Cal., stopping at Las Vegos Springs, New Mexico, Albuquerque. Before going further I took a trip to Chihuaha, Mexico. After visiting Los Angeles, I came to San Francisco where I now am. After starting from the lowest position in the Pacific Bank, I have worked my way up, until I am now at the head.

"On July 2 I was married to Miss Clara Belle Gardner of Carson City, Nevada, and we are now residing at 813 Sutton Street, San Francisco. Her father's name is Major M. C. Gardner. I belong to the Olympic Club and the California Pioneers."

WILLIAM HENRY McKENDRY.

"After leaving college I assumed the position of Assistant Superintendent of a zinc mine in New Hampshire. In the fall of 1883 I accepted an office from the U. S. Vapor Fuel Co. to superintend the application of their process to various iron and steel mills in the country, which position I hold at present. For the past year I have been located in Illinois but my residence here will not be permanent, and I expect to reach the Pacific coast before returning to the East."

WILLIAM THOMAS McKONE.

Has been studying and practising law, and has made no journeys except for pleasure and health. Studied at home in Andover, Mass., rather than in Cambridge, owing to illness. In April, 1883, entered the office of Hon. John K. Tarbox, Insurance Commissioner, in Lawrence, Mass., and remained there till June 1, 1884, when he passed examination for admission to the bar. He writes, "I have located in Lawrence, and propose to continue the practice of my profession here."

WILLIAM HOBBS MANNING.

"Having neither married nor written a book, I can hardly claim that my first three years since graduation have been eventful. I am living in Marquette, Lake Superior; my business is the care and sale of timber and mineral lands." Lands belonging to the estate of James C. Ayer of Lowell.

CHARLES FRANK MASON.

"When I left Cambridge I entered the Mexican Central Railway office in Boston. Was sent by that Company to Mexico in March, 1883. Returned in January, 1884, on account of ill health. From June 1, 1884, to March 1, 1885, I was in the Old Colony R. R. Superintendent's office in Fitchburg, from which place I obtained a transfer to my present address: General Freight Office, O. C. R R., Boston."

JOHN WHITING MASON.

Has been studying law at the Boston University Law School and expects to be admitted to the bar in June, 1885.

ALBERT MATTHEWS.

"1. I am not married, nor have I any intention of marrying.

"2. In February, 1883, thinking a short journey would benefit my health, I took a trip to the South. Going South I stopped at New York, Philadelphia, Washington, Richmond, Norfolk, Old Point Comfort, Jacksonville, St. Augustine, Palatka, Enterprise and, on my return, at Jacksonville, Savannah and Charleston. I was gone exactly four weeks, from the middle of February to the middle of March. I was very much interested in this trip, never before having been South. Of the cities which I visited, Washington, Richmond, Charleston, and St. Augustine pleased me and interested me most.

"3. So far my health has been too poor to permit my going into business or taking up a profession. Next autumn I expect to be well enough to do something—though what it will be I cannot even guess.

"4. I am a member of the Appalachian Mountain Club and of the Puritan Club."

GEORGE LOWELL MAYBERRY.

"I entered the Boston University Law School in October, 1882. Graduate in June, 1885. Was admitted to the Suffolk County Bar in December, 1884. Have since December, 1884, been in partnership with H. N. Allin, having law offices in Waltham and Court Street, Boston."

EDWARD PERCIVAL MERRITT.

Has been in the employ of Messrs. Blake Bros. & Co., Bankers, 28 State Street, Boston, since soon after Commencement. Went into the New York House of the same firm in the spring of 1885.

ALFRED EUGENE MILES.

"After getting my first report off my mind sailed for Liverpool with Leatherbee. After a flying trip through Scotland and back to London started for Flushing and then to Rotterdam, Amsterdam, Berlin and Dresden, and after a hard passage during which we were put out of a train at midnight with almost no money, because a conductor whom we had seduced by ample largesses to put us into the right car, put us into the wrong one and locked us in, we reached Vienna hungry and penniless. This did not last long, however, and we reached Venice all right. As we heard of floods in the neighborhood fled and were on the last train that was able to make the trip to Milan for several days. Found the hotels at Lugano one story under water and gave up the lakes and our overland trip through the mountains. Waited at Lucerne four days for fine weather and then to Heidelberg. Then down the Rhine. Brussels, Paris and London and back to America in November. After a few months of idleness obtained employment with Mr. F. S. Moseley, Note Broker, Boston, and hope to remain there."

SAM HENRY MORRILL.

"I was married November 16, 1884, to Miss Carrie Emily Barrington of Cambridge, daughter of Thomas and Elizabeth Barrington. I have established myself as concert pianist, composer and teacher of music, and am playing first violin in the Cambridge Orchestral Society. Have sold a song entitled "My Dream" to Oliver Ditson & Co. My compositions are as follows.

Opus 1. Three pieces for piano.
" 2. Three fugues.
" 3. Three songs.
" 4. Sonata in F for piano.
" 5. Three sacred vocal pieces.
" 6. Fantasie for piano on "The Tempest."
" 7. Concert valse in A flat.
" 8. Three songs.
" 9. Two Hungrarian dances, full orchestra. These dances have been played several times successfully.

Opus 10. Duo Concertanto for piano and 'cello.
" 11. Three songs.
" 12. Comic Opera "The Squire" brought out in Boston Music Hall, January 14, 1885, under the direction of the author of the libretto and part of the music, Mr. L. W. Thayer of Roxbury.

Opus 13. Overture in B flat (full orchestra).
" 14. Six arrangements for flute and strings with piano.
" 15. Comic Opera (not complete).
" 16. Set of four waltzes for orchestra.

"I am pursuing my study for Ph. D. with Professor Paine."

GARRETT EDWARD NAGLE.

"1. I have not married.

"2. My journeys have been through the United States and with no definite purpose.

"3. I have studied law in the Harvard Law School for two years and afterward in the office of Hon. H. W. Paine. Shall probably practice in Boston.

"4. I have gone into politics somewhat as I am a member of the Cambridge School Committee."

OLIVER ALLEN OLMSTED.

Has not been heard from but I am informed that shortly after leaving college he entered the office of the Wabash, St. Louis and Pacific Railroad Co., at Chicago.

HENRY THOMAS OXNARD.

"1. No.

"2. Travelled through this country for a few months after graduation; made a pleasure trip of it.

"3. Am engaged in the manufacture of sugar with my brothers (Fulton Sugar Refinery, Brooklyn, N. Y.), but am not yet a member of the firm. Shall probably continue to reside here.

"4. As you see by the above my life has been rather uneventful since I left college. I can only rejoice in the fact that although I have done nothing good, I have done nothing bad, *very bad*, I mean, and even that you have to take my word for."

WILLIAM ENOCH PAGE.

"During the Academic year 1882-83 I attended lectures at the Harvard Law School; since September, 1883, I• have been teaching school in Newport, Rhode Island. I do not propose to continue my law studies."

ROBERT TREAT PAINE.

"Since graduation I have been studying law two years in the Harvard Law School. This year I am in a law office in Boston. I expect to take the bar examination next fall."

IVAN NIKOLAYEVITSH PANIN.

"I still enjoy the blessed state of singleness. The time and place of my marriage I should be only too delighted to give you, but it requires two to fix the time and place, and whoever the lady is, as I have not the pleasure of knowing her, I cannot consult her at present conveniently about it. When I was young, a fortune teller gave me the exact name of my wife and her parents, but I regret to say that I did not make a memorandum of it.

"I have travelled West as far as Bismarck, Dakota, with a view of engaging there in some agricultural out-of-door pursuit, and looked over Eastern Dakota with that end in view. What I saw during that journey I have described at some length in the Albany Argus, of which I was then an occasional correspondent.

"3. On my return from the West, obliged on account of ill-health to lead an out-of-door life, I engaged in poultry-farming at Grafton, Mass., for a year and a half, which improved my health so much that I have returned to intellectual work, and am now Manager of "Law and Order," a weekly paper in Boston, devoted to the interests of the Citizens' Law and Order League Movement throughout the United States."

ELLIOTT HUNT PENDLETON.

"I studied law during the summer following graduation and entered the firm of Ramsey and Matthews here in Cincinnati, as a student, in the fall. I also attended the lectures at the Cincinnati Law School during the year 1882-83. The summer of 1883 I read by myself and in the fall returned to the Law School. On the fourth day of December, 1883, I was admitted to practice by the Supreme Court of Ohio, together with Rogers of our class. I then practised law until July, 1884, having my office still with Ramsay and Matthews. On the first of July I entered into partnership with Edward Barton under the partnership name of Pendleton & Barton, and am still practising law in conjunction with Mr. Barton. I still keep up my music and have the honor of being President of the Apollo Club of Cincinnati, which office I have held for three seasons."

Was married at Cincinnati, June 4, 1885, to Miss Isabelle Gibson Eckstein of that city.

*EDMUND SEHON PERIN.

Edmund Sehon Perin, the fourth son of Oliver Perin and Mary Nelson Perin, was born in Cincinnati, Ohio, November 16, 1859. At the age of sixteen years he left the High School of Cincinnati to prepare for college, and after a year at Phillips Exeter Academy entered the Senior Class at Adams Academy, Andover, and graduated with his class in June, 1878. By vote of the class at Adams he was chosen class orator.

It is not necessary for me to dwell upon his course in college, for he was almost universally known, and was a favorite with many of us who were intimate enough with him to know him well. In our Junior year he won the first Boylston Prize for Elocution, and at graduation was given "Honorable Mention" in Natural History.

We were shocked and greatly pained to learn within a month of Commencement Day that a severe hemorrhage from the lungs had prostrated him to such an extent that ultimate recovery was thought to be perhaps impossible, and so it proved, for in spite of every attention and all that human skill could do, he passed away December 5, 1882.

The news of his illness and death coming so soon after we had bade him good-bye as he started out in life with every prospect bright, with wealth, education and character such that, if applied as he gave us reason to feel sure he would apply them, must make his life profitable to his associates, made us feel keenly a great sorrow, and realize that in his death we had suffered a most distinct loss. Often, toward the end of his illness, he said to those around him, "I am resigned," and so must we be, and must perhaps believe that the lesson taught by his early death has done us good in learning it, but until our college recollections are effaced his figure will be prominent among them. He gave promise of a long and useful life and was the first of us as graduates to die. A.

GEORGE WILLIAM PERKINS.

"1. Not married.

"2. No 'Journeys.'

"3. The first two months after graduation I held the position of Assistant in Biology in Harvard University; at the same time I pursued the study of medicine at the Harvard Medical School and am now a member of the class that graduates in June, 1885. I obtained an appointment on the House Staff of the Boston City Hospital and on the 1st of January, 1885, I entered on an eighteen months' service there, choosing a Senior's service as House Surgeon.

"4. No books, etc. I am a member of the Boylston Medical Society of Harvard University.

JOHN WALTER PERKINS.

Since graduation has been in the Harvard Medical School.

ERNEST PERRIN.

Spent a year in Florida rusticating and engaged in planting an orange grove, and returned to New York in November, 1883, to enter the Columbia College Law School. Has been there since, reading also in an office. Received the degree of LL. B. May 27, 1885, and will probably practice law in New York.

McLAURIN JAMESON PICKERING.

"My life since graduation has been uneventful. In the fall of graduating year I took a trip West as far as Chicago and Northern Michigan, meeting several classmates during the trip. The months of April and May, 1884, were passed by me on the northern coast of Cuba on an English steamship enjoying myself very much. Have been employed in the shipping and steamship office of my father, in Boston (M. F. Pickering & Co.)."

WHIPPLE NAHUM POTTER.

"I have nothing of importance to report since I left college.

"August 1, 1882, I entered the employ of Silas Potter & Co., 109 High Street, to learn the wholesale boot and shoe business. The following spring, during February, March, April and May, I enjoyed an opportunity to visit the South and West as collector for the above firm.

"January 1, 1883, this firm dissolved, the partners retired from active business. For the next year I was not permanently settled anywhere. During January and February, 1884, Silas Potter & Co., my father and uncle, became interested in the organization of the Standard Cordage Co., and through them I have been able to obtain a most desirable position. The above company started to run about the last of June, 1884. By the first of September business had so increased that they were forced to double their number of spindles—to-day we are running two sets of workmen night and day, and are now established as the largest producers of Sisal Rope in the world—having a production of eight million pounds per year. The 5th of May I shall be married, the young lady's name being Miss Emily M. Howard. Shall be married in Hotel Kensington, Boston, which will be my address after May 1. Hoping the rest of the class have been prospered in like manner I am," etc.

JOHN PRESTON.

"After graduating I returned to New Ipswich (N. H.), where I still make my home. Went as delegate from New Ipswich to the last Congressional Convention. Am now engaged in teaching in the Appleton Academy (New Ipswich), and in the study of law."

WILLIAM LOWELL PUTNAM.

"I sailed for Europe immediately after graduation, leaving New York on Commencement Day, June 28, 1882. I travelled for fifteen months in England, Scotland, Holland, Germany, Austria, Italy, Spain, France and Switzerland.

"I came back to Cambridge in September, 1883, and entered the first year of the Harvard Law School, and I have remained in the Law School here till this date, taking the regular course. During the summer of 1884 I studied in the office of Ropes, Gray & Loring. During my two years at the Law School I have been a member of the Ames-Gray Law Club."

FREDERIC WILLIAM RHINELANDER.

"I am expecting to go into railway business before long, and am working here in Milwaukee with that end in view. I spent three months of the summer of 1883 abroad, dividing my time between England, Paris, Northern Italy, Switzerland, Germany, Holland and Belgium."

CHARLES MOEN RICE.

"With the exception of part of a year spent in post-graduate study at Cambridge, my attention has been given to the study of the law. Have not yet applied for admission to the Bar."

GEORGE MOREY RICHARDSON.

"I sailed for Bremen from New York September 9, 1882, to continue the study of classical philology in Germany. After a few weeks in Switzerland, I matriculated October 21 at the University of Jena, where I attended lectures during the winter semester, having by good luck Lothrop, '82, as a companion the whole time.

"In April, 1883, I removed to the University of Berlin, where I remained till the beginning of the summer vacation. This I spent in England, at the invitation of relatives. I travelled with an uncle through most of the western counties and in South

Wales, visiting the cathedral towns and the picturesque places on the coast. I was also some time in London. In October I returned to Germany and entered the University of Leipzig, where I am still working. The vacation of 1884 I was again in England, meeting my uncle at Scarborough, in Yorkshire. After two weeks here we took a trip through the east of England, ending with Cambridge and London.

"At odd times, I have managed to see the greater part of North Germany, and have had perhaps rather good advantages for forming an opinion of German society and character. In general, my stay in Germany has been a very pleasant one, but I would not intrude further details on such a cosmopolitan Class as '82. I shall return to America in 1886, or, at the latest, in 1887."

HERBERT AUGUSTUS RICHARDSON.

"Immediately after graduation I worked for the City of Boston as a civil engineer at the 'Improved Sewerage,' at Moon Island. In the fall of 1882 I returned to South Framingham (Mass.), where I have since been engaged in manufacturing ladies' straw hats. I am with Messrs. Emmons & Billings, manufacturers of straw goods, holding the position of superintendent of the bleachery, dye-houses and sewing halls, and have charge of one hundred and fifty girls and about fifty men. I expect to make South Framingham my home and manufacturing straw goods my business."

LUCIEN MOORE ROBINSON.

"I came to Philadelphia September, 1882, and entered Mr. H. H. Brown's (Harvard, '77) private school as teacher in mathematics. At the same time I began to study theology privately. I have also acted as private tutor, fitting two young men for Harvard. I am still in Mr. Brown's school, and hope to be ordained to the diaconate next year."

WILLIAM ARMSTRONG ROGERS.

December 4, 1883, was admitted to practice by the Supreme Court of Ohio, at Cincinnati.

Has not been heard from.

WILLIAM JOSEPH RUSHMORE.

"The first year after graduation I spent in the Boston Daily Advertiser office. The year following, I turned pedagogue and filled the position of assistant principal in the High School, Albion, N. Y. This year I am Sub-Master of the High School, Milford, Mass."

JOHN RUSSELL.

"After getting my degree, and keeping it through the dangers of Commencement, I went to Plymouth and killed time as best I could with guns and rods until October, 1882, when I went to the cranberry district near South Carver, and helped in keeping the cranberry accounts. Having got my hand in at bookkeeping, I undertook to keep the accounts of a foundry in Woburn, which was owned by the man whose bog I had been supervising. In June, 1883, I went to Woburn to live, and existed there until September, 1884, when I came to Boston. In January, 1884, the owner of the business died, and as there seemed to be no one who could take his place I took charge of the business, and still carry on the foundry at Woburn, and have an office in Boston."

HAROLD MARSH SEWALL.

"I have studied in the Harvard Law School, and shall graduate in June"(1885).

HENRY HAMILTON SHERWOOD.

"Am not married, 'though close onto it,' and may meet you at our Triennial in that capacity. Went into the importing and shipping business last summer, and am now a partner in the firm of Richards, Harrison & Sherwood, San Francisco."

HORACE EMMET SMITH.

"Married October 1, 1884, Lyda Dickson, daughter of James Dickson and Mary A. Dickson, of Indianapolis. While in Cambridge I took extra hours in the Law School during the three years I belonged to the Class, equal to just half of the Law School course. On my return to this place (Indianapolis), I entered the

Law School here, and stood my examinations. In the meantime was admitted to the bar of Marion County, Indiana, on motion of Pierce Norton, now Judge Norton of this place, in whose office I am yet in business, on the ninth day of September, 1882. I am already located here, and doing a very fair business for a young attorney. I am a member of no clubs of any kind, except the Indianapolis Light Infantry, which I re-joined after leaving college. This company has some reputation as a prize-drill team; we have won since I joined it again, in 1882, the sum of $2500 in prize money, and the best record ever reported to the War Department."

CHARLES ARMSTRONG SNOW.

"My doings since graduation may be summed up in very few words. I spent the two years directly after graduation in the law office of Gooch & Burdett (Boston), where I shall stay until fall. I expect to get admitted to the bar very soon, and will then try to support life in Boston's barren legal desert. If not sufficiently appreciated in Boston, I shall try some other city, whose name I cannot foretell."

GEORGE FREDERICK SPALDING.

"Soon after graduation I went into a shoe factory at Lynn to learn something about the manufacturing of shoes. After spending six months in the factory I began to sell shoes, and have continued to do so ever since. I have been as far west as Milwaukee, stopping at the largest cities on the way. Last winter I went to New Orleans on business. While there I visited the Exposition. Most of the time I am situated in Boston; two months of the year I am travelling, and my greatest pleasure at such times has been meeting members of '82."

ELIOT DAWES STETSON.

"Since Commencement I have resided at home in New Bedford, and have been occupied with the study of law, the first year in the office of Stetson & Greene, New Bedford, Mass., and the last two at the Harvard University Law School. I expect to settle in New Bedford."

CHARLES HERBERT STEVENS.

"In the fall of 1882, having determined upon the publishing business as the one I intended to pursue, I entered the University Press of John Wilson & Son, Cambridge, where I devoted myself to the printing business with special reference to its connection with publishing. In September of 1884, having completed a two years' term of hard work at the University Press, which I can truthfully say brought to light both the advantages and disadvantages of the printing business, I obtained a situation in the publishing house of James R. Osgood & Co. of Boston, where I now am. Since graduation I have neither married, made any extended journeys, nor written any books. In regard to the future, I cannot as yet make any definite statement; but I expect for the present to make Boston my headquarters."

EDWARD KNIGHTS STEVENS.

Was an assistant in the Chemical Department at Cambridge for a year, and then entered the employ of Messrs. Carter, Dinsmore & Co., Ink Manufacturers, Boston, and is at present with them. His work is in connection with the chemical part of the business.

FREDERIC MATHER STONE.

"After leaving college I travelled in Europe for a few months, and returned in the autumn to Cambridge to study for the degree of A. M. The summer of 1883 I spent in the law office of Stetson & Greene, New Bedford, Mass., and in the autumn returned to Cambridge to enter the Law School. The summer of 1884 I spent in the law office of Dexter, Herrick & Allen, Chicago, Ill., and returned to the Law School in the fall. I expect to leave Cambridge at the end of this year, and shall probably settle in Boston. Am neither married nor engaged."

WILLIAM ENOS STONE.

"In the autumn of 1882 I went to Dover, N. H., and spent nearly a year there in study of cotton manufacturing. In October, 1883, I came to North Carolina and became interested in a small way in a proposed railroad, which has not yet been completed. I may add that I have charge as lay reader of a small Episcopal Mission in this town (High Point, N. C.)."

JOHN HUMPHREYS STORER.

"Since graduation until this winter (1884-85), I have been in the Harvard Law School, taking the regular course of study. My summers have been passed studying law in the office of Ropes, Gray & Loring, of Boston. Now I am in the real estate business, in partnership with Richards M. Bradley of our class, under the firm name of Bradley & Storer. In January, 1885, I was admitted to the Suffolk Bar. Otherwise my life has been uneventful."

Was Secretary of the Rhode Island Harvard Club in 1883.

THOMAS CHANDLER THACHER.

Travelled in England, Scotland and on the continent of Europe for about three months after graduation, and has since been in the wool and cotton dealing business with his father's firm, H. C. Thacher & Co., Boston.

ROLAND THAXTER.

"As regards your questions I should prefer to say nothing, but suppose I must chronicle my highly interesting career since graduating. 1882-3, mostly lost through an accident at the end of my senior year which kept me practically on my back for nine months. Work done mostly biological in entomology; one or two short papers published.

"1883-4, entered Medical School in September, studied for a few months, when imperative duties demanding my continuous presence at home, obliged me, practically to discontinue my course. 1884-5, entered second class of Medical School as a formality, having passed sufficient examinations while considering the advisability of pursuing science as a profession, which course I decided upon on being appointed to the Harris fellowship. Have since been studying with a view to taking the degree of Ph.D., making botany a specialty."

GEORGE WARREN TOWNE.

"I have been instructor in mathematics at Dummer Academy, South Byefield, Mass., for the last three years, and I shall very probably remain here. The school is a fitting school for colleges, and especially for Harvard. It is under the charge of Mr. John W. Perkins, formerly principal of the Salem High School, Salem, Mass., and numbers thirty-five boys."

STEPHEN VAN RENSSELAER TOWNSEND.

"I began studying law the summer of 1882 at Albany, in the office of Marcus T. Hun. I have continued my studies at the Columbia Law School, and I expect to apply for admission to the Bar some time this year. I shall in all probability continue the profession here in New York. I have not written anything in the way of essays or the like, and am still a bachelor."

GUSTAVUS TUCKERMAN.

"During the year following graduation was engaged in tutoring: for two months at Newport, R. I., for ten months in England and Scotland. On return in September, 1883, entered Episcopal Theological School in Cambridge. Passed last summer on a cattle ranch in the north of Wyoming Territory. Have written a few verses for the newspapers, and published a few songs, both here and in England."

EDWARD LIVINGSTON UNDERWOOD.

Entered the employ of Messrs. E. Allen & Co. (wholesale woollen goods), Boston, immediately after graduation, and remained with them till May, 1884. Then connected himself with L. Beyer & Co., New York, in the same business. In November, 1884, began teaching at Rockport, Mass., and since then has been engaged in that vocation.

WILLIAM CUSHING WAIT.

"The story of my life since graduation is extremely short and simple—indeed, it consists mostly of negations. I have neither married, become a parent, been abroad, been admitted to practice in any profession, written any books, nor in any other way raised myself to distinction. With the exception of the months between September, 1882, and January, 1883, when I was at Newport in the office of Col. Geo. E. Waring, Jr., engaged in writing historical sketches for the U. S. Census of 1880, I have been at the Harvard Law School studying law. If there is anything since graduation which I have done that I think worth mentioning, it is simply this, that I had a hand in defeating Mr. Blaine last November. I was Secretary of a Town Committee at Medford, Mass. During my course at the Law School I have been a member of the Thayer Club and of the Pow-Wow. I hope to practice law in Boston, but am by no means sure my hopes will be gratified."

GUY WARING.

"From July, 1882, to May, 1884, was in the office of Col. G. E. Waring, Newport, as general assistant.

"On March 12, 1884, I married, in the town of Warwick, R. I., Mrs. Helen Clark Greene, relict of Dr. W. W. B. Greene, and daughter of George and Nancy Clarke. My wife has three children by her first marriage.

"On July 1 I left New York, with my family, for Portland Oregon, via Northern Pacific R. R. In Portland I was in the employ of the Comptroller's office of the O. R. and N. Co. for six weeks; at the end of that time I lost my place, owing to a reduction of the force instituted September 1, and although I was offered a position in another branch of the Company's service, I decided to go into farming in some part of the Northwest. From that time I have travelled over a large part of Oregon and Washington Territory travelling in all about four thousand miles. I left Portland after a residence of six months, and have made Port Townsend, W. T., my headquarters since December 9 (1884). Recently I purchased a Ranch west of the Okanagon River, in Stevens County, W. T., and about twelve miles south of the forty-ninth parallel. There I shall go into stock raising. I now expect to leave Sprague, W. T., on May 1, with my family, for my new home. The journey will be made by wagon and although only two hundred and twenty miles I am told that it will occupy about three weeks to accomplish. My Post Office address will be Marcus (on the maps old Fort Colville on the Columbia), Stevens County, W. T. I may say here that the Post Office is one hundred and forty miles from my house. If any of my classmates come out to this country I should be delighted to have them visit me, and I can promise them the best of hunting and fishing."

HENRY ELDRIDGE WARNER.

"I have been at the Harvard Law School since we graduated and I expect to remain there during all of this Academic year (1884-85). I was admitted to practice in the Suffolk Bar in January, 1885. I joined the Puritan Club, Boston, in 1884"

FREDERIC WARREN.

Went into the shipping business with Warren & Co., Liverpool, proprietors of the Warren Line of Steamships.

FREDERIC LEONARD WASHBURN.

After graduating and spending the succeeding summer in camping on the Maine coast with a friend, took a trip through Morocco, Spain, France, Italy, Greece and Turkey, and after a very interesting journey returned in February, 1883, to Boston and after a two months' stay took a trip to Texas to see the country—a prospecting tour— but returned to Chicago in May of the same year and entered a lumber office, where he remained until October, 1883. Then entered a lumber office in Minneapolis, but withdrew to accept a position in the Library of the city, and to become Curator of the Museum of the Minnesota Academy of Sciences, which position he now holds.

"Have written nothing unless it be an article or two for the papers."

PHILIP MOEN WASHBURN.

"In the fall after graduation I went to New York City and spent the winter of 1882-83 there as a member of the Union Theological Seminary, at that time in University Place. I remained there until the end of the Seminary year, in May, 1883, and on the 5th of June I was married in Brooklyn, New York, to Miss Miriam Phillips Storrs, the youngest daughter of the Rev. Richard S. Storrs, D. D. of that city. On the 20th of June accompanied by my wife I sailed for Europe. After a summer spent in travel in Switzerland I went to Berlin, Germany, and remained there as a student at the 'Friedrich-Wilhelm' University for two semesters, eight weeks in the spring between the semesters being spent in a journey to Italy. Leaving Berlin in August I reached England in the latter part of September, having spent the intervening time in travel on the Continent. I came to Cambridge (England) in October and have been here since as a member of the University. On the 3rd of December, 1884, a daughter was born to us, her name being Mary Washburn. I have been studying for ordination in the Episcopal Church in the diocese of Massachusetts, and expect to be ordained in the fall. At present I have no idea where I shall be after that time."

JOHN SYDNEY WEBB.

"I have not married, nor made any journeys, nor been admitted to practise law, nor written anything of the nature of essays, books, etc.

"Two years' work at law in Washington at the National University, resulted in the degree of LL.B. Admission to the bar in the District requiring three years' study, I came to Harvard for the third year, and am now special student in the Law School.

"My intention is to settle in Washington."

J. EDWARD WELD.

"1. I am not married, nor likely to be.

"2. I sailed from New York in June, 1884, to Antwerp, and after a detour to Paris went up the Rhine from Cologne, and on to Heidelberg. There I studied German for a month, attending a few lectures at the University and doing my utmost to become a veritable Deutcher. The warm weather drove me to Switzerland, where I made an extensive pedestrian tour of six weeks, crossing almost all the famous passes and several glaciers, but not attempting a more ambitious height than the Görner Grat (10,500 ft.). As the cholera quarantine prevented my reaching Italy, I then visited South Germany and took a long sail on the Danube to Vienna. Procuring a passport I travelled north through Poland to St. Petersburg and then down to Moscow. Being alone and somewhat unfamiliar with the Russian language, I had many peculiar adventures until I obtained a smattering of the dialect, at one time being examined as a Nihilist—again obliged to resort to the pictorial art to obtain the necessities of life, etc., etc. Afterward I made an excursion through Finland and crossed the Baltic Sea to Stockholm. The language of the Fins was utterly beyond my comprehension and my abilities. Frozen out in Scandinavia, I returned by way of Denmark to North

Germany and then passed through Holland and across to England, reaching home in time for Christmas and thinking the most remarkable event of my trip was that I had not encountered a single '82 graduate.

"3. I entered Columbia Law School in 1882, and graduated in May, 1884. During this time I was a student in the law office of Messrs. Wheeler and Souther, both Harvard graduates. I passed my examinations for admission to the New York Bar in May, 1884, but was not sworn in till after my return from Europe in December. Am now practising law in New York City and propose to remain there.

"4. The only association I belong to at present is the 'Harvard Alumni' of New York."

EVERT JANSEN WENDELL.

Has not been heard from.

Travelled in Europe, India, etc., for something over a year, a part of the time in company with Rev. Phillips Brooks. On returning took a short course in a commercial college in New York, and then entered the employ of a banking and brokerage house in New York.

ELMER ELLSWORTH WENTWORTH.

"After the usual summer vacation following Commencement, and made more necessary by the severe labors of Class Day and Commencement, I spent some weeks connected with my father's business. Some time after his death I began teaching as Sub-Master in the Watertown (Mass.) High School. Entered upon my work there in January, 1883, and in October of that year resigned to go into work in Boston. Not many months passed before I found myself back in the work of teaching, which now engages what time I do not give to study. My plans still have "an anchor to windward" in the direction of law. Have travelled into no foreign countries except Cape Cod, and am neither father nor husband. My authorship embraces only a few stray poems, in which the world has failed to see any especial merit. I don't blame the world."

ISAAC SPAULDING WHITING.

Has been in the Harvard Law School since graduation. For further information consult the Secretary of 1881.

RUSSELL WHITMAN.

"Since graduating my life has been uneventful. In the summer of 1882 I accepted a position as teacher at Adams Academy, Quincy, and stayed at the Academy two years. Besides the work of the school, I had several private pupils, and made a beginning, also, at studying law. In the autumn of 1884, I came to New York and registered at the Columbia Law School where I attended such lectures as seemed profitable. I also entered a lawyer's office as student, spending my mornings at office work, my afternoons and evenings at the school. If the practice of law proves as interesting as the study of it, I see no reason for supposing that I shall regret my choice of a profession."

SAMUEL WILLISTON.

"In February, 1882, I left college to take a position as private secretary to Professor R. Pumpelly, then at the head of the northern Transcontinental Survey, the object of which was to make a general survey of the whole Northwest in the interest of the railroads which supported it—the Northern Pacific and the Oregon Railway and Navigation Co.

"In June, 1882, I returned to Cambridge, passed my 'annuals' and took my degree with the class. I continued as secretary to the Northern Transcontinental Survey for the next two years, living in Newport, R. I., where I saw many Harvard men—not a few from the class of 1882; and once a year the dinner of the Harvard Club of Rhode Island united us.

"In 1884 this survey was discontinued and soon after I left Professor Pumpelly. In September of that year I took a position as teacher in 'S. C. Shortlidge's Media Academy,' thirteen miles west of Philadelphia, and I am now there teaching chiefly French and German."

OWEN WISTER.

Sailed for Europe upon graduation, and returned in December, 1883. Was a clerk in the Union Safe Deposit Vaults of Boston, from that time until January, 1885. Is at present studying law in Philadelphia.

FREDERICK CLINTON WOODBURY.

"I went abroad soon after graduating and spent the months of July, August and September in travelling on the Continent, making quite an extensive walking trip through the Eastern Alps and Dolomites. Came back in the fall of 1882 and entered the Harvard Medical School where I have been ever since. Became a member of the Boylston Medical Society in 1883, and received the appointment of Medical Interne at the Massachusetts General Hospital in the spring of 1885. Was recently elected a member of the Puritan Club in Boston."

HERBERT GRAFTON WOODWORTH.

"In October, 1882, I entered the tea business in Boston as a clerk and salesman, and a very few weeks' experience convinced me that the first year out of college is an anti-climax. The next year, however, when my experience had doubled with my salary, I began to get engrossed in my business, and throughly to enjoy it, and close application since has not been without its results. On the 29th of October, 1884, I was married to Miss Grace G Taylor, daughter of the late T. Albert Taylor, of this city (Boston). In all probability I shall continue in the importing tea business, and on the first of June, 1885, I shall be admitted to membership in the firm of Robinson & Woodworth."

JOSEPH RUGGLES WORCESTER.

"1. I have not married.

"2. I have made no journeys whatever, Philadelphia being the furthest point from Boston which I have reached since graduation.

"3. My time has been entirely occupied in the Boston Bridge Works which I entered as a draughtsman in May, 1882. My time of entering the office proved very fortunate, for opportunities for advancement offered themselves just as fast as I was able to grasp them. In the fall of 1883 I took charge of the designing department, and in September, 1884, I was made 'Engineer of the concern.'"

TEMPORARY MEMBERS.

HERBERT AUSTIN.

"On leaving college, I entered the wholesale iron business with my uncle, F. B. Austin & Co., Boston, where I am still situated."

I copy the above from the Secretary of 1881, and would refer to him for further information.

CHARLES SIDNEY AVERILL.

On leaving college, which was on account of poor health, he took a vacation of two years to recruit. His health being then considerably improved, he began to teach and last year accepted the position of Principal in the Jackman Grammar School, Newburyport, Mass. Last January he was attacked by severe illness from which, at the time of writing, he has not recovered but is still very ill.

I just now learn, June 15, that he died May 17, 1885. A sketch of his life will be published in the next report.

RENE BACHE.

Was employed on the New York *Sun* as reporter for a while after leaving Cambridge, but has given up his position, and has not been heard from. I think he is living in Philadelphia.

GEORGE EDWIN BACHELDER.

"Immediately after leaving college I commenced the study of law in the office of David B. Kimball, Esq., at Salem. I continued with him and at the Law School of Boston University for about three years and six months. I was admitted to the bar in Essex Co. in December, 1883, and at once opened an office and commenced the practice of my profession at Salem, where I have continued since. May 31, 1883, I was married at Amesbury,

Mass., to Isabel, daughter of John Hume, a carriage manufacturer of that place. I have one child, a daughter, born April 30, 1884.'

I copy this from the Secretary of 1881, to whom I would refer for further information.

CHARLES HAMMATT BARTLETT.

"1. Was married June 3, 1885, at Bangor, Maine, to Miss Virginia D. Hight.

"2. Have not travelled.

"3. Admitted to the practice of law at the Penobscot Bar, at Bangor, Me., November 18, 1883, where now settled in practice.

"Answer to question 4,— no works; no clubs."

CHARLES WESLEY BIRTWELL.

" In the first half of our senior year ill health obliged me to discontinue my studies. In the fall of 1882, my health being restored, I devoted myself to private tutoring in Boston, principally to preparing pupils for Harvard. I soon cancelled some of my engagements, however, and resumed study at the college, with a view to completing my course. But sickness again interrupted my work, and I went to Florida, where I spent the winter and spring, visiting various places along the St. John's River, spending part of the time on the lakes and in the backwoods farther south, and concluding the trip with a stay of some length on the seacoast at St. Augustine. From the spring of 1883 to the fall of 1884, I devoted my time to further rest and travel. In the fall of 1884, having regained firm health, I returned to Cambridge to finish my college course. I shall be enrolled as a graduate of the Class of '82 at the end of the current academic year."

FRANK TAYLOR BROWN.

"I am still located in Carbon Co., Wyoming, in sheep and cattle raising business, and expect to continue a few years more Shall put on a bunch of brood mares this summer."

WILLIAM CHALFANT.

"Studied law two years, and am now in my uncle's office (T. W. Marshall), endeavoring to learn the banking and brokerage business, all in West Chester (Pa.). I expect to remain here."

STEPHEN CUTTER CLARK.

In July, 1881, went to Germany, and for a half semester attended lectures at the Leipzig University. After a trip to Italy and France, returned to America in June, 1882, and joined the class of 1883 in October. After completing the college course with that class, in September, 1883, organized and took charge of the J. Tyler Barker Free School, in West Boxford, Mass.

JAMES PENDLETON CRUGER.

"Spent the spring of 1880 travelling in Texas. Sailed for Europe in July, spending the summer in Biarritz, and the fall in Pau, France. Travelled from December until May, 1881, in France and Italy. Was married May 3, 1881, at London, England, to Amy, daughter of Alexander W. and Ann E. Shepard, of Brooklyn, N. Y. A son, James Jauncey Cruger, was born January 13, 1883. Is at present engaged in the sheep business at Silver Lake Ranch, Bracketville, Texas."

I copy the above from the secretary of 1881 to whom I would refer for further information.

JOHN POMEROY DABNEY.

I have not heard from him directly but am informed that he is still in the employ of the Taunton Tack Company, at Taunton, Mass.

HIRAM IRVING DILLENBACK.

"In the summer of 1881 I entered the journalistic profession actively as special correspondent at the White Mountains of the Boston *Globe*, Boston *Times*, New York *World* and several smaller papers. In October, 1881, I became assistant editor of the East Boston *Argus*, and in the spring of 1882 I became managing editor of the Boston *Express*. The following summer was passed as the previous ones, and in the service of the same papers. In October, 1882, I became assistant editor of the Boston *Times* and remained in that position until January, 1883, when I purchased the Times in partnership with Edward C. Davis, its former business manager. I have been, since that time, editor of this paper, and my partner retired in September, 1884, taking with him the *Yankee Blade*, which we originally purchased in conjunction with the *Times*. Am the author and composer of a song, published by Blair and Lydon of this city, entitled 'My Blue-eyed Geraldine,' and a number of songs which have been sung upon the stage but which have not been printed."

JAMES JOSEPH DOOLING.

Entered the class of 1884, and after leaving college went into the catering business and is at present at Doolings, restaurateurs and caterers, Temple Place, Boston.

HILAND HULBURD DUNLEVY.

"Nothing worthy of note has taken place in my life since June, 1882, except that after two years' preparation I was admitted to the Illinois Bar in March, 1885. I am at present practising law in Chicago with the firm of Edward S. Isham and Robert S. Lincoln."

CHARLES HAMLIN DUNTON.

Was for some time a clerk at 338 Washington Street, Boston, but is at present travelling in Europe.

CLINTON JOHNSON EDGERLY.

Studied law in the office of Wadleigh, Fish & Wellman, in Boston, and on admission to the bar in Suffolk County, opened an office at 31 Milk Street, Boston. Removed to an office corner of Pemberton Square and Tremont Row, in the autumn of 1884.

Was married in Jersey City, on Easter Sunday, 1885, to Miss Rose Coghlan of New York.

FREDERICK LARNAC ELDRIDGE.

"Since our former catalogue came out I have been with Messrs. H. B. Hollins & Co., Stock Brokers, 74 Broadway, New York. I leave, however, to-day, February 26, 1885, to go into the cattle-feeding business near Stanton, Nebraska, with Mr. Wm. T. Blodgett (of the class of 1880), and Mr. N. H. Thorp of New York, under the firm name of Wm. T. Blodgett & Co; we expect to devote ourselves to this business for some years to come."

DANIEL BUTLER FEARING.

"I left the shipping business and am now a salesman in the city trade of the above house (Wm. Turnbull & Co.), which will also be my address until further notice. In reply to your questions I can only say—

"1. I am unmarried.

"2. On the 1st of October, 1883, in company with a friend, I left New York for Colon, Isthmus of Panama, on my way to Japan, via San Francisco, touching at several Central American and Mexican ports on the way up. I passed five or six most interesting weeks in Japan, and then went through the Inland Sea to Shanghai, China, where I stopped for a week's steeple chasing and hunting. Hong Kong and Canton, Foo Chow, Macao and other ports of China then attracted me for a few weeks until I had to start on again. I touched at Singapore and Penang and passed two very pleasant weeks in Ceylon. When the balmy breezes grew too warm I left for Calcutta, touching at Madras on the way; from Calcutta I made the overland trip across India, touching and stopping for longer or shorter periods at Benares, Agra, Delhi, Jeypore, and other points of interest, ending at Bombay from where I took steamer for Malta, having a flying glimpse of Egypt in transit. After leaving Malta my trip was the usual humdrum affair of every European traveller. In closing, my advice to each member of '82 is, go to Japan even if you have to walk half way but *go*, somehow.

"3. My purpose is to settle here in New York.

"4. I can not lay claim to any 'printed matter.' I am a member of the Knickerbocker Club, Calumet Club, Seawanka Yacht Club."

EDWIN THAYER FEARING.

"In reply to your questions will say: On the 10th of June, 1884, was married in Watertown, Mass., to Alice C. Ingraham, daughter of William H. and Caroline B. Ingraham. Have been in the same business as in the last report (with H. L. Fearing & Co., Boston, Cordage, etc.), and in the way of travelling have only done what was necessary in my business, going East and West. Shall continue to do business in Boston, and am at present living in Newton."

EDWARD ASHLEY FERGUSON.

"Am still in a state of single blessedness. My wanderings have been mainly such as were necessitated by business, and I have been unable to scribble my name on the roll of Fame by the publication of anything literary or musical: though I have several musical efforts committed to manuscript which I intend to have published as soon as I have time to attend to it. When I left college in 1880, I took a position as clerk in the office of Merrell & Ferguson, Detroit, Mich., General Agents for the Northwest of the Mutual Life Insurance Company of New York. Am now acting as Superintendent of Agencies for them, and most of my time is employed in wandering over their territory and taking charge of their agents."

JOHN QUINCY ADAMS GRIFFIN.

"After studying law for three years I was admitted to the bar in Suffolk County and am practising at 44 Court St., Rooms 9 and 10, in Boston. I have not married and have no present intention of doing so. Have travelled through the Southern States and Texas, and the British Provinces in Nova Scotia, New Brunswick, etc."

ALMON WHITING GRISWOLD.

I copy from the Secretary of 1881 with which class Mr. Griswold took his degree.

"My residence has been 131 East 56th Street, New York City. I have been studying law at the Columbia College Law School, where I graduated in the spring of 1883. In July, 1883, I went to Europe, where I remained until the last of December, 1883, travelling through England, Belgium, Holland, Germany, Switzerland, Italy and France, in the order named."

RAMON BENJAMIN GUITERAS.

"After graduating at the Harvard Medical School in 1883, I started for Vienna to continue my studies there. I spent the fall and winter of 1883-84 there and in the spring of 1884 started out on a tour, travelling through Spain, Southern France, Italy, Greece, Asiatic and European Turkey, Bulgaria, Roumania, Servia, Hungary and back to Vienna. After staying a short while in Vienna, I started out again and travelled through Austria, Bohemia, Germany and Denmark to Norway, where I spent the summer, fishing and travelling about through the Fjords. I then went to Stockholm and embarked for Finland where I spent some time travelling. After this I went through Russia, visiting the fair at Nijni Novgorad and going down the Volga to Razan. I then returned via Stockholm to Germany and spent the winter of 1884-85 in Berlin and Paris, and am at present stopping here in New York. As to future plans I shall probably either enter the U. S. Navy or practice medicine in Colorado."

PERCIVAL SMITH HILL.

Left college in April, 1880, and owing to the illness of his brothers who were in the jobbing-carpet business in Philadelphia, went into the business to look after their interests. After winding up their affairs continued the business in his own name, changing it gradually to that of selling cotton and woolen yarns chiefly to carpet manufacturers.

Was married April 3, 1883, to Cassie Rowland Milnes of Philadelphia, and with his wife spent three months in travel in Europe. On returning continued his business as before till December 1, 1883, when he gave it up to become junior partner in the firm Boyd, White & Co., Philadelphia, Dealers in Carpetings.

"The uneventful tenor of my life was interrupted on October 22, 1884, by the birth of a son, George W. Hill, Jr., but the novelty of this change has now nearly worn off and from present indications my ship is floating gently on the sea of life, moored to its present location, and there seems to be no prospect of my spreading its sails to the winds to seek new pastures."

FRANCIS MARION HOLDEN.

Has been studying medicine in Boston. For further information consult the Secretary of 1880.

CHARLES HARVEY HOLMAN.

"Shortly before the close of the senior year, on March 13, 1882, I married, at Philadelphia, Miss Florence Lippincott, daughter of the late George and Mary Greenough Lippincott, of that city. Almost immediately afterward I severed my connection with the University and devoted myself to journalism, in which I had been engaged during most of my college course, and also began the study of law. In the fall of 1882, I entered the law school of Boston University, and in connection with a younger brother established a weekly newspaper, The Roxbury *Advocate*, which has become favorably known among family journals. An irreparable calamity overtook me in the death of my wife on the second day of December, 1882, and led to the abandonment of my legal studies and a sad ending of my plans for the future. Since that time I have travelled extensively in this country, more especially in the South, and have contributed to my own paper and to more than a score of others, articles on social and industrial topics, suggested by events that occurred within the range of my observation. With the exception of my regular editorial work and contributions to various periodicals in all parts of the country, I have accomplished little literary work. I am a member of the Bostonian Society, of the Boston and Massachusetts Bicycle Clubs, of the Roxbury City Guard, and of a number of social organizations. I became connected with the Masonic order at Roxbury, and am a member of Washington Lodge, located there. I have also taken degrees and been admitted to membership in St. Paul's Royal Arch Chapter, of Boston, and King Hiram's Council of Royal and Select Masters, of Rockland, Maine."

FRANK WHITEHOUSE HOWE.

Left the class soon after it was formed, on account of illness, and travelled for about four months in the West, going as far as the Pacific coast. After regaining his health returned to Lowell, Mass. "I started in the lumber business with my father's firm, beginning as an outside 'lumper' and followed it quite closely for three years until our old firm was reorganized and I was admitted into partnership, February 1, 1883 (Howe Bros. & Co.)."

Has spent the last three winters in the South both for business

and pleasure. He writes that he has but one bad blot on his
record, and that is that he allowed "his name to be used" at a
caucus and was unfortunate enough to be elected a member of
the City Council of Lowell.

WILLIAM ADDISON HOWE.

"Was managing his farm at Boston, Mass., until 1883. He
then went to New York and in October, 1882, went to Oregon,
where, in company with Mills ('81), he is now engaged in farming." I copy from the Secretary of 1881 to whom I would refer
for further information.

WOODBURY KANE.

Has not been heard from.

Spent one summer in Europe and has since been living in New
York City.

*GEORGE CLARK KENNETT.

I regret not being able to give a sketch of his life here. As
in preparing my first report, I depended on a classmate to write
one, with the same unfortunate result.

*WILLIAM AMOS LAMPREY.

Was born at Exeter, N. H., August 8, 1858, and having formed
at an early age the desire to become a physician, entered college
with our class in 1878 to prepare himself for his profession; but a
hemorrhage from the lungs, in October, 1879, forced him to postpone his college course. Owing to steadily failing health he
reluctantly gave up the purpose of gaining a college education,
but continued to study, never relinquishing his purpose to become
an educated man. In the summer of 1880 his health improved
and he began studying regularly in the office of a physician, but
the improvement was of short duration, and in June, 1882, he
was again stricken down and gradually declined till his death in
Somerville, Mass., August 3, 1882.

He was with us at college only a short time—too short for many
of us to learn to know him well, but his continued illness and
suffering command our sympathy, and his energy and firmness

in pursuing his chosen course while the victim of disease which tended constantly to dishearten him deserve our highest respect

COURTNEY LANGDON.

Was married January 2, 1884, at Olean, N. Y. to Julia H. Bolles, daughter of the Hon. D. H. Bolles of that place. November 3, 1884, at Bedford, Pa., a little girl was born and named Eglantine Courtney (Langdon), but died February 26, 1885.

In September, 1881, accepted the position of teacher of French, German, and Spanish at the Episcopal Academy of Connecticut, near New Haven. After a year was appointed Instructor in Modern Languages at Lehigh University. Shortly after the beginning of his third year there accepted an invitation to take entire charge of the education of the sons of Mr. T. Harrison Garrett of Baltimore. Has been with them since, and in connection with his tutoring has been pursuing the study of Languages and History at Johns Hopkins University, and next year expects to become connected with it officially as a special student under Dr. Adams of the Historical Department.

PRESCOTT LAWRENCE.

Since 1882 has been travelling for pleasure, mostly in Europe. Has not been engaged in any business nor in studying for any profession. At the time of writing is in the midst of a yachting trip with Leeds '77, Curtis, '77, Burnham, '77, and Lyman, '83, to the West Indies and the neighborhood.

*CLINTON HILL LORD.

Died in Newton, Mass., January 30, 1880. See first report.

CHARLES WASHINGTON LUCK.

"Upon leaving our class in April, 1881, I was employed as private tutor in a family living in Boston, with whom I remained a year. On the 27th of April, 1882, I married Miss Adella Matilda Luce, daughter of Capt. George L. Luce and Sophia M. Luce. Our only child, Charles Arthur Luck, was born February 28, 1883. In the fall of 1882 I went to Guatemala, Central

America, in the employ of the Tropical Products Co. of Boston. Having obtained certain privileges from the government of Guatemala in behalf of the company, I selected lands and began a plantation on the Atlantic Coast near the town of Livingston. In the spring of 1884, I left the employ of the Company and engaged in the lumber business in the same country. Abandoning this in December I returned home to pursue the purpose of my life in the study of Theology. I am at present a junior in Andover Theological Seminary, which Institution I entered last January (1885)."

GEORGE WILLIAM McCOLL.

"Since 1880 has been engaged in sheep farming in Texas and has been connected with the firm of McColl Bros. of New York, in the California fruit business. Is at present at El Paso, Texas, in the mining business."

I copy from the Secretary of 1881, to whom I would refer for further information.

CHARLES HERBERT McFEE.

"I left college at the end of the junior year to accept a position as principal of Washington Academy, at Wickford, R. I. In the fall of 1881 I was elected principal of Consolidated Schools in this town (Woonsocket, R. I.). This position I have held ever since with a constant increase of salary. I have taken a somewhat active part in the politics of the town, being a member of the Democratic Committee. At the end of the present year, June, 1885, I am to begin the study of the law and it is my intention to practise in Woonsocket."

CHARLES HENRY MAHON.

I have not heard from him directly, but am informed that he lived in Lynn, Mass., for a time after leaving college but is at present in Canada.

ERNEST HOMER MARIETT.

"I left the class of '82 at the end of my sophomore year to enter in the following year as special student in Philosophy.

The following year I entered the middle class of the Episcopal Theological School, Cambridge, and graduated there in the class of '82. I was ordained Deacon at the Seminary Chapel, June, 1882. In July, 1882, was appointed Missionary at Fall River, in charge of St. Mark's and St. James's Episcopal Missions and also Assistant Minister to the Rev. A. St. John Chambré, D. D., Rector of the Church of the Ascension, Fall River. I was married June 25, 1882, to Alice Elizabeth Carter of Franklin, Mass. In December, 1884, I resigned the charge of St. Mark's Mission and am now Rector of St. James's Episcopal Church, Fall River. In October, 1884, I began to build a new church in Fall River, for the Parish of St. James. This new church will be finished during the month of May (1885)."

CHARLES ANDREWS MITCHELL.

Joined the class of 1881 and graduated with them. I am indebted to the Secretary of that class for the information that in August, 1881, he was elected to the position of teacher of Greek in the Cleveland High School, but that it is his intention to study law at Cambridge after his third year in his present position.

JOHN KEARSLEY MITCHELL.

I copy from the Secretary of 1881 to whom I would refer for further information.

"When I left college I entered the Medical School of the University of Pennsylvania, in the autumn of 1880. I staid there three years, diversified by one European trip in the summer of 1882, when my brother and I walked through the Tyrol for a month. I graduated April 13, 1883. I was chosen Resident Physician to the Children's Hospital of Philadelphia, and went on duty immediately after graduation. I remained the whole term of six months and then tried for a similar position as Resident at the Episcopal Hospital, where I now am and shall be until next April. I have not contributed much to literature unless occasional verses, or scraps in 'Life' and 'Puck,' or a review for the Medical Journals may be looked on in that way."

SOLLACE MITCHELL.

Graduated from Harvard with the class of 1883, and from the Bellevue Medical College, New York City, March 8, 1885, standing first in a class of 134, and consequently obtained an appointment to the Bellevue Hospital where he will remain at least eighteen months, that being the term of service at the Hospital.

HENRY WHITING MUNROE.

Has remained in the Banking House of Munroe & Co., Paris, and is now a member of the firm. Visited America early in 1885, but will probably remain in Paris permanently.

HUGH KINSLEY NORMAN.

Has been engaged most of the time during the past three years in the business of building and superintending water works, and is at present Superintendent of the Water Works at Gloucester, Mass.

RICHARD CHAPPELL PARSONS.

"After leaving college I spent the winter of 1881-82 in California, going over the entire southern portion of it on horseback, riding through all the great 'Ranches' and enjoying on many of them the almost unequalled shooting they afford. I returned to the East in June, in time to see the Class graduate at Cambridge. The summer of 1882 was spent at different points along the Atlantic coast. The winter of 1882-83 was passed in reading law in Cleveland until February, when I went South on a hunting expedition, spending two or three months in Florida. During the summer following I was again on the Atlantic coast, and later in the woods of Michigan, a part of the time on business connected with the Marquette, Houghton and Ontonagon R. R., and part of the time fishing and shooting on the shores of Lake Superior. The winter of 1883-84 I read law in Cleveland. The summer found me once more on the Atlantic coast. In December, 1884, I entered into an agreement with Messrs. E. K. Willard & Co., Brokers, of New York, by which I was to take charge of the Cleveland branch of their house." Is still in this position.

WILLIAM HERBERT PRESCOTT.

Has been studying medicine since leaving college, most of the time at his home in Concord, Mass.

FREDERICK HENRY PRINCE.

After leaving college entered the office of C. E. Fuller & Co., Bankers and Brokers, State Street, Boston, and remained there until January 1, 1885, when he succeeded to the business of the above firm and is now established in the same office as the head of the firm of F. H. Prince & Co.

Married Miss Norman, daughter of Geo. H. Norman, Esq., of Boston, and has one child, a son.

HAZEN KIMBALL RICHARDSON.

"For four years after I left the Class in 1879, I was in business. Since then I have been studying in Cambridge and shall take a degree in all probability, next June (1886.)"

Intends to study law.

HUBERT ST. PIERRE RUFFIN.

Is practising law at 13 Court Square, Boston.

EDWARD DAVID SCOTT.

Has not been heard from.

HENRY DWIGHT SEDGWICK.

During the year 1884-85 has been in the Harvard Law School. Before that studied law in an office in Boston.

ARCHIBALD LOWERY SESSIONS.

"After graduating in 1883 I came at once to New York, and began my preparation for admission to the bar, and was admitted in May, 1884. Since then I have been doing as most young professional men do. It is my intention to practise here in New York."

*HENRY SHIPPEN.

Died at Jamaica Plain, Mass., July 28, 1879. See first report.

DENISON ROGERS SLADE.

"Has been 'connected with the telephone business, since November, 1881, most of the time in Boston."

I copy from the Secretary of 1881, and beg to refer to him for further information.

CHARLES INCHES STURGIS.

"1. Am not married.

"2. Entered the employ of the C. B. and Q. Ry. Co., at Chicago, in October, 1880; was transferred to Denver, Colorado, the following spring. Spent three years there and returned to Chicago, August 1, 1884, where I am now, in the employ of the same railroad. Expect to remain in Chicago.

"3. Have been once to California going by way of New Mexico and Arizona and returning through Nevada and Utah."

WILLIAM ELDREDGE THAYER.

The last report stated that he was in business with H. F. Thayer & Co., Manufacturing Chemists, Boston. He writes that he afterwards went into the employment of Messrs. Peterson, Read & Wayne, Manufacturers Agents, India St., Boston. "With this firm I remained until 1883 when I entered the employment of the Prang Educational Co., Publishers, Manufacturers and Importers, in which firm my position at first was that of entry clerk. About a year ago, however, I became cashier and bookkeeper of the Company, and this position I still hold. Am unmarried."

FRANK HARRISON THOMPSON.

After leaving college was engaged in manufacturing in Cambridge, and still lives there though he has not been heard from directly.

EDWARD JAMES TILTON.

Entered the class of 1885 and has been with them four years. Expects to graduate with them in June.

Please consult the Secretary of 1885 for further information.

CHARLES EVERETT TORREY.

Has not been heard from.

GEORGE MACBETH TRENHOLM.

"I have resided in Charleston, S. C., since leaving college. In January, 1880, I entered the law office of Mitchell and Smith, as a student, and in May, 1881, at my examination before the Supreme Court, I was admitted to practise law in all the courts of this State. Some time later I was admitted to practise in the United States Courts. In January, 1883, I opened an office of my own and have since practised law on my own account. I was married November 17, 1881, at Charleston, to Claudia A., daughter of J. B. Bissell, Esq., of Charleston."

I copy from the Secretary of 1881, to whom I would refer for further information.

*GEORGE CHRYSTIE VAN BENTHUYSEN.

Died in Boston, June 24, 1882. See first report.

CHARLES MICHAEL VAN BUREN.

"After leaving college travelled abroad for a year, most of the time in Germany, returning in the fall of 1881. He then entered the Boston University Law School. In the fall of 1882 removed to Patterson, N. J., where he has since continued the study of law."

I copy from the Secretary of 1881, to whom I would refer for further information.

MARS EDWARD WAGAR.

See the triennial report of the Secretary of 1881. Mr. Wagar writes "The only change I have to make is, that upon the organization of the Schlather Brewing Co. (Cleveland), I was elected Secretary."

WILLIAM BERNARD WARING.

Is still in China. Has not been heard from.

EDWARD FREEMAN WELLS.

"My doings since leaving college have been rather uneventful and in brief are about as follows. I have not married. In the fall of 1882 I went to St. Paul, Minn., and took a position in the Land Department of the Northern Pacific R. R. After six months' confining office work, my health compelled me to resign. After a few months' rest I went into the Real Estate business for myself, in St. Paul; that, too, proved too much for me and I soon had to give it up. Since that time I have been travelling in the North and West and in Canada. Horace Greeley had a level head when he said, 'young man, go West!' it is the place for him. About the first of January last (1885), I was called home to go into business with my father in the above firm (Bosworth, Wells & Co., Wholesale Grocers, etc., Marietta, Ohio). Here I shall probably stay for a few years, any way. While in St. Paul I was a member of the St. Paul Dramatic Club, St. Paul Choral Society, St. Paul Bicycle Club."

GORDON WENDELL.

After gaining his health entered the Commission Dry Goods business in New York, with Jacob Wendell & Co. and has remained there, but is at time of writing travelling in Europe.

ALFRED JEROME WESTON.

Graduated with the class of 1883. Spent the following winter in Demarara, and the West Indies. Returning to New York, went into business in New York with Caldwell, Weston Bros. & Watts, Wholesale Coal Miners and Shippers, in which firm he was a partner. Is still in business in New York being a member of the firm of Weston Bros. & Agnew, successors to the old firm, and doing a general commission business with the West Indies, "exporting all the products of this country and importing sugar, coffee, pimento, cocoa, etc." Is not married and is a member of the Calumet Club, of New York.

HENRY WHITE.

Is practising law at 23 Court Street, Boston.

GEORGE WALTON WILLIAMS.

"I was married April 4, 1883, to Margaret M. Adger, daughter of J. E. Adger of this city (Charleston S. C.). We have one child, Margaret Adger Williams, born February 25, 1884. I have been to Europe twice but have done nothing which would be of interest to any one. I have been actively engaged in business since I left college (after a year in Europe). Am associated with my father in the banking business (Geo. W. Williams & Co.) and am a member of the Cotton & Commission House of Robertson, Taylor & Co.

"For the present I shall live in South Carolina. The South at this time offers, in my judgment, better inducements to a young man than the overcrowded North and East. As to the future I have no plans. I shall probably make this city my home as far as I can see. I am probably a fixture in Carolina or Georgia."

FRANK HERBERT YOUNG.

Has been and is now in the "Clothiers and Tailors Trimmings" business at 56 Summer Street, Boston.

CLASS BABY.

"In reply to your letter asking for information about myself, I will say that my name is Charles Peabody Averill, I was born in Essex, Massachusetts, on the 17th of March, 1884. One day when I was five or six weeks old papa brought home a lovely cradle trimmed with pretty blue ribbon, having a silver plate at the head on which is written my name and below the name the words 'Class Baby.' Papa called it a 'Class Cradle.' I don't know what he means by a class baby and a class cradle, but papa says that the cradle is a present to me from the Class of 1882, and that I ought to be proud of it. I am proud of it and thank the Class for sending me such a beautiful present. I am thirteen months old now, and can almost walk alone, and I weigh just twenty-five pounds.

"Papa says I have written enough for a little boy, so I will close. I will write a longer letter next time."

CLASS BABY.

Our class baby, Charles Peabody Averill, was born at Essex, Mass., March, 17, 1884.

After a reasonable time, in which no one disputed the claim and no one entered any other claim, I sent to him the Class Cradle appropriately marked. His reply to my circular asking for information will be found in the body of this report.

CLASS MEETINGS.

But one class meeting has been held since graduation, and that was in Boylston Hall on Commencement Day, 1883. The report of the Secretary was read and accepted. It was voted:—

That the action of the Class Committee, in preparing resolutions and sending them to the members of the Class, upon the death of Edmund Sehon Perin and William Amos Lamprey, is approved, and that they be requested to act in the same way in the future rather than to call a class meeting to take action.

DEATHS.

Since graduation we have lost by death one regular member, Edmund Sehon Perin, who died December 5, 1884, and two temporary members, William Amos Lamprey, August 3, 1882, and Charles Sidney Averill, May 17, 1885.

News of the death of the latter came too late for me to prepare a sketch of his life for this report.

COMMENCEMENT ENTERTAINMENTS.

The Class has occupied Rooms 19 and 20 in Hollis, on Commencement Day. The entertainment provided has been punch, lemonade, sandwiches, etc. At the request of President Eliot we broke away from the custom of entertaining the graduating class in 1883. The question whether we shall have rum punch at Commencement has not been laid before the class for consideration.

RESIDENCE.

The following table shows the changes in residence since 1882:

	1882	1885
Azores	1	1
California	2	5
Colorado	0	1
Connecticut	0	1
District of Columbia	2	3
England	0	1
Florida	1	0
Germany	0	1
Illinois	5	5
Indiana	1	1
Iowa	1	1
Maine	6	5
Massachusetts	115	100
Michigan	0	1
Minnesota	2	3
Missouri	0	1
New Hampshire	4	5
New Jersey	1	1
New York	28	28
North Carolina	2	2
Ohio	4	2
Pennsylvania	2	5
Rhode Island	3	1
Scotland	0	1
South Carolina	1	1
Vermont	2	3
Virginia	0	1
Wisconsin	0	1
Wyoming	0	1
Deceased	0	1
	183	183

OCCUPATION.

The following table shows the *probable* occupation in 1882, and the actual occupation now.

	1882	1885
Business	56	57
Law	49	50
Undecided	22	5
Medicine	20	18
Teaching	11	21
Journalism	5	8
Study	1	5
Ministry	6	4
Chemistry	6	4
Physical Science	1	0
Library work	0	1
Music	0	3
Engineering	0	2
Farming	0	2
Architecture	0	1
Landscape Gardening	0	1
Others	6	0
Deceased	0	1
	183	183

The class is divided among the different occupations as follows : —

BUSINESS. — Anderson, Baker, Baldwin, Blodgett, Bowen, Boyd, Bradley, Brown, Buell, Bullard, Burt, Chapin, W. G. Chase, Cheney, Clement, Crehore, Cunningham, Cunningham, Cutler, Dabney, Dean, Dickey, G. B. Dunbar, French, Gilman, Goddard, Goodnough, Gordon, Haupt, Heywood, Hubbard, Leatherbee, Leavitt, Lyons, McArthur, R. H. McDonald, McKendry, Manning, C. F. Mason, Merritt, Miles, Olmsted, Oxnard, Pickering, Potter, Rhinelander, H. A. Richardson, Russell, Sherwood, Spalding, C. H. Stevens, W. E. Stone, Storer, Thacher, Warren, Wendell, Woodworth, — 57.

LAW. — Allen, Andrews, Babson, Baird, Barlow, Beale, Bryant, Codman, Cook, Copeland, Creesey, W. H. Dunbar, Eaton, Elliot, Emerson, F. S. Hall, Hardon, Hoar, Hopkins, Hoyt, Hunt, Keep, Knowles, Lane, Lothrop, McCoy, McKone, J. W. Mason, Mayberry, Nagle, Paine, Pendleton, Perrin, Preston, Putnam, Rice, Rogers, Sewall, Smith, Snow, Stetson, F. M. Stone, Townsend, Wait, Warner, Webb, Weld, Whiting, Whitman, Wister,—50.

UNDECIDED. — Cabot, Fellows, Flagg, B. R. Kittredge, Matthews,—5.

MEDICINE. — Babcock, H. L. Chase, Clark, Cochrane, Crockett, Danforth, Delaney, Fiske, Francis, Gage, Gillespie, Harlow, Herrick, Jennings, E. U. McDonald, Perkins, Perkins, Woodbury,—18.

TEACHING. — Averill, Bishop, Blair, Boynton, Burnham, Bush, Coolidge, Dakin, Davis, Dickerman, Goldthwaite, Greenough, Jones, G. L. Kittredge, Page, Robinson, Rushmore, Towne, Underwood, Wentworth, Williston,—21.

JOURNALISM.—Burton, Fernald, Firman, Fuller, Kingsbury, Luce, Ludlow, Panin,—8.

STUDY. — Cole, A. Hall, Howard, G. M. Richardson, Thaxter, —5.

MINISTRY. — Foster, Garrett, Tuckerman, P. M. Washburn,—4.

CHEMISTRY. — Bancroft, Comey, Hartshorn, E. K. Stevens,—4.

LIBRARY WORK. — F. L. Washburn,—1.

MUSIC.— C. F. Bacon, Cumming, Morrill,—3.

ENGINEERING. — J. H. Bacon, Worcester,—2.

FARMING. — Gardner, Waring,—2.

ARCHITECTURE. — Kent,—1.

LANDSCAPE GARDENING. — Eliot,—1.

MARRIAGES, BIRTHS AND DEATHS.

MARRIAGES.

Allen	Hannah C. Smith	Cincinnati, Ohio, March 26, 1885.
Averill	Clara Ada McKay	New York City, December 25, 1882.
Blodgett	Emma S. Garfield	Fitchburg, Mass., October 9, 1882.
Burton	Winnifred N. Baxter	Malden, Mass., February 14, 1885.
Crehore	Alicia V. Robson	Boston, Mass., September 6, 1883.
Dakin	Estella True	Natick, Mass., January 17, 1884.
Elliott	—— Pugh	Washington, D. C., September 9, 1884.
Garrett	Lily Selmes	Boston, Mass., September 1, 1883.
Goldthwaite		
Heywood	Hattie D. Jennings	East Orange, N. J., December 18, 1884.
Howard	Anna Heflrigl	Merau, Tyrol, July 1, 1884.
Ludlow	Harriet Frances Putnam Carnochan	New York City, January 16, 1879.
McDonald, R. H.	Clara Belle Gardner	Carson City, Nevada, July 2, 1884.
Morrill	Carrie Emily Barrington	Cambridge, Mass, November 16, 1884.
Pendleton	Isabelle Gibson Eckstein	Cincinnati, Ohio, June 4, 1885.
Potter	Emily M. Howard	Boston, Mass., May 5, 1885.
Smith	Lyda Dickson	Indianapolis, Ind., October 1, 1884.
Waring	Helen Clark Greene	Warwick, R. I., March 12, 1884.
Washburn, P. M.	Miriam Phillips Storrs	Brooklyn, N. Y., June 5, 1883.
Woodworth	Grace G. Taylor	Boston, Mass., October 29, 1884.
Bachelder	Isabel Hume	Amesbury, Mass., May 31, 1883.
Bartlett	Virginia D. Hight	Bangor, Maine, June 3, 1885.
Cruger	Amy Shepard	London, England, May 3, 1881.
Edgerly	Rose Coghlan	Jersey City, N. J., April 5, 1885.
Fearing, E. T.	Alice C. Ingraham	Watertown, Mass., June 10, 1884.
Hill	Cassie Rowland Milnes	Philadelphia, Pa., April 3, 1883.
Holman	Florence Lippincott	Philadelphia, Pa., March 13, 1882.
Langdon	Julia H. Bolles	Olean, N. J., January 2, 1884.
Luck	Adella Matilda Luce	—— April 27, 1882.
Mariett	Alice Elizabeth Carter	Franklin, Mass., June 25, 1882.
Prince	—— Norman	Boston, Mass., ——
Trenholm	Claudia A. Bissell	Charleston, S. C., November 17, 1881.
Williams	Margaret M. Adger	Charleston, S. C., April 4, 1883.

BIRTHS.

Averill	Charles Peabody	Essex, Mass., March 17, 1884.
Blodgett	Emily Louise	Cambridge, Mass., July 6, 1883.
Goldthwaite	Harry Wales	—— July 13, 1877.
"	Ralph Harvard	St. Albans, Vt., September 17, 1882.
Ludlow	Julia Elektra Livington	Athens, Greece, October 29, 1879.
"	Thomas William	New York City, April 15, 1881.
"	Henry Gouverneur Corbett	Yonkers, N. Y., November 7, 1882.
"	Lewis Walton Morris	Yonkers, N. Y., May 17, 1884.
Wasburn, P. M.	Mary	Cambridge, England, December 3, 1884.
Bachelder	A daughter	Salem, Mass, April 30, 1884.
Cruger	James Jauncey	Bracketville, Texas, January 13, 1883.
Hill	George W.	Philadelphia, Pa., October 22, 1884.
Langdon	Eglantine Courtney	Bedford, Pa., November 3, 1884.
Luck	Charles Arthur	Guatemala, February 28, 1883.
Prince	A son	Boston, Mass., ——.
Williams	Margaret Adger	Charleston, S. C., Feb. 25, 1884.

DEATHS.

Perin	Colorado	December 5, 1882.
Averill	——	May 17, 1885.
Kennett	——	——
Lamprey	Somerville, Mass.,	August 3, 1882.
Lord	Newton, Mass.,	January 30, 1880.
Van Benthuysen	Boston, Mass.,	June 24, 1882.

CLASS FUND.

CLASS FUND.

A. E. MILES, IN ACCOUNT WITH THE CLASS OF 1882.

December 5, 1881, to June 30, 1882.

1882.   Dr.

February	23.	Sale of Stamps,		$1.14
May	3.	E. S. Perin,	½ of First Instalment,	50.00
"	3.	R. M. Bradley,	First Instalment,	10.00
"	3.	R. H. McDonald,	" "	10.00
"	3.	J. W. Babcock,	" "	10.00
"	4.	Ernest Perrin,	" "	40.00
"	4.	G. H. Eaton,	" "	10.00
"	4.	F. L. Washburn,	Subscription in full,	50.00
"	4.	A. Hall,	First Instalment,	10.00
"	5.	F. C. Woodbury,	" "	20.00
"	5.	H. Clement,	" "	10.00
"	5.	J. P. Clark,	" "	10.00
"	6.	F. W. Howe,	" "	20.00
"	6.	H. G. Woodworth,	" "	10.00
"	6.	G. L. Cabot,	Subscription in full,	40.00
"	9.	H. L. Chase,	First Instalment,	10.00
"	9.	A. Matthews,	" "	20.00
"	9.	H. W. Cunningham,	" "	20.00
"	10.	W. Kane,	" "	20.00
"	10.	C. W. Andrews,	" "	15.00
"	10.	C. F. Mason,	" "	5.00
"	10.	C. W. Birtwell,	" "	3.00
"	11.	R. P. Dabney,	" "	10.00
"	12.	H. M. Sewall,	⅔ of Subscription,	50.00
"	18.	S. Williston,	First Instalment,	5.00
"	18.	G. W. Towne,	" "	3.00
"	22.	S. Hoar,	" "	20.00
"	22.	F. Warren,	" "	30.00
"	22.	L. S. Anderson,	" "	5.00
"	22.	G. H. Francis,	" "	20.00
"	22.	G. W. Dickerman,	" "	3.00
"	23.	A. P. Averill,	" "	2.00
"	23.	Sale of Stamps,		.45
"	23.	R. B. Guiteras,	First Instalment,	5.00
"	24.	J. R. Worcester,	" "	5.00
		Carried forward,		552.59

CLASS FUND.

A. E. MILES, IN ACCOUNT WITH THE CLASS OF 1882.

December 5, 1881, to June 30, 1882.

Cr.

1881.			
Dec.	5.	Postal cards and envelopes,	$1.00
"	13.	100 three cent stamps,	3.00
1882.			
Feb.	14.	Collation for Election meeting,	30.00
"	16.	Stamps,	2.00
"	16.	Blank book,	.75
"	16.	Letter file,	.50
May	3.	W. H. Wheeler, miscellaneous printing,	35.75
"	5.	T. Groom & Co. Class Life blanks,	21.00
"	5.	Stamps,	1.00
"	11.	Account book,	.37
"	12.	J. Wilson & Son, printing,	24.00
"	12.	Amee Bros., blocks and ballots for election meeting,	2.70
"	19.	Stamps,	.50

Carried forward, $122.57

		Brought forward.		552.59
May	25.	J. W. Bowen,	First Instalment,	30.00
"	25.	J. W. Bowen,	On Account of Second,	20.00
"	26.	J. W. Perkins,	First Instalment,	5.00
"	26.	G. E. Nagle,	" "	20.00
"	26.	E. K. Stevens,	" "	10.00
"	27.	A. D. Elliott,	" "	4.00
"	29.	P. M. Washburn,	" "	10.00
"	29.	A. F. McArthur,	" "	20.00
"	30.	F. A. Dakin,	" "	5.00
"	30.	M. J. Pickering	" "	10.00
"	31.	M. A. Crockett,	" "	10.00
"	31.	Guy Waring,	" "	5.00
June	1.	J. M. Cochrane,	" "	10.00
"	2.	G. M. Richardson,	" "	10.00
"	2.	W. C. Wait,	" "	10.00
"	5.	W. W. Kent,	" "	10.00
"	5.	G. C. Van Benthuysen,	" "	5.00
"	5.	A. F. Lane,	" "	10.00
"	7.	E. L. Underwood,	" "	10.00
"	8.	C. M. Rice,	" "	20.00
"	10.	B. R. Kittredge,	" "	10.00
"	12.	I. S. Whiting,	" "	4.00
"	12.	W. H. Herrick,	" "	6.00
"	12.	Robert Luce,	" "	10.00
"	13.	J. M. Foster,	" "	25.00
"	13.	H. W. Hardon,	" "	10.00
"	14.	W. H. McKendry,	" "	10.00
"	14.	A. P. Lothrop,	" "	8.00
"	14.	J. E. Bullard,	" "	5.00
"	15.	W. I. McCoy,	⅔ of First Instalment,	20.00
"	16.	M. S. Crehore,	First Instalment,	25.00
"	16.	R. Codman,	Subscription in full,	100.00
"	19.	A. M. Allen,	First Instalment,	10.00
"	21.	H. H. Sherwood,	" "	20.00
"	21.	C. H. Keep,	" "	10.00
"	21.	I. N. Panin,	First & Second Instalment,	4.00
"	22.	W. J. Rushmore,	First Instalment,	3.00
"	22.	H. M. Hubbard,	" "	10.00
"	22.	J. W. Mason,	" "	5.00
"	22.	G. W. Perkins,	" "	3.00
"	24.	W. H. Dunbar,	" "	10.00
"	24.	C. J. Brown,	" "	1.00
"	24.	A. A. Howard,	" "	20.00
"	26.	G. L. Mayberry,	" "	5.00
"	26.	F. G. Cook,	" "	4.00
		Carried forward,		1124.59

Account from December 5, 1881, to June 50, 1882.

		Brought forward,	$122.57
May	30.	F. A. Dakin, for stationery,	.50
June	7.	Envelopes,	1.80
"	13.	W. H. Wheeler, on account, printing,	50.00
"	13.	Stamps,	.37
"	14.	A. P. Lothrop, for expense,	1.00
"	20.	Blank book,	.25
"	22.	Allen Danforth, Bursar, for use of Holden Chapel for Class Meeting,	1.00
"	24.	R. M. Pulsifer & Co., for notice of death of Van Benthuysen,	2.10

Carried forward, $179.59

Account from December 5, 1881, to June 30, 1882.

	Brought forward,		$1124.59
June 26.	R. Delaney,	First Instalment,	5.00
" 26.	E. W. Baker,	" "	5.00
" 26.	H. A. Richardson,	" "	5.00
" 26.	J. P. Gardner,	Subscription in full,	150.00
" 26.	J. H. Hopkins,	First Instalment,	5.00
" 27.	G. W. Williams,	1st, 2d and ½ of 3d Instal't,	25.00
" 28.	W. L. Putnam,	First Instalment,	15.00
" 28.	H. C. French,	" "	20.00
" 29.	F. E. Heywood,	" "	20.00
" 29.	J. S. Bryant,	" "	5.00
" 30.	W. I. McCoy,	" "	10.00
" 30.	A. M. Comey,	" "	10.00
" 30.	R. T. Babson,	" "	5.00
Total to July 1, 1882,			1404.59

The total is made up as follows:

First Instalment, due May 1, 1882,	$1059.00	
Second " " " 1, 1883,	115.00	
Third " " " 1, 1884,	88.00	
Fourth " " " 1, 1885,	73.00	
Fifth " " " 1, 1886,	68.00	
Sale of Stamps	1.59	
	$1404.59	

July 1, 1882, to January 1, 1883.

1882. **Dr.**

July 1.	Balance brought forward,			$1009.30
" 1.	H. E. Smith,	First Instalment,		5.00
" 1.	T. C. Thacher,	" "		20.00
" 1.	H. M. Sewall,	Balance of Subscription, ⅓,		25.00
" 7.	G. L. Kittredge,	First Instalment,		5.00
" 12.	Class Day Committee, balance from sale of Class			
	Day Tickets,	664.88		
	Paid out,	1.50	663.38	

	Carried forward,	$1727.68

Account from December 5, 1881, to June 30, 1882.

		Brought forward,	$179.59
"	29.	G. W. Pach, for photographs for W. C. Wait of the Class Day Committee,	44.80
"	29.	W. A. Bancroft, unpaid bill of Class Crew for coaching,	70.00
"	30.	G. W. Pach, photographs, for E. J. Wendell of the Class Day Committee,	43.40
"	30.	G. W. Pach, for photographs for A. E. Miles, Secretary,	50.50
"	30.	Young's Hotel, for Magnum of Champagne sent to the Class of '69 at their dinner,	7.00
		Total to July 1, 1881,	$395.29

The total is made up as follows:

Postage,	$8.87	
Stationery, etc.,	27.87	
Printing,	109.75	
Catering,	37.00	
Crew debt,	70.00	
Photographs,	138.70	
Miscellaneous,	3.10	395.29
Balance to July 1, 1882,		1009.30
		$1404.59

July 1, 1882, to January 1, 1883.

1882.   **Cr.**

July	3.	H. D. Parker & Co. for Class Dinner,	$328.00
"	3.	Postage stamps,	.50
"	7.	W. H. Wheeler, Printing book containing Oration, Poem, etc.,	83.75
"	8.	Boston Transcript Co., Advertisement of Class Dinner,	3.00
"	10.	Amee Bros., Cards used at Class Dinner, etc.,	13.47
"	11.	Boston Daily Advertiser, Miscellaneous Class Notices,	6.60
"	11.	Wrappers for mailing Reports,	1.00
"	12.	W. H. Wheeler, Printer, on account,	50.00
"	12.	Harvard Daily Echo, for printing the Class Song,	3.00
"	18.	W. H. Wheeler, balance for printing Class Report,	86.80
"	18.	Expense in Cambridge in getting out Report,	20.00
		Carried forward,	$596.12

		Brought forward,		$1727.68
June	25.	W. G. Fellows,	First Instalment,	20.00
"	25.	Blue book, Class Day exercises,		.25
"	28.	" " " " "		.25
"	28.	6 Blue books, " " "		1.50
"	28.	C. F. Cutler,	First Instalment,	5.00
"	29.	Blue book, Class Day exercises,		.25
"	31.	J. H. Storer,	First Instalment,	30.00
July	31.	F. M. Stone,	" "	15.00
August	7.	F. W. Rhinelander,	" "	8.00
"	10.	John Preston,	" "	5.00
"	16.	Blue book, Class Day Exercises,		.25
"	21.	John Russell,	First Instalment,	10.00
"	26.	W. E. Stone,	" "	5.00
September	25.	H. G. Leavitt,	" "	50.00
November	11.	W. H. Burnham,	" "	2.00
"	21.	R. T. Paine,	" "	10.00
December,	2.	R. Whitman,	" "	12.00
"	2.	Class of 1884, Balance due for Class Shell, Part paid to the Captain of the Crew and used for the Crew,		85.00
"	5.	R. Cumming,	First Instalment,	5.00
"	5.	F. N. Goddard,	" "	5.00
"	5.	W. H. Danforth,	" "	10.00
"	8.	H. D. Sedgwick,	" "	10.00
"	11.	E. H. Pendleton,	" "	20.00
"	12.	J. Gillespie,	First and Second Instal'ts	12.00
"	19.	W. B. Fiske,	First Instalment,	5.00
"	25.	R. Cumming,	Second Instalment,	5.00
"	27.	F. L. Creesy,	First Instalment,	10.00
"	28.	C. R. Dean,	" "	10.00
"	30.	L. M. Miles, Interest on $500.00 for 5 months at 4 per cent, on note paid this day,		8.33

Total to January 1, 1883, $2087.51

The total is made up as follows:

First Instalment, due May 1, 1882,	$283.00	
Second " " " 1883,	11.00	
Fourth " " " 1885,	10.00	
Fifth " " " 1886,	15.00	
Class Day Committee,	663.38	
Sale of Class Shell,	85.00	
Interest,	8.33	
Sale of Class Day Books	2.50	
	1078.21	
Balance from preceding six months,	1009.30	$2087.51

Account from July 1, 1882, to January 1, 1883.

		Brought forward,	$596.12
July	19.	Labor and packing,	3.75
"	19.	Stamps for reports and assistance in mailing them,	15.00
"	26.	Blanchard & Brown, Printing circulars, Class Fund dues,	1.25
"	26.	Expressage,	.50
"	28.	W. H. Wheeler for printing Report, extra work beyond contract,	4.41
"	28.	Oak Hall, G. W. Simmons & Son, Unpaid bill left by Class Crew,	6.20
"	28.	Herdic,	1.00
"	28.	Labor,	2.50
"	31.	Stamps,	.15
"	31.	Two Horse Car tickets,	.10
August	10.	Stamps,	1.00
"	25.	Geo. Smyth, Labor in putting boat in order,	14.00
"	25.	Car tickets,	.25
"	28.	Wrappers and stamps,	1.00
October	23.	J. Ford & Son, Printing,	2.55
November	15.	Blanchard & Brown, Printing,	4.75
"	15.	Boston Transcript, Notice,	1.38
"	22.	R. Whitman, Expense incurred,	3.98
"	22.	Postage,	.62
December	5.	Stationery,	1.05
"	5.	Postage Stamps,	.15
"	9.	" "	.06
"	14.	" "	.12
"	19.	" "	.13
"	27.	" "	.06
		Total to January 1, 1883,	662.08

The total is made up as follows:

Postage,	$22.79	
Stationery,	1.05	
Printing,	249.98	
Catering.	328.00	
Crew debt,	20.20	
Miscellaneous.	40.06	662.08
Balance to new account,		1425.43

$2087.51

January 1, 1883, to July 1, 1883.

1883.   **Dr.**

Jan. 1.	Balance brought forward,			$1425.43
" 14.	Mrs. Mary J. Perin on account of Subscription of E. S. Perin,			
		Balance of First Instalment,	20.00	
		Second Instalment,	70.00	
		On acct. of Third Instalment,	60.00	150.00
" 19.	Geo. B. Dunbar,	First Instalment,		10.00
" 26.	W. H. Manning,	" "		20.00
" 30.	J. H. Beale,	" "		5.00
" 30.	J. H. Beale,	Second Instalment,		5.00
Mar. 22.	H. C. French,	" "		20.00
Apr. 30.	H. W. Cunningham,	" "		20.00
May 2.	J. S. Bryant,	" "		5.00
" 5.	G. M. Richardson,	" "		10.00
" 5.	F. N. Goddard,	" "		5.00
" 7.	E. P. Merritt,	First and Second Instal'ts,		20.00
" 8.	J. E. Bullard,	Second Instalment,		5.00
" 8.	W. L. Putnam,	" "		15.00
" 8.	J. H. Hopkins,	" "		5.00
" 8.	J. S. Webb,	First Instalment,		10.00
" 8.	Russell Whitman,	Second Instalment,		12.00
" 9.	G. W. Towne,	" "		3.00
" 10.	J. W. Bowen,	Bal. of 2d Instal't $10. ½ of 3d $15.		25.00
" 10.	E. H. Pendleton,	Second Instalment,		20.00
" 10.	W. H. Danforth,	" "		10.00
" 11.	F. A. Dakin,	" "		5.00
" 11.	F. W. Rhinelander,	" "		8.00
" 11.	H. E. Smith,	" "		5.00
" 12.	J. P. Clark,	" "		10.00
" 22.	B. R. Kittredge,	" "		10.00
" 23.	R. H. McDonald,	" "		10.00
" 29.	C. W. Birtwell,	" "		3.00
" 29.	J. M. Cochrane,	" "		10.00
" 31.	S. Williston,	2d, 3d, 4th and 5th Instal'ts,		20.00
June 2.	S. Hoar,	Second Instalment,		20.00
" 2.	John Russell,	" "		10.00
" 2.	F. Warren,	" "		30.00
" 5.	F. C. Woodbury,	" "		20.00
" 9.	Homer Gage,	First and Second Instal'ts,		20.00
" 11.	H. L. Chase,	Second Instalment,		10.00
	Carried forward,			$1991.43

January 1, 1883, to July 1, 1883.

	1883.	**Cr.**	
Jan.	11.	Fitchburg Sentinel Co., Notices of death E. S. Perin,	6.00
"	11.	254 one cent stamps,	2.54
"	24.	Circulars, Fitchburg Sentinel Co.,	2.50
"	24.	Envelopes,	.60
"	24.	250 one cent stamps,	2.50
Mar.	24.	Eight Stamps,	.24
April	20.	Stationery,	2.10
"	20.	Stamps,	.75
"	20.	Telegram, to R. Whitman,	.27
"	24.	Three stamps,	.09
"	29.	R. R. tickets, Boston and return to Fitchburg,	2.00
May	2.	Circulars, Class Fund Notices,	1.25
"	4.	150 Stamped Envelopes,	4.83
"	8.	R. Whitman, Telegram,	.25
"	8.	Stamps,	.17

Carried forward, $26.09

		Brought forward,		$1991.43
June	12.	W. de L. Cunningham,	First and Second Instal'ts,	20.00
"	12.	W. de L. Cunningham,	Interest on the above,	.75
"	14.	H. G. Woodworth,	Second Instalment,	10.00
"	15.	M. S. Crehore,	" "	25.00
"	16.	G. W. Perkins,	" "	3.00
"	19.	Guy Waring,	" "	5.00
"	19.	H. W. Harlow,	First and Second Instal'ts,	50.00
"	20.	R. T. Babson,	Second Instalment,	5.00
"	22.	C. F. Cutler,	" "	5.00
"	22.	T. C. Thacher,	" "	20 00
"	26.	A. M. Allen,	" "	10.00
"	27.	I. S. Whiting,	" "	4.00
"	27.	E. K. Stevens,	" "	10.00
"	27.	H. A. Richardson,	" "	5.00
"	27.	A. Matthews,	" "	20.00
"	27.	J. R. Worcester,	" "	5.00
"	27.	F. G. Cook,	" "	4.00
"	27.	M. J. Pickering,	" "	10.00
"	27.	G. F. Spalding,	First Instalment,	10.00
"	27.	L. S. Anderson,	Second and Third Instal'ts,	10.00
"	27.	H. W. Hardon,	Second Instalment,	10.00
"	27.	E. V. McDonald,	First and Second Instal'ts,	10.00
"	27.	W. H. McKendry,	Second Instalment,	10.00
"	27.	G. H. Francis,	" "	20.00
"	27.	C. J. Brown,	" "	1.00
"	28.	G. C. Buell,	First and Second Instal'ts,	40.00
"	28.	A. A. Howard,	Second Instalment,	20.00
"	28.	W. H. Herrick,	" "	6.00
"	29.	J. W. Mason,	" "	5.00

              Total to June 30, 1883, $2345.18

The total is made up as follows :

First Instalment, due May 1, 1882.				155.00	
Second	"	"	" 1883.	669.00	
Third	"	"	" 1884.	85.00	
Fourth	"	"	" 1885.	5.00	
Fifth	"	"	" 1886.	5.00	
Interest,				.75	
Balance from preceding 6 months,				$1425.43	$2345.18

Account from January 1, 1883, to July 1, 1883.

		Brought forward,	$26.09
June 12.		Stamps,	.45
"	15.	M. S. Crehore, to pay him for money lent to Class Crew. I credit him with payment of Second Instalment of his subscription. No money was changed between us,	25.00
"	15.	Stamps,	.04
"	19.	"	.06
"	21.	"	.06
"	21.	Check Stamps,	.04
"	21.	Stamp.	.02
"	21.	Boston Daily Advertiser, Advertising for Commencement,	4.00
"	27.	Matches at Commencement,	.50
"	27.	J. H. Hubbard, on account for Class Punch,	80.00
"	27.	C. Eastman, Services, etc., on Commencement Day,	14.00
"	28.	Postage Stamps,	.95
"	28.	Envelopes,	.20
		Total to July 1, 1883,	$151.41

The total is made up as follows:

	Postage,	$12.70	
	Stationery,	2.90	
	Printing,	9.75	
	Catering, etc.,	94.50	
	Class Crew,	25.00	
	Miscellaneous,	6.56	151.41

Balance to new account,	2193.77
	$2345.18

July 1, 1883, to January 1, 1884.

1883.   **Dr.**

		Balance brought forward,		$2193.77
July	1.	F. E. Heywood,	Second Instalment	20.00
"	6.	G. W. Dickerman,	Second Instalment,	3.00
"	6.	G. T. Hartshorn,	First and Second Instal'ts,	20.00
"	8.	G. E. Nagle,	Second Instalment,	20.00
"	10.	H. M. Hubbard,	Bal. of First $10, Second $20.	30.00
"	10.	C. F. Mason,	Second Instalment,	5.00
"	24.	W. E. Stone,	" "	5.00
"	24.	H. D. Sedgwick,	" "	10.00
"	31.	P. Lawrence,	First and Second Instal'ts,	100.00
Aug.	10.	A. Hall,	Second Instalment,	10.00
Sept.	12.	A. M. Comey,	" "	10.00
Oct.	5.	C. M. Rice,	" "	20.00
"	5.	E. W. Baker,	" "	5.00
"	20.	H. Clement,	" "	10.00
"	20.	October Coupon F. R. R. bond,		25.00
Nov.	1.	W. W. Kent,	Second Instalment,	10.00
"	13.	R. T. Paine,	" "	10.00
"	29.	W. A. Blodgett	First and Second Instal'ts,	40.00
"	30.	J. M. Foster,	Second Instalment,	25.00
Dec.	26.	R. P. Dabney,	" "	10.00
		Total to January 1, 1884,		$2581.77

The total is made up as follows :

First Instalment, due May 1, 1882,	90.00	
Second " " " 1883,	273.00	
Interest,	25.00	
Balance from preceding 6 months,	$2193.77	$2581.77

January 1, 1884, to July 1, 1884.

1884.   **Dr.**

Jan.	1.	Balance brought forward,		$2429.54
"	1.	Interest on Saving's Bank deposit,		50.80
"	4.	H. G. Leavitt,	Second Instalment,	50.00
"	23.	Owen Wister,	First and Second Instal'ts,	40.00
Feb.	8.	C. H. Keep,	Second Instalment,	10.00
Mar.	15.	F. A. Fernald,	First and Second Instal'ts,	10.00
"	29.	A. P. Averill,	Second and Third Instal'ts,	4.00
		Carried forward,		$2594.34

July 1, 1883, to January 1, 1884.

1883.		**Cr.**	
July 1.		H. I. Wallace, for borrowed money to tip the Commencement waiter,	$1.00
" 9.		Smith Bros, Catering at Commencement,	38.78
" 9.		J. H. Hubbard, Balance for Punch and Cigars at Commencement,	62.25
" 31.		P. Lawrence, Money owed by the Crew, Subscription being $250.00 on condition that this be paid him. See opposite page,	50.00
Oct. 20.		Postage Stamps,	.20

Total to January 1, 1884,   152.23

The total is made up as follows:

Postage,	.20	
Catering, etc.,	102.03	
Class Crew,	50.00	152.23

Balance to January 1, 1884,   2429.54

$2581.77

January 1, 1884, to July 1, 1884.

1884.		**Cr.**	
Jan. 21.		Check book,	$0.50

Carried forward, $0.50

Account from January 1, 1884, to July 1, 1884.

			Brought forward,	$2594.34
Apr.	14.	Asaph Hall,	Third Instalment,	10.00
"	30.	H. W. Cunningham,	" "	20.00
"	30.	April Coupon F. R. R. bond,		25.00
May	1.	H. G. Woodworth,	Third Instalment,	10.00
"	3.	E. L. Underwood,	Second and Third Instal'ts,	20.00
"	3.	P. M. Washburn,	" " " "	20.00
"	5.	J. H. Storer,	" " " "	60.00
"	6.	J. S. Bryant,	Third Instalment,	5.00
"	6.	H. G. Leavitt,	" "	50.00
"	6.	G. W. Williams,	" "	5.00
"	6.	R. M. Bradley,	Second and Third Instal'ts,	20.00
"	8.	W. H. McKendry,	Third Instalment,	10.00
"	9.	F. A. Dakin,	" "	5.00
"	10.	J. G. Flagg,	First and Second Instal'ts,	10.00
"	10.	A. F. McArthur,	Second and Third Instal'ts,	40.00
"	10.	R. Cumming,	Third Instalment,	5.00
"	10.	Guy Waring,	" "	5.00
"	10.	Sale of Class Oars,		20.00
"	12.	G. W. Towne,	Third Instalment,	3.00
"	13.	J. P. Clark,	" "	10.00
"	13.	J. E. Bullard,	" "	5.00
"	13.	W. H. Dunbar,	Second and Third Instal'ts,	20.00
"	14.	R. H. McDonald,	Third Instalment,	10.00
"	17.	John Preston,	Second and Third Instal'ts,	10.00
"	17.	J. M. Cochrane,	Third Instalment,	10.00
"	17.	R. B. Guiteras,	Second and Third Instal'ts,	10.00
"	19.	R. P. Dabney,	Third Instalment,	10.00
"	20.	H. E. Smith,	" "	5.00
"	21.	W. H. Danforth,	" "	10.00
"	24.	John Russell,	" "	10.00
"	24.	W. H. Burnham,	Second and Third Instal'ts,	4.00
"	26.	W. L. Putnam,	3d, 4th, and 5th Instal'ts,	15.00
"	26.	G. W. Dickerman,	Third Instalment,	9.00
"	26.	F. Warren,	" "	30.00
June	1.	I. S. Whiting,	" "	4.00
"	2.	F. A. Fernald,	" "	5.00
"	11.	W. G. Fellows,	2d, 3d, 4th and 5th Instal'ts,	80.00
"	13.	H. H. Sherwood,	Second and Third Instal'ts,	40.00
"	14.	B. R. Kittredge,	Third Instalment,	10.00
"	14.	A. M. Allen.	" "	10.00
"	14.	G. W. Perkins,	" "	3.00
"	15.	John Gillespie,	" "	6.00
"	18.	H. D. Sedgwick,	" "	10.00
"	19.	W. H. Herrick,	" "	6.00
			Carried forward,	$3279.34

	Brought forward,	$0.50
April 21.	W. H. Wheeler, Printing,	3.00
" 30.	200 Stamps, at two cents,	4.00
" 30.	Envelopes,	.50

Carried forward,	$8.00

		Brought forward,		
June 20.	G. E. Nagle,	Third Instalment,		20.00
" 20.	C. W. Birtwell,	" "		3.00
" 21.	A. P. Lothrop,	Second and Third Instal'ts,		16.00
" 25.	J. J. Greenough,	1st, 2d and 3d Instalments,		15.00
" 25.	H. A. Richardson,	Third Instalment,		5.00
" 25.	F. G. Cook,	" "		4.00
" 25.	Geo. F. Spalding,	Second "		10.00
" 25.	J. H. Beale,	Third "		5.00
" 25.	M. J. Pickering,	" "		10.00
" 28.	G. M. Richardson,	" "		10.00
" 28.	G. L. Kittredge,	Second and Third Instal'ts,		10.00

Total to June, 30, 1884,   3387.34

The total is made up as follows:
Balance from preceding 6 months,				$2429.54	
First Instalment, due May 1, 1882,				35.00	
Second	"	"	" 1883,	262.00	
Third	"	"	" 1884,	519.00	
Fourth	"	"	" 1885,	23.00	
Fifth	"	"	" 1886,	23.00	
Interest,				75.80	
Sale of Oars,				20.00	$3387.34

July 1, 1884, to January 1, 1885.

1884.   **Dr.**

July 1.	Balance brought forward,		$3345.84
" 1.	Accrued interest at Union Safe deposit Vaults,		9.40
" 1.	Accrued interest on Savings Bank deposit,		21.00
" 10.	J. W. Mason,	Third Instalment,	5.00
" 14.	G. F. Hartshorn,	" "	10.00
Sept. 2.	F. A. Fernald,	Fourth and Fifth Instal'ts,	10.00
" 19.	J. H. Hopkins,	Third Instalment,	5.00
" 25.	H. Clement,	" "	10.00
Oct. 4.	Geo. H. Francis,	" "	20.00
Nov. 8.	Russell Whitman,	" "	12.00
" 28.	October Coupon on F. R. R. bond,		25.00

Total to January 1, 1885,   3473.24

The total is made up as follows:
Balance from preceding 6 months,				$3345.84	
Third Instalment, due May 1, 1884,				62.00	
Fourth	"	"	" 1885,	5.00	
Fifth	"	"	" 1886,	5.00	
Interest,				55.40	$3473.24

Account from January 1, 1884, to July 1, 1884. 107

		Brought forward,	$8.00
May	3.	100 receipts,	.50
"	6.	Wakefield Rattan Co., for Class Cradle,	31.00
"	13.	50 Stamps, two cents,	1.00
June	23.	Boston Daily Advertiser, Notice about Commencement Day,	1.00
		Total to July 1, 1884,	41.50

The total is made up as follows:

Postage,	$5.00	
Stationery,	1.50	
Printing,	4.00	
Class Cradle,	31.00	41.50

Balance to new account,	3345.84
	$3387.34

July 1, 1884, to January 1, 1885.

1884. **Cr.**

July	5.	J. H. Hubbard, Commencement Punch, etc.,	40.50
"	5.	Leavitt & Peirce, Cigars,	12.75
"	5.	W. L. Shepard, Class Punch,	71.45
"	5.	D. Jewett, Services,	7.60
"	5.	Smith Bros., and waiters, $38.55 + 3.00,	41.55
Sept.	3.	Bill File,	.75
Oct.	1.	100 Stamps at 2 cents,	2.00
Dec.	2.	Thos. Groom & Co., Blank book,	3.50
"	15.	250 One cent Stamps,	2.50
		Total to January 1, 1885,	182.60

The total is made up as follows:

Postage,	4.50	
Stationery,	4.25	
Catering, etc.,	173.85	182.60

Balance to new account,	3290.64
	$3473.24

January 1, 1885, to June 15, 1885.

1885.		**Dr.**	1885.
		Balance from preceding six months,	$3290.64
Jan.	1.	Accrued interest Union Safe Deposit Vaults,	5.64
"	1.	Accrued interest on Savings Bank Deposit,	21.42
"	24.	J. E. Weld, First Instalment,	5.00
Feb.	6.	Feb. Coupon Denv. Ex. 4 per cent bond,	20.00
Mar.	4.	J. W. Bowen, balance ½ of subscription,	75.00
"	4.	H. L. Chase, Third Instalment,	10.00
"	4.	C. M. Rice, Third "	20.00
"	4.	C. F. Cutler, Third "	5.00
"	6.	E. H. Pendleton, Third and Fourth Instalments,	40.00
"	11.	C. J. Brown, " " " "	2.00
"	11.	M. S. Crehore, Third Instalment,	25.00
"	11.	E. K. Stevens, " "	10.00
"	14.	T. C. Thacher, " "	20.00
"	16.	A. A. Howard, " "	20.00
"	16.	F. W. Rhinelander, Third and Fourth Instalments,	16.00
"	26.	J. R. Worcester, " " " "	10.00
"	30.	C. D. Burt, First Instalment,	10.00
"	31.	Charles Eliot, " "	20.00
"	31.	W. H. Herrick, Fourth and Fifth "	12.00
April	4.	W. I. McCoy, Second Instalment,	30.00
"	4.	Woodbury Kane, " and Third "	40.00
"	6.	A. M. Comey, Third " Fourth "	20.00
"	14.	W. B. Fiske, Second " Third "	10.00
"	16.	H. W. Hardon, Third Instalment,	10.00
"	16.	G. C. Buell, " "	20.00
"	20.	F. H. Prince, First Second & Third Instalments,	60.00
"	23.	H. C. French, Third and Fourth Instalments,	40.00
"	25.	April coupon F. R. R. bond,	25.00
May	2.	H. G. Woodworth Fourth Instalment,	10.00
"	2.	W. H. Burnham, " "	2.00
"	2.	H. L. Chase, " "	10.00
"	2.	F. A. Dakin, " "	5.00
"	2.	W. H. Danforth, " "	10.00
"	4.	F. C. Woodbury, Third "	20.00
"	4.	J. J. Greenough, Fourth "	5.00
"	5.	C. W. Birtwell, " "	3.00
"	5.	F. Warren, " "	30.00
"	8.	Sherman Hoar, ½ Third "	10.00
"	8.	R. Cumming Fourth "	5.00
"	8.	G. W. Williams, " "	10.00
"	9.	John Gillespie, " "	6.00
"	9.	J. S. Bryant, " "	5.00
		Carried forward,	$4023.70

January 1, 1885, to June 15, 1885.

	1885.	**Cr.**	
Jan.	9.	Blair and Hallett, Printing,	$6.25
Feb.	9.	" " " "	6.25
"	9.	250 one cent Stamps,	2.50
March	2.	100 two cent Stamps,	2.00
"	4.	Blair and Hallett, Printing,	4.50
"	16.	G. G. Bradford, for College papers,	2.50
"	17.	50 Postal Cards,	.50
"	17.	Paper and envelopes,	1.00
"	17.	Letter file,	.25
"	20.	Three Blocks of paper, at 12 cents,	.36
"	20.	Second Letter file,	.25
"	24.	100 one cent Stamps,	1.00
"	31.	50 Postals and 25 two cent Stamps,	1.00
April	6.	Letter file,	.25
"	6.	Blair and Hallett, 500 envelopes and printing,	1.75
"	17.	100 two cent Stamps,	2.00
May	4.	100 " " "	2.00
"	5.	Blair and Hallett, 50 postals and printing,	2.10

Carried forward, $3646.

Account from January 1, 1885, to June 15, 1885.

		Brought forward,		$4023.70
May	11.	W. C. Wait,	Second, Third, and Fourth Instalments,	30.00
"	11.	G. W. Towne,	Fourth Instalment,	3.00
"	13.	John Preston,	" "	5.00
"	13.	Geo. H. Eaton,	Second Instalment,	10.00
"	13.	John Russell,	Fourth Instalment,	10.00
"	15.	R. H. McDonald,	" "	10.00
"	16.	J. E. Bullard,	" "	5.00
"	18.	H. W. Cunningham,	Fourth and Fifth Instalments,	40.00
"	19.	C. F. Cutler,	Fourth Instalment,	5.00
"	22.	J. M. Cochrane,	" "	10.00
"	23.	H. H. Sherwood,	" "	20.00
"	28.	A. F. McArthur,	" "	20.00
"	28.	H. M. Hubbard,	Third and Fourth Instalments,	40.00
June	1.	M. A. Crockett,	2d, 3d, 4th and 5th "	40.00
"	5.	M. J. Pickering,	Fourth Instalment,	10.00
"	5.	Mrs. M. J. Perin,	Balance of subscription $350, of E. S. Perin,	150.00
"	5.	Edwards Cheney,	First and Second Instalments,	10.00
"	5.	I. S. Whiting,	Fourth Instalment,	4.00
"	15.	A. P. Averill,	" "	2.00
		Total to June 15, 1885,		$4447.70

The total is made up as follows :

First Instalment,	due May 1,	1882,	$60.00	
Second	"	"	"	1883,	110.00	
Third	"	"	"	1884,	344.00	
Fourth	"	"	"	1885,	435.00	
Fifth	"	"	"	1886,	136.00	
Interest					72.06	1157.06
	Balance from preceding 6 months,					3290.64
						$4447.70

Balance as above,		$4307.35
Deposit in Worcester North Savings Institution, Fitchburg, Mass.,	$1000.00	
Accrued interest on the same,	93.22	
Fall River Railroad Co. 5 per cent first mortgage $1000 bond,	1060.28	
Denver Extension (C., B. & Q.) 4 per cent bond,	858.83	
Cash on hand,	1295.02	$4307.35

Account from January 1, 1885, to June 15, 1885.

	Brought forward,	$36.46
May 19.	20 two cent Stamps,	.40
" 20.	100 two cent Stamps,	2.00
" 22.	W. H. Wheeler, on account for printing Triennial Report,	100.00
" 27.	50 one cents Stamps,	.50
June 13.	Telegram to W. H. Wheeler,	.24
" 13.	150 Cards for Triennial Dinner,	.75
	Total to June, 15, 1885,	140.35

The total is made up as follows:

Postage,	14.40	
Stationery,	2.11	
Printing,	120.35	
Catering,	.75	
Miscellaneous,	2.74	140.35

Balance to June 15,	4307.35
	$4447.70

CLASS FUND.

A statement of our assets is given on page 110. The deposit in the Worcester North Savings Institution draws interest at 4 per cent. The Fall River Railroad bond is a first mortgage bond, due in April 1, 1895. The interest is guaranteed by the Old Colony Railroad Co. until the bond is paid. I put it in at the gross cost, *i. e.* 105 and interest. At this price it pays about $4\frac{3}{8}$ per cent. The Denver Extension bond is put in at gross cost, *i. e.* $85\frac{1}{2}$ and interest. At this price it pays about $4\frac{7}{8}$ per cent. Since it was purchased it has appreciated and is now quoted at 96.

The cash on hand is deposited in the Union Safe Deposit Vaults, of Boston, and draws interest at 2 per cent. The balance at present is unusually large, as a large amount will be needed to pay for the Class Dinner, this report, and the Commencement Entertainment.

Our fund as subscribed at graduation was $9695. A few subscriptions have been made since, and it is now $9935. You will remember that subscriptions were to be paid in five annual instalments, beginning May 1, 1882. The payments have been as follows:

	First Instalment.	Second Instalment.	Third Instalment.	Fourth Instalment.	Fifth Instalment.
Paid	$1682.	$1440.	$1098.	$551.	$252.
Unpaid	305.	547.	889.	1436.	1735.
	$1987.	$1987.	$1987.	$1987.	$1987.

If the instalments had been paid promptly when due, I think we should have been able to live on our income or nearly so, and should not have been obliged to spend so much of the principal. If any of you would like to increase your subscriptions please do so. Those who have not subscribed are invited to send in their subscriptions at any time.

COLLEGE FUND.

Our college fund was the smallest for a number of years, at graduation, and I regret that nothing has been added to it, and very little paid in since Commencement, 1882. The following account shows the receipts:

1882.				
May	22.	S. Hoar,	First Instalment,	$10.00
June	2.	W. C. Wait,	" "	5.00
"	12.	W. H. Herrick,	First and Second Instal'ts,	4.00
"	12.	R. Luce,	First Instalment,	5.00
"	14.	A. P. Lothrop,	" "	3.00
"	14.	J. E. Bullard,	" "	5.00
"	22.	W. H. Dunbar,	" "	5.00
"	26.	B. M. Firman,	" "	10.00
"	26.	J. P. Gardner,	Subscription in Full,	50.00
July	2.	J. P. Lyons,	First Instalment,	5.00
Dec.	5.	A. Matthews,	First Instalment,	5.00
1883.				
Jan.	7.	Geo. H. Eaton,	First Instalment,	5.00
"	19.	G. B. Dunbar,	" "	5.00
August	31.	B. M. Firman,	Second Instalment,	10.00
1884.				
March	15.	F. A. Fernald,	First and Second Instal'ts,	5.00
June	2.	F. A. Fernald,	Third Instalment,	2.50
1885.				
March	31.	W. H. Herrick,	Balance of Subscription,	16.00
April	4.	F. A. Fernald,	" " "	17.50
May	10.	J. E. Bullard,	Second and Third Instalments,	10.00
		Total to June 15, 1885,		$178.00

I feel that we ought to pay promptly what we have subscribed, especially when the subscription is so small ($700.). The only expense has been $2. for printing, postage, etc., and the balance over expenditures is therefore $176. This has been paid over to the custodian of the fund, Mr. A. B. Silsbee. In the future as fast as money comes in I will pay it over to him. I earnestly urge you to increase the subscription, and to pay your instalments more promptly, as the "Class Subscription Fund" is much needed.

ADDRESSES.

[So few of you have heeded my request for information of changes and mistakes in your addresses that it is, I fear, of very little use to ask you to please notify me of any change and to keep me informed of your addresses. I will distribute another list as soon as I am informed of a reasonable number of changes.]

ALLEN, A. M., Greendale, Hamilton Co., Ohio.

ANDERSON, L. S., Quincy, Mass., or Old Colony, R. R. Freight Dept., Boston, Mass.

ANDREWS, C. W. 110 James St., Syracuse, N. Y.

AUSTIN, HERBERT, 9 Arlington St., Boston, Mass.

AVERILL, A. P., Bolton, Mass.

BABCOCK, J. W., Chester, South Carolina.

BABSON, R. T., Gloucester, Mass.

BACHE, RENE, Philadelphia, Pa.

BACHELDER, G. E., Salem, Mass.

BACON, CHAS. F., Lock Box 19, Newton, Mass.

BACON, JAMES H., Wilmington, N. C.

BAIRD, CHAMBERS, Jr., 285 16th Street, Denver, Colorado.

BAKER, EDWARD W., Brookline, Mass.

BALDWIN, C. A., care of C. Adolphe Low & Co., San Francisco, California; or 560 5th Avenue, New York, N. Y.

BANCROFT, CLARENCE, Manchester Mills, Manchester, N. H.

BARLOW, GEO. F., 62 Temple Court, New York, N. Y.

BARTLETT, CHARLES H., Bangor, Maine.

BEALE, JOSEPH H., Jr., Train St., Dorchester, Mass.

BIRTWELL, CHARLES W., 281 Broadway, Lawrence, Mass.
BISHOP, JOHN R., Princeton, N. J.
BLAIR, W. A., High Point, Guilford Co., North Carolina.
BLODGETT, W. A., 16 Trowbridge Street, Cambridge, Mass.
BOWEN, J. W., Hotel Brunswick, Boston, Mass.
BOYD, ALEXANDER, Jr., care James Boyd & Sons, Boston, Mass.
BOYNTON, C. E., 29 White St., Haverhill, Mass.
BRADLEY, R. M., 40 State Street, Boston Mass.
BROWN, CHARLES J., 100 Mulberry Street, Worcester Mass.
BROWN, F. T., Carbon, Carbon Co., Wyoming Ter.
BRYANT, JOHN S., 236 Niagara Street, Buffalo, N. Y.
BUELL, G. C., Jr., Rochester, N. Y.
BULLARD, JOHN ELIOT, 149 Beacon Street, Boston, Mass.
BURNHAM, W. H., Dunbarton, N. H.
BURT, CHARLES D., 40 Somerset Ave., Taunton, Mass.
BURTON, F. R., Boston Post, Boston, Mass.
BUSH, WALTER N., Oakland, California.
CABOT, G. L., 11 Park Square, Boston, Mass.
CHALFANT, W., Jr., West Chester, Pa.
CHAPIN, H. G., Chapin & Gould, Springfield, Mass.
CHASE, H. L., Park St., Brookline, Mass.
CHASE, W. G., 21 Hamilton St., Boston, Mass.
CHENEY, EDWARDS, P. O. Box 218, Lowell, Mass.
CLARK, J. PAYSON, 385 Marlboro St., Boston, Mass.
CLARK, S. C., West Boxford, Essex Co., Mass.
CLEMENT, H., 131 Newbury St., Boston, Mass.
COCHRANE, J. M., 14 State St., Cambridgeport, Mass.
CODMAN, ROBERT, Jr., 17 Brimmer St., Boston, Mass.
COLE, F. N., Marlboro, Mass.
COMEY, ARTHUR M., 4 Granite St., Somerville, Mass.

Cook, F. G., 6 Hollis Hall, Cambridge, Mass.; or, Warsaw, Wyoming Co., N. Y.

Coolidge, J. A., Coolidge Ave., Cambridge, Mass.

Copeland, C. T., Calais, Maine.

Creesy, F. L., Brookline, Mass.

Crehore, M. S., H. G. Jordan & Co., 82 Water St., Boston, Mass.

Crockett, M. A., Medford, Mass.

Cruger, J. P., Silver Lake Ranch, Bracketville, Kinney Co., Tex.

Cumming, Robert, care of Lysson Gordon, 7 Chestnut Court, Somerville, Mass.

Cunningham, H. W., 31 St. James Ave., Boston, Mass.

Cunningham, W. de L., care J. W. Cunningham & Bro., 11 Wall St., New York, N. Y.

Cutler, Chas. F., 89 Broad St., Boston, Mass.

Dabney, John P., Taunton Tack Works, Taunton, Mass.

Dabney, R. P., Care Chas. W. Dabney & Sons, Fayal, Azores.

Dakin, F. A., St. Johnsbury, Vt.

Danforth, W. H., Plymouth, Mass., Lock Box 370.

Davis, W. P., 634 Post St., San Francisco, Cal., or Florence, Mass.

Dean, C. R., Box 3, Taunton, Mass.

Delaney, Richard, Woodville, Mass.

Dickerman, Geo. W., 6 East 44th St., New York, N. Y.

Dickey, Chas. D., Jr., Care Messrs. Brown Bros. & Co., Wall St., New York, N. Y.

Dillenback, H. I., The Sunday Times, Boston, Mass.

Dooling, J. J., Temple Place, Boston, Mass.

Dunbar, Geo. B., 14 Highland St., Cambridge, Mass.

Dunbar, Wm. H., 14 Highland St., Cambridge, Mass.

Dunlevy, H. H., 1812 Indiana Ave., Chicago, Ill.
Dunton, Chas. H., Allston, Mass.
Eaton, Geo. H., Lawrence, Mass.
Edgerly, Clinton J., Belmont, Mass.
Eldridge, Fred'k L., Care H. B. Hollins & Co., 74 Broadway, New York, N. Y.
Eliot, Charles, Quincy St., Cambridge, Mass.
Elliot, A. D., Care of Senator Jas. L. Pugh, Washington, D.C.
Emerson, F. W., Newton, Mass.
Fearing, D. B., Care W. Turnbull & Co., 57 & 59 Worth St., New York, N. Y.
Fearing, E. T., 91 & 93 Commercial St., Boston, Mass.
Fellows, Gordon, 584 Fifth Ave., New York, N. Y.
Ferguson, Edw. A., Bank Chambers, Detroit, Mich.
Fernald, F. A., 3 Bond St., New York, N. Y.
Firman, B. M., Boston Daily Advertiser, Boston, Mass.
Fiske, W. B., 9 Clinton St., Cambridgeport, Mass.
Flagg, J. G., 31 East 40th St., New York, N. Y.
Foster, J. M., Bangor, Maine.
Francis, Geo. H., Brookline, Mass.
French, H. C., French, Potter & Wilson, Chicago, Ill.
Fuller, F. E., Boston Daily Advertiser, Boston, Mass.
Gage, Homer, Worcester, Mass.
Gardner, J. P., Hamilton, Mass.
Garrett, Rev. D. C., Davenport, Iowa.
Gillespie, John, 27 Pinckney St., Somerville, Mass.
Gilman, Henry H., Haverhill, Mass.
Goddard, F. Norton., 516 Broadway, New York, N. Y.
Goldthwaite, C. H., St. Albans, Vt.
Goodnough, X. H., Brookline, Mass.

GORDON, LYSSON, 7 Chestnut Court, Somerville, Mass.
GREENOUGH, JAS. JAY., Brewster Place, Cambridge, Mass.
GRIFFIN, J. Q. A., 44 Court St., Boston, Mass.
GRISWOLD, A. W., Jr., 21 Courtland St., New York, N. Y.
GUITERAS, R. B., 134 E. 24th St., New York, N. Y.; or Bristol, R. I.
HALL, ASAPH, Jr., 18 Gay St., Georgetown, D. C.
HALL, F. S. Winthrop St., Taunton, Mass.
HARDON, H. W., Care of Evarts, Choate & Beaman, New York City.
HARLOW, H. W., Augusta, Maine.
HARTSHORN, G. T., care Chas. W. Hartshorn, Esq., Taunton, Mass.
HAUPT, F. S., 312 Summit Ave., St. Paul, Minn.
HERRICK, W. H., Care of W. A. Herrick, Esq., 3 Niles Block, 33 School St., Boston, Mass.
HEYWOOD, F. E., P. O. Box 923, Worcester, Mass.
HILL, P. S., 1805 Spring Garden Street, Philadelphia, Pa.
HOAR, SHERMAN, Concord. Mass.
HOLDEN, FRANCIS M., 77 Poplar St., Boston, Mass.
HOLMAN, C. H., 2336 Washington St., Boston, Mass.
HOPKINS, J. H., Barnstable, Mass.
HOWARD, A. A., Leipzig, Germany.
HOWE, F. W., Care Howe Bros. & Co., Lowell, Mass.
HOWE, W. A., Bolton, Mass.
HOYT, H. R., Care Alfred M. Hoyt, Esq., 15 State St., New York, N. Y.
HUBBARD, H. M., 387 La Salle Ave., Chicago, Ill.
HUNT, F. T., Weymouth, Mass.
JENNINGS, Dr. C. G. R., Bennington Centre, Vermont.
JONES, WILLIAM, 305 North Duke St., Lancaster, Pa.
KANE, WOODBURY, Care H. S. Ely, 22 Pine St., New York, N. Y.
KEEP, CHAS. H., 302 Franklin St., Buffalo, N. Y.

Kent, W. W. Care H. H. Richardson, Brookline, Mass.; or 274 Delaware Ave., Buffalo, N. Y.

Kingsbury, A. B., Jr., Daily News, Chicago, Ill.

Kittredge, B. R., Peekskill, N. Y.

Kittredge, G. L., Exeter, N. H.

Knowles, C. F. S., Yarmouthport, Mass.

Lane, A. F., Care Gaston & Whitney, 28 School St., Boston, Mass.

Langdon, Courtney, Johns Hopkins University, Baltimore, Md.

Lawrence, Prescott, Groton, Mass.

Leatherbee, Geo. H., 122 East Dedham St., Boston, Mass.

Leavitt, H. G., 1 East 40th St., New York, N. Y.

Lothrop, A. P., Care T. J. Lothrop, Esq., Taunton, Mass.

Luce, Robert, Boston Globe, Boston, Mass.

Luck, Chas. W., Andover, Mass.

Ludlow, T. W., Cottage Lawn, Yonkers, N. Y.

Lyons, John P., Naval Office, New York, N. Y.

McArthur, A. F., 275 Ashland Ave., Chicago, Ill.

McColl, E. W., Care of McColl Bros., New York, N. Y.

McCoy, W. I., Troy, N. Y.

McDonald, E. V., Fall River, Mass.

McDonald, R. H., Jr., Pacific Bank, San Francisco, Cal.

McFee, Chas. H., P. O. Box, 433, Woonsocket, R. I.

McKendry, W. H., Canton, Mass.

McKone, Wm. T., North Andover Depot, Mass.

Mahon, C. H., Lynn, Mass.

Manning, W. H., Marquette, Michigan.

Mariett, Rev. E. H., 98 East North Main St., Fall River, Mass.

Mason, C. F., Old Colony R. R. Freight Office, Boston, Mass.

Mason, J. W., Brookline, Mass.

Matthews, Albert, 145 Beacon St., Boston, Mass.

MAYBERRY, G. L., Waltham, Mass.
MERRITT, E. P., Care Blake Bros. & Co. New York, N. Y.
MILES, A. E., 51 State St., Boston, Mass.
MITCHELL, C. A., 413 Pearl St., Cleveland, Ohio.
MITCHELL, JOHN K., Care Dr. S. Weir Mitchell, Philadelphia, Pa.
MITCHELL, DR. SOLLACE, 21 East 21st St., New York, N. Y.
MORRILL, SAM HENRY, 58 Mt. Auburn St., Cambridge, Mass.
MUNROE, H. W., Care Munroe & Co., 7 Rue Scribe, Paris, France.
NAGLE, G. E., 815 Main St., Cambridge, Mass.
NORMAN, H. K., Gloucester, Mass.
OLMSTED, O. A. Wabash, St Louis & Pac. R. R., Chicago, Ill.
OXNARD, H. T., Fulton Sugar Refinery, Brooklyn, N. Y.
PAGE, W. E., 87 Washington St., Newport, R. I.
PAINE, R. T., 46 Mt. Vernon St., Boston, Mass.
PANIN, I. N., Hampton, Virginia.
PARSONS, R. C., Jr., Cleveland, Ohio.
PENDLETON, ELLIOTT H., Jr., Pendleton & Barton, Cincinnati, Ohio.
PERKINS, GEO. W., Topsfield, Mass.
PERKINS, JOHN W., Hyde Park, Mass.
PERRIN, E. N., 70 William St., New York, N. Y.
PICKERING. M. J., 71 Magazine St., Cambridge, Mass.
POTTER, W. N., Jr., Standard Cordage Co., Boston, Mass.
PRESCOTT, W. H., Concord, Mass.
PRESTON, JOHN, New Ipswich, N. H.
PRINCE, F. H., 2 State St., Boston, Mass.
PUTNAM, W. L., Care of Geo. Putnam, Esq., 35 Court St., Boston, Mass.
RHINELANDER, F. W., M. L. S. & W. R. R. Co., Milwaukee, Wis.

RICE, C. M., Care W. W. Rice, Esq., Worcester, Mass.

RICHARDSON, G. M., Care F. J. Stimson, 209 Washington St., Boston, Mass.

RICHARDSON, H. A., South Framingham, Mass.

RICHARDSON, H. K., Middleton, Mass.

ROBINSON, L. M., 1805 Pine St., Philadelphia, Pa.

ROGERS, W. A., P. O. Box 613, Dacatur, Ill.

RUFFIN, H. St. P., 13 Court Square, Boston, Mass.

RUSSELL, JOHN, Plymouth, Mass.

RUSHMORE, W. J., 22 Mt. Auburn St., Cambridge, Mass.

SCOTT, EDWARD D., 1222 North 2nd St., Richmond, Va.

SEDGWICK, H. D., Jr., 31 Pemberton Sq., Boston, Mass.

SESSIONS, A. L., 32 Pine St., New York, N. Y.

SEWALL, H. M., Bath, Maine.

SHERWOOD, H. H., Richards, Harrison & Sherwood, San Francisco, Cal.

SLADE, D. R., Care W. H. Fearing, 24 Broad St., New York, N. Y.

SMITH, H. E., 48½ East Washington St., Indianapolis, Ind.

SNOW, CHAS. A., 41 Rutherford Sq., Boston, Mass.

SPALDING, GEO. F. Care Davis & Crafts, Haverhill, Mass.

STETSON ELIOT D., New Bedford, Mass.

STEVENS, C. H., 308 Harvard St., Cambridge, Mass.

STEVENS, E. K , Care Carter, Dinsmore & Co., Boston, Mass.

STONE, F. M., Cottage St., New Bedford, Mass.

STONE, W. E., High Point, North Carolina.

STORER, JOHN H., 40 State St., Boston, Mass.

STURGIS, C. I., Pay Dep't. C. B. & Q. R. R. Co., Chicago, Ill

THACHER, T. C., 16 Pearl St., Boston. Mass.

THAXTER, ROLAND, Kittery Point, Maine.

THAYER, W. E., 7 Park St., Boston, Mass.
THOMPSON, F. H., Cambridgeport, Mass.
TILTON, E. J., care of the Secretary.
TORREY, C. E., care of the Secretary.
TOWNE, G. W., So. Byefield, Mass.
TOWNSEND, S. V. R., 46 West 9th St., New York, N. Y.
TRENHOLM, GEO. M., Charleston, S. C.
TUCKERMAN, GUSTAVUS, Gloucester, Mass., Care of R. T. Babson.
UNDERWOOD, E. L., 55 East Newton St., Boston.
VAN BUREN, C. M., Patterson, N. J.
WAGAR, MARS E., York & Carroll Sts., Cleveland, Ohio.
WAIT, W. C., 28 Holyoke St., Cambridge, Mass,
WARING, GUY, Port Townsend, Wyoming Ter.
WARING, W. B., St John's College, Shanghai, China.
WARNER, HENRY E., Cambridge, Mass.
WARREN, F., Jr., Warren & Co., Alexandra Building, Liverpool, Eng.
WASHBURN, F. L., Academy of Science, Minneapolis, Minn.
WASHBURN, P. M., 36 Elm St., Worcester, Mass.
WEBB, JOHN S., 1918 F. St., Washington, D. C.
WELD, J. EDWARD, 128 Pearl St., New York, N. Y.
WELLS, E. F., Marietta, Ohio.
WENDELL, E. J., 8 East 38th St., New York, N. Y.
WENDELL, GORDON, 8 East 38th St., New York, N. Y.
WENTWORTH, E. E., 16 Tremont St., Chelsea, Mass.
WESTON, A. J., Weston Bros. & Agnew, 15 to 25 Whitehall St., New York, N. Y.
WHITE, HENRY, 23 Court St., Boston, Mass.
WHITING, ISAAC S., Wilton, N. H.
WHITMAN, RUSSELL, Plymouth, Mass.

WILLIAMS, GEO. W., Jr., Charleston, S. C.
WILLISTON, S., Harvard Law School, Cambridge, Mass.
WISTER, OWEN, Branchtown P. O., Philadelphia, Pa.
WOODBURY, F. C., 3 Mt. Vernon St., Boston, Mass.
WOODWORTH, H. G., 31 Central St., Boston, Mass.
WORCESTER, J. R., Waltham, Mass.
YOUNG, F. H., 56 Summer St., Boston, Mass.

ADDENDA.

Since the body of the report was printed I have received the following:

WILLIAM ARMSTRONG ROGERS.

Since June, 1882, I have read law. Was admitted to the bar in this state (Ohio) in December, 1883, and have since been practising in Cincinnati. I expect to locate here permanently."

EVERT JANSEN WENDELL.

"After leaving college I went abroad with the intention of spending only the summer; but after three months spent in travelling, took apartments in Berlin with the intention of studying German there," but gave it up to accept the invitation of Mr. Phillips Brooks to accompany him to India. Sailed from Venice, December 1, 1882, for Bombay.

At Delhi was attacked by small-pox, but soon recovered and resumed travelling. About the end of March parted from Mr. Brooks to go to Palestine by the way of Egypt, and arrived at Jerusalem on the evening of Easter Sunday. After a short stay in Palestine went to Constantinople by way of Asia Minor; and then to Athens, and finally, after fifteen months of travel sailed from Liverpool for home.

"After getting home it took me a little while to settle down, and finally, about a year ago, I entered the office of John Paton & Co., Bankers to learn the business.

"I am now with them and am enjoying my work very much."

www.ingramcontent.com/pod-product-compliance
Lightning Source LLC
Chambersburg PA
CBHW032143230426
43672CB00011B/2430